CHILDREN OF FANTASY

To Dennis,
A fellow worker in
the historical vineyards
& Schaeffer Hall sufferer.

Robert Humphrey

Children of Fantasy

The First Rebels of Greenwich Village

ROBERT E. HUMPHREY

A RONALD PRESS PUBLICATION

JOHN WILEY & SONS, New York • Chichester • Brisbane • Toronto

Library of Congress Cataloging in Publication Data

Humphrey, Robert E.
    Children of fantasy.

    Bibliography: p.
    Includes index.
    1. Greenwich Village, New York (City)
2. Bohemianism—New York (City)—Greenwich Village.
3. Intellectuals—New York (City)—Greenwich Village—
Biography.   I. Title.

HN80.N5H85   974.7′1   77-28242
ISBN 0-471-42100-6

Printed in the United States of America

10 9 8 7 6 5 4 3 2 1

For

ROBERT GUYLER HUMPHREY

1914-1976

Preface

Between 1910 and 1920, Greenwich Village became a gathering place for men and women who wished to express and act out a rebellion against social conformity and middle-class culture. Although these nonconformists came from varying backgrounds and circumstances, they shared an aversion for ordinary pursuits and bureaucratic organizations. They assumed that a colony of like-minded rebels, existing on the edge of society, could promote freedom, liberate women, enjoy warm relationships, nourish talent, and set an example for the rest of society. They considered it possible and advantageous to combine a bohemian style of living with artistic achievement and radical politics. This book analyzes the events and activities that molded a common identity, and it assesses the political and artistic accomplishments of those writers, artists, and journalists who viewed themselves as the cultural vanguard in America.

To understand and evaluate Greenwich Village more fully, I thought it necessary to examine the careers of five individuals who participated in the bohemian revolt. Hutchins Hapgood, George Cram Cook, Max Eastman, John Reed, and Floyd Dell grew up in small towns that seemed backward, restrictive, and monotonous. During childhood and adolescence they developed a romantic view of reality; it became the hallmark of their rebelliousness and initiated their search for a world where love, adventure, and freedom flourished. They settled in Greenwich Village with the hope that the bohemian "community" would fulfill their dreams and needs. This study attempts to discover whether life in the Village was a satisfying and productive experience.

Since participants and historians have often exaggerated the vitality and creativity of the prewar Village, a critical perspective seemed justified. I did not want to glamorize the past nor add to the enduring mythology about Greenwich Village. I hope that I have judged the Villagers on the basis of their expectations, claims, and ac-complishments. If, as I conclude, Village rebels failed to achieve their most ambitious objectives, nevertheless they popularized iconoclastic ideas about art, politics, feminism, sex, and psychology while furthering personal freedom for men and women. Since Villagers led the assault against Victorian morality and culture, they are worthy of our attention.

Iowa City, Iowa
January 1978   Robert Humphrey

Acknowledgments

In writing this book I have needed the kindness of strangers and the generosity of friends. Linda Kerber, Sydney James, and Ellis Hawley offered advice and encouragement during the initial stages of preparation. Kenneth R. Chamberlain and Edmond M. Cook answered questions about their experiences, and Virginia Marberry shared information from her research. Eric Valentine selected the manuscript for publication and astutely commented on its shortcomings. Christopher Lasch, an inspiring teacher, read an early draft and raised some important questions. Keith Rageth, Robert McCown, and Wayne Rawley of the University of Iowa Library provided special assistance, and Mary Strottman was a conscientious typist.

Special debts of gratitude are owed to Michael J. Hogan, Paul and Nicole Mazgaj, Robert J. Klaus, and John A. Stack who read the manuscript and suggested improvements. In supplying cogent advice, perceptive criticism, and good humor, Jon Kinnamon, Jerald Kinnamon, and above all Edward E. Deckert proved invaluable allies. I greatly appreciate the gallant effort of these individuals to save the author from himself.

Finally, I thank my wife Beverly for her unfailing support and loving company.

R. E. Humphrey

Contents

Introduction, 1

Chapter 1 The Bohemian Revolt in Greenwich Village, 14

Chapter 2 Hutchins Hapgood and the Art of Personal Relations, 54

Chapter 3 George Cram Cook: A Bohemian in Search of Classical Greece, 84

Chapter 4 John Reed: The Poet on Horseback, 119

Chapter 5 Max Eastman: Social Engineer and Moral Reformer, 158

Chapter 6 Floyd Dell: The Bohemian as Romantic Lover, 207

Chapter 7 Greenwich Village: The Playground of Utopia, 236

Select Bibliography, 256

Index, 265

CHILDREN OF FANTASY

Introduction

In the years preceding American entry into World War I, an area of New York City known as Greenwich Village became famous for its unconventional inhabitants. These nonconformists included men and women who pursued the arts and some who merely wished to associate with artists. There were white-collar professionals (journalists, editors, teachers, social workers, lawyers) of both sexes who dabbled in high culture, "society" women bored with upper-class life, educated idlers, disgruntled anarchists, eccentrics, alcoholics, European expatriates, and actors. Although few in number, these rebels projected the image that made Greenwich Village synonymous with bohemia.[1]

The emergence of an artistic community in New York was not unique; colonies also appeared in Chicago, St. Louis, New Orleans, San Francisco, and Carmel. That Greenwich Village surpassed all in importance is not surprising; New York was the cultural capital of America. Once an isolated hamlet, Greenwich Village was now encircled by New York City. Located on the lower west side of Manhattan, its approximate borders were Fifth Avenue (including Washington Square, the symbolic center), Fourteenth Street, Houston Street, and the Hudson River. Primarily a residential area of three-and-four-storied eighteenth-century houses, the Village was the oldest surviving section of the city, and it retained something of the charm and atmosphere of the early republic. Because its narrow, oblique streets did not conform to the prevailing gridiron pattern, the Village was separated to some extent from the rest of New York.

1

Providing a small-town environment within the city, it seemingly offered an ideal setting for freedom and art.[2]

The well-to-do had once settled parts of Greenwich Village, and their stately mansions, particularly the red-brick Greek Revival homes on the north side of Washington Square, survived the influx of Irish immigrants. In 1900, a few blacks still lived near the Square, but the rest moved into Harlem as Italians inched their way upward from the crowded regions of lower Manhattan. The general decline in real estate values made the Village accessible to both the immigrant and the artist. Some writers and artists already lived there; many more followed in the early years of the new century to take advantage of cheap rents and inexpensive restaurants. Avoiding the larger tenement buildings, bohemians lived on the south side of Washington Square or to the north and west in remodeled stables or old houses that had been divided into apartments and studios. Stripping their quarters to bare essentials, the bohemians rejected bourgeois conveniences and Victorian affectations.[3]

Washington Square North in 1905. Courtesy of the New York Historical Society, New York.

The popularity of bohemian nonconformity was related to a dissatisfaction with middle-class society. Young, educated men and women objected to the restraints of respectability and denounced the competition for material goods. For women who found domestic life too confining and for men who objected to customary roles, the Village beckoned as a haven of freedom and adventure. These nonconformists came in search of a new perspective and a new identity. They wanted to create a mode of existence that would maximize creativity and self-fulfillment. They hoped to find love and enjoy simple pleasures in a colony of artists and writers.

Villagers were among those Progressive Era critics who demanded political, social, and economic reform. In contrast to other reformers, Village rebels spoke of a radical reorganization of society to provide social justice, sexual equality, and personal freedom. Wanting to dissociate themselves from the middle classes, bohemians spurned traditional morality, which they considered as oppressive as economic injustice. Since censorship, sexual repression, political corruption, and economic exploitation seemed to be integrally related, the rebels thought it necessary to attack all forms of social oppression.

Historically, artists and writers had been subsidized by governments and wealthy benefactors, enduring a dependency that sometimes circumscribed their work and behavior. In advanced western European countries the popularity of newspapers, books, and public exhibitions compensated for the gradual disappearance of patronage. In the nineteenth century most writers and artists supported themselves by producing for a mass market, a consequence of spreading affluence and literacy. This development enabled literary and artistic journeymen to live and work in communities of their own choice.[4] To establish an identity, artists and writers created bohemia and erected their own social barriers.

The term "bohemia" implies a loosely-bound community of artists who disregard conventional dress codes, sexual taboos, and work habits. In France the word "bohemian" originally referred to wandering gypsies who supposedly came from Bohemia, a kingdom in central Europe. The "bohemian" label was appropriated by nineteenth-century Romantic artists who called themselves vagabonds. In the 1840s a few struggling Parisian painters and poets experimented with bohemianism in the Latin Quarter, an undertaking popularized by one of the garret-dwellers, poet-journalist Henri Murger. Bohemians like Murger and his friends lived precariously, devoting their energies to art, drinking, romantic adventures, and the trials of surviving without regular employment or patronage.[5] Poverty was celebrated and identified with bohemianism; it was the price of independence and the consequence of obscurity.

By the end of the century a bohemian tradition had evolved in the Latin Quarter, a development which in part explained why Paris became the experimental center of the art world.[6] Aspiring American artists, initiating the era of expatriation to France, visited Paris and were influenced by their European counterparts. Some students returned to Greenwich Village, where they attempted to recapture a style of life found in Paris.[7]

In New York in the 1850s a small group of writers, painters, and poets met regularly at Pfaff's beer cellar on Broadway to drink and engage in lively conversation. But this self-styled bohemianism did not outlive its participants. In the 1890s bohemianism gained considerable notoriety, especially after the publication and staging of George Du Maurier's *Trilby,* a melodrama about an artist's model and her experiences in Paris. Writer Stephen Crane and art-student friends frolicked at Buchignani's on Third Avenue near Fifteenth Street while music critic James G. Huneker dined with the avant-garde at Mouquin's on Sixth Avenue. Rebellious writers and journalists frequented foreign restaurants and taverns to partake of a freer, more exotic milieu. Although this recreation was not confined to any one area, the Village's convenient location and numerous cafés made it a favorite spot for bohemian activities.[8]

Since the middle of the nineteenth century painters had lived in Greenwich Village, renting inexpensive rooms in the old New York University building or in hotels on Washington Square. In the first years of the twentieth century their numbers increased. Among the newcomers were William Glackens, Everett Shinn, George Luks, John Sloan, Glenn Coleman, George Bellows, and Stuart Davis, members of the so-called Ash Can School who offended established art critics by painting lifelike scenes of the city and its inhabitants. Portraying the poor and disreputable in ordinary situations, the Ash Can painters expressed a new social consciousness in their rebellion against academic standards and rules in general.[9]

The discovery of urban poverty and the urge to see life beyond the sheltered confines of middle-class culture gave rise to social work among the poor. The first New York settlement house was established on Delancey Street in 1893; another, the Greenwich House, opened nine years later at 26 Jones Street in the heart of the Village. These settlement houses attracted middle-class college graduates who wanted to help immigrants and to gather material for realistic fiction.[10] In 1902, Ernest Poole, the son of a wealthy Chicago family, arrived at the University settlement on the Lower East Side and found William English Walling, J.G. Phelps, Howard Brubaker, and Arthur Bullard who "came there to write" about life in the tenements.[11] First-hand contact with filth, disease, drunkenness, and prostitution convinced them that drastic reforms were needed and they became socialists.

Headquarters for Branch One of the Socialist party was in the Rand School of Social Science on East Nineteenth Street, an institution established in 1905 to study social problems and provide free education for the poor. John Sloan, Max Eastman, Sinclair Lewis, William E. Walling, cartoonist Art Young, and poet Louis Untermeyer attended Socialist party meetings there. Untermeyer recalled that the basement restaurant was "a gathering place of all the Utopians, muckrakers, young intellectuals, and elderly malcontents south of Forty-Second Street."[12]

Other "institutions" also brought artists and radicals together and created a sense of common purpose and a spirit of rebellion. Alfred Stieglitz's "291" Gallery on Fifth Avenue near Thirty-First Street provided a center for avant-garde art while the anarchist Ferrer School attracted rebels and artists who lectured to immigrants. Radicals gathered in the offices of Emma Goldman's Mother Earth, painters at the McDowell Club on West Fifty-Fifth Street, and reformers at the Liberal Club in Gramercy Park.[13] Although these groups often met outside Greenwich Village, they contributed to the revolt against traditional authorities. This convergence of writers, painters, socialists, reformers, and feminists gave the Village its distinctive mixture of art, radicalism, and unconventional social behavior.

The growth of urban bohemias in larger cities was enhanced by the general exodus from the countryside. America had advanced beyond the frontier stage when sons and daughters were needed at home. Society had developed sufficiently to permit the pursuit of impractical occupations, and the artistically inclined could survive marginally in large cities. The small-town eccentric could become the urban bohemian.

Greenwich Village was heavily populated by men and women from small towns and cities who knew something of culture and wished to escape the restrictions of provincialism. Artistic rebels left for a university or the nearest city to enlarge their circle of friends and improve the quality of their lives. Some arrived in New York by way of Chicago, St. Louis, or San Francisco; others came after four years at college.

In moving to the city, these exiles from the provinces encountered the confusing disorder of an urban environment. Detached from the moorings of class, family, and social institutions, they tried to create more familiar surroundings by living in the same area of New York and frequenting the same cafés. Floyd Dell, who had grown up in Illinois and Iowa, felt "alien and a little frightened" in New York City.[14] Consequently, he preferred to stay in Greenwich Village where friendly faces gave him a sense of belonging. Max Eastman, a refugee from upstate New York, told the *New York Tribune* in 1914 why he lived in Greenwich Village:

> I want to be very close to that exciting current of life and business that flows north and south on the main avenues. I want to be able to rush into it for pleasure or profits on a moment's notice. But I don't want to live right in it, because I can't stand the strain. And so I seek out the little low-roofed cove. . . where only an occasional backwater eddy of the mainstream reaches me, and I live in complete quietness, with air and sunshine that I couldn't find elsewhere on Manhattan Island south of Riverside Drive.[15]

Here was the best of both worlds: the tempo and security of the small town, the excitement and adventures of a great city.

To journalist Mary Heaton Vorse, who had spent her childhood in Amherst, Massachusetts, the Village offered an attractive alternative to middle-class urban life and an escape from "the curse of conformity." "Uptowners," bound by "some unwritten decalogue of dress, conduct and manners," only associated with other members of the middle class. By contrast, Vorse maintained, in the Village one knew people of "all classes" and interests, and everyone spent "their time more in the realities of life than in that soul-racking game known as keeping up appearances."[16] Cartoonist Art Young thought that one avoided the "conventional atmosphere of business civilization" in Greenwich Village. Here a "man felt something like his raw self, though he knew well that he had been cooked to a turn by the world's conventions."[17] Presumably the "real" individual, not the social personality, had a chance to develop in bohemia. By tearing away social masks, Villagers hoped to establish a more honest basis for social intercourse. They expected that this process would lead to the discovery of the true self and the building of a real community.

The bohemian vision of the good society harked back to preindustrial settings. Bohemians imagined that the Village had its antecedents in classical Greece. Identifying with legendary figures offered historical justification and prestige to their undertaking. Stressing the importance of a favorable milieu, rebels attributed their own lack of artistic creativity to American society. They anticipated talent would finally gestate in Greenwich Village.

Reacting against the insularity and pretense of middle-class society, Villagers upheld the superiority of a simple life. Existence, Dell recalled, "was quaintly enriched by our poverty. How otherwise, except by being very poor, should we ever have learned to make the most of those joys that are so cheap, or that cost nothing at all, the joys of comradeship and mere childlike fun?"[18] The ingenious enjoyment of ordinary pleasures showed up the middle class and its extravagant amusements. Living in want reassured the Villager of his commitments; it evoked images of the neglected artist living for art's sake and of the radical sharing the fate of social outcasts. When applied self-consciously this image produced the supercilious attitude that bohemians were morally superior to other men. But social conditions in the Village were "quaint," not oppressive, and voluntary poverty was not permanent destitution.

Within Greenwich Village artists and writers were a small minority scattered amongst poor ethnic groups and an assortment of prostitutes, petty criminals, and bums. The bohemians were outsiders, many not even from New York, with little previous exposure to immigrants or derelicts. They became only superficially acquainted with ethnic families and social outcasts; the Villagers traded with local merchants, ate at foreign restaurants, and drank in local taverns. For the most part sons and daughters of the middle class, they acted out their rebellion against respectability by living close to the submerged classes. Ironically, their compatriots, the authoritarian lower classes, favored repression more than the middle class did. But the poor were idealized as outcasts who endured poverty and social inferiority. Besides, the Irish and the Italians were unprepared to impose their standards on the irreverent strangers in their midst. Bohemians could live cheaply and freely in an exotic world of their own choosing.

Not a self-governing or a self-sufficient community, Greenwich Village existed as a subculture within the larger society. The Village defined itself as an island of art and freedom surrounded by a hostile world of crass materialism and hypocritical respectability. Greenwich Village had no formal institutions to regulate social behavior and wanted none. Acceptance within the group required affirmation, by word or deed, of a Village code that celebrated creativity and rejected conventions. Villagers could extol a negative conception of freedom, which would eliminate institutions and their constraints, because they need not uphold the social order. While Villagers gathered at favorite meeting places, participated in common activities, and shared certain values, they hardly formed a unified or ongoing community.

The Villagers suffered no social discrimination for their transgressions; on the contrary, members of the *haute bourgeoisie* praised them for sinning openly. Unlike most social deviants, Village rebels acclaimed their own nonconformity. Besides, in dress, manners, and tastes, deviations from middle-class norms were not extreme. Unless excessively eccentric or uncouth, a Villager could move back and forth across the line between chic respectability and bohemianism. Mabel Dodge's salon, symbolically located on the edge of Greenwich Village, functioned as the social intersection of Fifth Avenue sophisticates and bohemians.

    Characteristically, historians have lumped all young, rebellious intellectuals and artists of this period in a single group. These rebels, so the argument runs, attacked the prevailing social, cultural, and political standards of their time, demanded equality for women, and sang the praises of psychoanalysis, progressive education, avant-garde art, and socialism. Using accounts supplied by the participants, historians have concluded that the prewar community in Greenwich Village was a thriving intellectual community.

    In 1916 Floyd Dell, one of bohemia's leading citizens, first publicized the idea that Greenwich Village was a delightful playground. He saluted the Village rebels because they were free from middle-class hypocrisy, materialism, and conformity; they enjoyed intimacy, candor, love and "the aristocratic use of leisure" without money. Already, however, Dell feared the catastrophe that threatened to devastate utopia, for the "great wave . . . of ordinariness, of law and order, of middle class virtue" was poised to descend upon bohemia. Two years later, with the extension of Seventh Avenue through the Village, he announced that the fatal blow had been struck. He rued the passing of "those old, forgotten, far off days" when Greenwich Village had been "a quiet island . . . where the pace of life slowed down a bit and left time for dreams and friendships and art and love." The "barbarians to the north," the bored middle classes, ruined his paradise by driving the Villagers, like persecuted "Christians," into hiding.[19]

    In *Exile's Return* (1934), Malcolm Cowley, who did not arrive in the Village until 1919 and stayed less than a year, revived Dell's notion of a lost utopia. Distinguishing between those who arrived before and after the First World War, Cowley argued that the prewar Villagers "read Marx and all the radicals had a touch of the bohemian."[20] The war, however, destroyed Village interest in political action and talk about revolution gave way to talk about psychoanalysis. Having lived through the war and its aftermath, Cowley and other members of his "generation" could no longer accept prewar illusions or fight for social reform.

    Some years later, Dell incorporated Cowley's analysis of bohemia and its demise in a new version of the Greenwich Village story. Dell reported that indeed the war had wrecked a flourishing "intellectual" community. Before 1917, he explained, the "intelligentsia was socially dominant,

[and] social reform was its keynote." With American intervention, however, all "group boundaries" dissolved and intellectual life disappeared:

> Artists, writers, intellectuals, liberals, radicals, IWWs, bohemians, well-to-do patrons,onlookers—all were hurled into a miscellaneous social melee in which earnestness and frivolity were thoroughly intermingled. The 'real' Village . . . was swept away in the flood.[21]

Stressing the intellectual, not the social accomplishments of the Village, Dell again maintained that outside forces, not internal inadequacies decimated his utopia.

Historians have not questioned Dell's assertion that there was an intellectual Camelot in Greenwich Village. In *The End of American Innocence* (1959), Henry F. May argued that a "cultural revolution" involving an assault on gentility occurred in the years preceding World War I; it was led by youthful rebels, including those who resided in Greenwich Village.[22] In *Writers on the Left* (1961), Daniel Aaron discovered in Village bohemianism "the origins of a more serious rebellion to come." He viewed the Village as a "Mecca" where "the intellectual and cultural and even political revolution was brooded over, if not hatched and here came young rebels from all over America to be free, to flout convention, to live vibrantly and indecorously."[23]

The idea of a "renaissance" in Greenwich Village appeared more recently in James Gilbert's *Writers and Partisans: A History of Literary Radicalism in America* (1968). Gilbert maintained that in Greenwich Village before the War "more than anyplace else, . . . the character of the American radical intellectual was determined." There the "radicalism of Marx and the anarchism of the I.W.W. met and mixed with the new experiments in literature and art." Gilbert did not, however, explain what this alleged union of "political radicalism, experimental art, and bohemian life" produced nor what disastrous consequences followed from the postwar fragmentation of intellectual life.[24] In *The Agony of the American Left* (1969), Christopher Lasch agreed with Gilbert's assessment and sadly concluded that the War destroyed America's only intellectual community. *The Masses,* Lasch argued, "the highest product of the prewar rebellion, owed its distinctive vitality to a combination of socialism and 'paganism.' " He too deplored the postwar separation of art and politics because it furthered the "poverty of social criticism in the United States."[25]

Historians and commentators have not shown that the combination of art, radical politics, and bohemianism created a cultural renaissance or that Greenwich Village was its nucleus. There existed an inherent conflict between artistic freedom and ideological politics that Villagers never successfully resolved; artists either ignored politics or subordinated their talents to political causes. Villagers advocated political and cultural reforms without heeding the contradictions in their program. Bohemian rebels often confused their needs with those of the poor. But what was liberating for the Villagers—for example, informal personal relations, freedom of expression, sexual liberation, and an unregulated social life—was irrelevant to laboring-class families struggling for existence. The ease with which psychoanalysis, socialism, syndicalism, feminism, progressive education, cubism, and free love were tossed together was an indication of intellectual confusion and the importance of rebellion for its own sake. Moreover, the loosening of social and sexual restraints, praised as a revolutionary assault on conventionality, often deflected rebels from artistic and political endeavors. Exhilarated by the opportunity to live freely and to shock respectable opinion, many Village rebels became absorbed in the pursuit of affairs, personal relations, and social antics. Interest in psychology and self-discovery often nurtured self-indulgence and diverted the imagination of aspiring artists, writers, and social critics.

To understand Greenwich Village it is necessary to examine the careers of the most prominent bohemians. These individuals edited and contributed to *The Masses,* participated in Mabel Dodge's salon, amused themselves at the Liberal Club and bohemian haunts, and established the Provincetown Players, an amateur theatrical group that first staged the plays of Eugene O'Neill. These men and women determined Village norms and reflected its values. Because they left historical records, they must serve as spokesmen for the "community." Those who did not write, the nameless, and those who survive only as names, must remain in the background. Other members of the avant-garde were excluded because they did not actively pursue Village activities. Walter Lippmann, William Carlos Williams, and Alfred Stieglitz, to name a few, lived and worked in and about New York City but had only passing involvement with the center of Village life.

Although Theodore Dreiser periodically resided in the Village, had affairs with "liberated" women, drank at the Hotel Brevoort and ate at Polly's Inn, he objected to the bohemian label. When H.L. Mencken accused him of becoming like the "childish, red ink bunch" who wrote for *The Masses,* the Village's radical journal, Dreiser protested his innocence:

I hold no brief for the 'parlor radical'. . . . I sometimes think that because
I have moved into 10th Street and am living a life not suitable to the
home streets of Baltimore that you think I have gone over to the red ink
family and the 'brothers of the hollow skull.'[26]

Similarly, Eugeen O'Neill, an important member of the Provincetown
Players, preferred to mingle with criminals and alcoholics instead of the
Village crowd.[27] Dreiser and O'Neill stood apart from the rest; genius and
self-discipline made the preservation of their independence necessary
and possible.

This book focuses on five significant individuals who were attracted to
bohemianism, who influenced their companions, and who in turn were
affected by Greenwich Village. Hutchins Hapgood, George Cram Cook,
Max Eastman, John Reed, and Floyd Dell had much in common before
and after their arrival in New York. These rebels were not refugees from
factory towns or immigrant ghettoes and they suffered emotional, not
physical hardships. To offset the loneliness and alienation of childhood
and adolescence, they read books and dreamed about a world in which
freedom, poetry, and love abounded. Idealists trapped in a world
dominated by practical concerns, they sought out those who shared their
romantic sensibilities and artistic interests. In Chicago and New York
they discovered the existence of outsiders like themselves. They became
optimistic about the prospects of building a new way of life, buoyed up
by their mutual self-discovery, their secret sense of superiority, and the
excitement of doing something rebellious, possibly revolutionary.

Villagers harbored utopian ideas; they dreamed of reorganizing society, expanding artistic achievement, liberating the individual, and
establishing a community of equals. Extravagant expectations demanded
miraculous powers, but in Greenwich Village even ordinary will power
was in short supply. Settlers in the Village sought to escape a society
unreceptive to their dreams and needs. But in retiring to a community of
like-minded rebels, they kept their adolescent fantasies in good health
beyond the usual life expectancy.

NOTES

1. Albert Parry, *Garrets and Pretenders: A History of Bohemianism in America* (New York, 1960), pp. 267-315.
2. Egmont Arens, *The Little Book of Greenwich Village* (New York, 1918), pp.1-25. *New York City Guide* (New York, 1939), pp. 124-143.
3. Carolyn Ware, *Greenwich Village, 1920-1930* (New York, 1965), pp. 12-15.
4. Leo Lowenthal, *Literature, Popular Culture and Society* (Englewood Cliffs, N.J., 1961), pp. 52-65. Cesar Grana, *Bohemian Versus Bourgeois: French Society and the French Man of Letters in the Nineteenth Century* (New York, 1964), pp. 31-36.
5. Grana, *Bohemian Versus Bourgeois,* p. 67, pp. 21-27. Henri Murger, *Vie de Bohemia,* trans. Norman Cameron (London, 1960). Robert Baldrick, *The First Bohemian: The Life of Henry Murger* (London, 1961).
6. Roger Shattuck, *The Banquet Years: The Origins of the Avant Garde in France, 1885 to World War I* (New York, 1968), pp. 3-28. R. H. Wilenski, *Modern French Painters,* Vol. 2 (New York, 1966), pp. 25-71.
7. Barbara Rose, *American Art Since 1900: A Critical History* (New York, 1967), p. 14, pp. 30-34. Jo Davidson, *Between Sittings: An Informal Autobiography* (New York, 1952). Werner Haftmann, *Painting in the Twentieth Century,* Vol. 1 (New York, 1965), pp. 155-161.
8. Parry, *Garrets and Pretenders,* pp. 14-61, pp. 66-75, pp. 87-109.
9. John Baur, *Revolution and Tradition in Modern American Art* (Cambridge, Mass., 1966), pp. 11-19. *John Sloan's New York Scene: From the Diaries, Notes and Correspondence, 1906-1913,* ed. Bruce St. John (New York, 1965).
10. Allen F. Davis, *Spearheads for Reform: The Social Settlements and the Progressive Movement, 1890-1914* (New York, 1967).
11. Ernest Poole, *The Bridge: My Own Story* (New York, 1940), p. 73.
12. Louis Untermeyer, *From Another World* (New York, 1939), p. 37.
13. Van Wyck Brooks, *The Confident Years: 1885-1915* (New York, 1952), pp. 475-495.
14. Floyd Dell, *Homecoming: An Autobiography* (New York, 1933), p. 250.
15. *New York Tribune.* (December 20, 1914), Sec. 4, p. 2.
16. *Ibid.*
17. Art Young, *On My Way: Being the Book of Art Young in Text and Picture* (New York, 1928), p.129.
18. Floyd Dell, "The Rise of Greenwich Village," *Love in Greenwich Village* (New York, 1926), p. 33.
19. Floyd Dell, "Out of the World," *Looking At Life* (New York, 1924), pp. 66-67. Floyd Dell, "Lost Paradise," *Looking at Life,* pp. 125-127.
20. Malcolm Cowley, *Exile's Return: A Narrative of Ideas* (New York, 1934), p. 76.
21. Floyd Dell, "Rents Were Low in Greenwich Village," *American Mercury,* Vol. 65 (December, 1947), p. 665.
22. Henry F. May, *The End of American Innocence: A Study of the First Years of Our Own Time, 1912-1917* (New York, 1959). Contrary to standard interpretations, Greenwich Village was not strictly a rebellion of youth. If 1914 is used as a bench mark, the forty most prominent Villagers were not that young. Of the forty, thirteen were in their twenties, twenty in their thirties, and seven in their forties.
23. Daniel Aaron, *Writers on the Left: Episodes in American Literary Communism* (New York, 1961), pp. 10-12.

24. James B. Gilbert, *Writers and Partisans: A History of Literary Radicalism in America* (New York, 1968), p. 18, pp. 48-87.

25. Christopher Lasch, *The Agony of the American Left* (New York, 1969), p.47.

26. H. L. Mencken to Theodore Dreiser (April 22, 1915), Theodore Dreiser to H. L. Mencken (April 26, 1915), in *Letters of H. L. Mencken,* ed. Guy Forgue (New York, 1961), pp. 67-69.

27. Barrett Clark, *Eugene O'Neill* (New York, 1926), p. 29.

CHAPTER ONE

The Bohemian Revolt in Greenwich Village

In 1913 the establishment of three "institutions" in Greenwich Village brought together assorted rebels who developed the fashions of bohemianism. The Liberal Club, Mabel Dodge's salon, and the offices of *The Masses* provided important meeting places where insurgents exchanged opinions and enjoyed each other's company. In addition, two events, which occurred outside the Village, brought rebels into conflict with conventional society and shaped their bohemian identity. The Armory Show, an astonishing exhibition of international art, and the Paterson strike, a conflict between immigrant silk workers and New Jersey mill owners, captured the attention and support of Village rebels. Participation in these episodes, which Villagers infused with revolutionary significance, helped to mold a self-conscious, bohemian community.

The International Exhibition of Modern Art opened February 17, 1913, in the 69th Regiment Armory at Lexington Avenue and Twenty-Fifth Street. Organized by a group of independent artists who were led by painters Arthur Davies, Walter Kuhn, and Jerome Myers, the Armory Show, as it came to be known, was an attempt to introduce the American public to the latest developments in painting and sculpture. It also represented a revolt against the conservative National Academy of Design and established art dealers who refused to exhibit unconventional paintings.[1]

Interior of Armory Show. Smithsonian Institution.

Most of the works on display, especially the American entries, did not depart radically from traditional artistic standards. But the exhibition also included a selection of paintings and statues from the Continental avant-garde who created nonrepresentational works of art. It was this group, particularly the geometric Cubist paintings and the expressive studies of Henri Matisse, that caused an immediate sensation. The Show received extensive publicity and thousands of people attended in order to see the most startling European exhibits. Although Pablo Picasso, Georges Braque, Vincent van Gogh, and Paul Gauguin were represented, the public was drawn to Marcel Duchamp's *Nude Descending a Staircase,* which became the most celebrated exhibit in the Show.[2] It was the incongruity of the title with the artist's novel representation that caused an uproar, producing merriment and ridicule among the Armory visitors.

Unwilling to accept abstraction or postimpressionism as serious art, conventional critics and viewers sneered at modernism and its supporters. *American Art News* sponsored a contest to find the "nude" in Duchamp's paintings while derisive commentators amused themselves by proposing alternative titles — two suggestions were "an explosion in a shingle factory" and "a staircase descending a nude."[3] The *New York Tribune* stated that the exhibition included "some of the most stupidly ugly pictures in the world and not a few pieces of sculpture to match them."[4] Other commentators reacted with disgust and fear. *Current Opinion* quoted one mother who warned: "If I caught my boy Tommy making anything like them, I'd certainly give him a good spanking."[5] Frank Jewett Mather, Jr., professor of art history at Princeton University, was even more abusive. He advised laymen to "dismiss on moral grounds an art that lives in the miasma of morbid hallucination or sterile experimentation and denies in the name of individualism values which are those of society and life itself."[6] Theodore Roosevelt, who visited the Show on March 4, instead of attending the inauguration of Woodrow Wilson, thought Duchamp's "picture of a misshapen nude woman repellent from every point of view." Comparing the Cubist paintings with his Navajo rug, he decided that the rug had more "decorative value and artistic merit."[7]

Despite a reaction that was generally whimsical and adverse, insurgent artists were heartened by the large attendance, and some perceived that the Show won over visitors who had originally intended to jeer. Sculptor Jo Davidson recalled:

. . . before the trumpets of the avant-garde, prejudice crumbled like the walls of jericho. Never had art in America attracted so much attention. People came in droves. The smart set gave dinner parties and brought their guests to the Armory Show; and some who came to scoff remained to praise.[8]

Painter William Zorach, who was converted to abstraction by the Show, thought that "art was stirred up as it never had been before." From that period on, he contended, the artist freed himself from the bonds of tradition by seeing "the world with a view as primitive and unsophisticated as a child."[9] On that point Zorach's attitude coincided with the opinions of disparaging critics who argued that modern art resembled the scribblings of children.

Although the Armory Show organizers wanted to give the public a glimpse of modern art, the exhibition impressed on American artists that Europe was the source of creative originality. William Glackens, an American Realistic painter, concluded that "we have no innovators here.

Everything worthwhile in our art is due to the influence of French art. We have not yet arrived at a national art."[10] Intended in part to demonstrate the accomplishments of American rebels, the Armory Show had the unforeseen effect of heightening a dependence on Europe. It prompted some American artists to adopt the techniques of modernism without understanding its principles.[11] Eclectic incorporation of the latest cultural fashions from Europe became an accepted practice in the Village.

The Armory Show's contribution to art was of secondary importance to Village rebels who adopted and subverted the exhibition for their own ends. Mabel Dodge, who contributed five hundred dollars and borrowed paintings from wealthy patrons, felt that the exhibition belonged to her:

It became, overnight, my own little Revolution. I would upset the old order of things. . . . I was going to dynamite New York and nothing would stop me. Well, nothing did. I moved forward in my role of Fate's chosen instrument, and the show certainly did gain by my propulsion.[12]

To Mabel the Show signified the beginning of a "new spirit" that would "shake up and make over the fixed patterns of life."[13] Villagers regarded modern art as an expression of bohemian values, and they delighted in the electrifying effect it had on conventional opinion. The futuristic value of the Armory exhibition was incentive enough for the short journey uptown. By visiting the Show and affirming the new art styles, Villagers asserted their avant-garde status. This experience provided an esoteric subject for discussions and strengthened a sense of common purpose. Hanging abstract paintings in bohemian meeting places and decorating Village apartments in garish colors became a favorite method of displaying one's membership in the vanguard.

In viewing the Armory Show as an agent of revolution, Villagers assigned political value to a collection of modern paintings. Painter John Sloan remarked in his diary that "Matisse, the neo-Impressionists, and the Cubists" were "a splendid symptom, a bomb under conventions. Some of the painters are nothing but flying splinters imagining themselves highly explosive forces but the explosive force is there—revolution it is."[14] Other Villagers concurred that the exhibition represented an attack on American society. Hutchins Hapgood, a Village habitué and a part-time journalist, believed that modern art disturbed the "pillars of routine" and "respectable Anglo-Saxon[s]." Comparing "post-impressionist" artists to the Industrial Workers of the World, he thought that the labor war, "boiling beneath the entire surface of society," was "paralleled by the unrest in art." Artists and workers wanted to "loosen up the old forms and traditions," and "get down deeper" to underlying natural laws.[15] Together, he envisioned, they would sweep away inhibiting traditions and revitalize art and life.

Village rebels and conventional critics alike confused art with politics and exaggerated the revolutionary potential of artistic works. When Theodore Roosevelt referred to the Cubists and the Futurists as a "lunatic fringe," he expressed a prejudice shared by most Americans toward foreign artists, immigrants, and "European extremists."[16] On March 16, one day after the Armory Show closed, the New York Times expressed its disdain for modern artists, who were linked to free-verse poets and political anarchists:

> It should be borne in mind that this movement is surely part of the general movement, discernible all over the world, to disrupt and degrade, if not destroy, not only art, but literature and society, too . . . . [T]he cubists and futurists are own cousins to the anarchists in politics, the poets who defy syntax and decency, and all would-be destroyers who with the pretense of trying to regenerate the world are really trying to block the wheels of progress in every direction. . . . They have no true message to impart, but there is no room, nevertheless, to doubt the potency of their appeal to many of the disheartened, embittered, and discontented, as well as the mentally ill-balanced.[17]

To defenders of the status quo the subversion of traditional artistic standards meant cultural and social anarchy. Village rebels believed that these critics were correct in their assessment. Mabel Dodge told Gertrude Stein that the Exhibition was "the most important public event" since the Declaration of Independence and it was "of the same nature." There would be, she predicted, "a riot and a revolution and things will never be quite the same afterwards."[18]

The simultaneous outbreak of a silk workers' strike in Paterson, New Jersey, an industrial city twenty miles from New York City, was eyed by Village rebels as additional evidence of social unrest and the need for revolutionary change. Labor sympathizers anticipated that the Paterson strike would follow a pattern begun in Lawrence, Massachusetts, where textile workers walked out of the factories during the early weeks of 1912. In Lawrence, the Industrial Workers of the World (the I.W.W. or Wobblies), a militant organization preaching revolution and industrial democracy, had directed the strikers. William ("Big Bill") Haywood, Elizabeth Gurley Flynn, Arturo Giovannitti, and other Wobbly leaders had welded twenty thousand workers, comprising twenty-five nationalities, into a peaceful but powerful force. After nine weeks of bitter struggle the strikers won a small increase in wages.[19]

The triumph at Lawrence, which Eastman called the "biggest human victory of recent years in America," greatly bolstered the prestige of the I.W.W. in the East.[20] Formed in 1905, the I.W.W. advocated the formation of one giant union that would encompass all workers. Wobblies envisioned that a general strike would lead to the overthrow of capitalism. In forming industrial unions and favoring violence, the I.W.W. was at odds with the Socialist party, which hoped to accomplish its goal through peaceful participation in the democratic system. At Lawrence, however, the Wobblies had shown that they were capable of employing the tactics of peaceful resistance to obtain piecemeal gains.

With the arrival of Haywood and other Wobbly leaders in Paterson the strike spread to all the mills and upwards of twenty thousand workers, for the most part Italian and Jewish immigrants, manned picket lines to discourage strike-breakers. In the months that followed, the police repeatedly harrassed the strikers, jailing hundreds on nuisance charges. Local authorities attempted to eliminate the Wobblies, who were considered dangerous firebrands, and break the strike, which they viewed as potentially revolutionary.[21]

Excited by the spectacle of industrial strife in proximity to Greenwich Village, the rebels adopted the Paterson strike as their special cause. Villagers visited Paterson and filed news dispatches or drew cartoons about the strike. Others received their information from Bill Haywood, who was lionized as a proletarian intellectual. Inviting Haywood and other labor radicals to the Village provided a chance to associate with those who were directly involved in working-class struggles. Wobbly radicals, poet Harry Kemp recalled, exhibited "an inextinguishable courage that contagiously bore us along with them." Rubbing shoulders with labor organizers served to establish radical credentials. Kemp confessed: "We sang the songs of the Wobblies with gusto, but there was an unsmoothed vigor or rough balladry about the verses, a direct contact with life, as invigorating as strong drink that took us captive."[22] The opportunity to link themselves with radicals who challenged conventional society was as appealing as contributing to a working-class victory.

Hutchins Hapgood reported that Villagers used Wobblies to provide vicarious excitement. When Haywood visited painter Robert Henri's studio, those in attendance "gathered about him and made him talk about the strike" because they "wanted new life. They wanted Haywood's life."[23] But workers also had a stimulating affect on Hapgood. To him the strikers represented a spiritual movement, a phalanx "inspired and sustained" by group "enthusiasm." Visiting the strike in April, he told his readers in the *New York Globe:* "I wish that everybody could spend a day at Paterson feeling the spirit of the silk workers."[24] Other Villagers thought that the strike set the stage for a social conflagration. Writer Wilbur D. Steele told Mary Heaton Vorse and Joe O'Brien:

> I missed West Virginia [the coal miners' strike] . . . and I'm afraid I'm going to slip up on Paterson, but believe me, that is the last.
> You folks want to hurry up and come home [from Europe] or you're going to miss the Revolution. Now take it from Cousin Wilbur, things are going to happen in the U.S.A. before many generations have passed. Everything is getting ripe all together. And the tariff is going to be the spark to set off the powder. Lawrence, West Virginia, Paterson, Little Falls [New York] Buffalo and the rest have done their work, and now wait and see the fireworks when the manufacturers begin trying to cut down the wages when the tariff goes in.[25]

Although Villagers talked about revolution, few condoned the use of violence. Max Eastman, editor of *The Masses,* thought the Wobblies were useful as shock troops to startle those "privileged by the possession of capital." A "belligerent, somewhat negative and unresponsible" [sic] organization, the I.W.W. could agitate capitalists and "awaken the workers to the philosophy of socialism," but they would not "usher in the day of industrial democracy."[26] Village rebels approved of the I.W.W.'s unstructured organization and the Wobblies' suspicious attitude toward authority. They liked to imagine the fear that Wobbly leaders produced in conventional circles and they urged labor radicals to use strikers for this purpose. After a mass rally in Paterson, Harry Kemp chided Bill Haywood for his failure to arouse the workers. Haywood replied: "Hell, Harry, I'm not running this strike as a show for Greenwich Village."[27]

Village participants assumed that reality existed beyond the bounds of respectability where the disreputable lived. The search for the hidden side of life seldom, however, entailed prolonged contact with social outcasts. Few Villagers sought intimate relations with immigrants, workers, blacks, and criminals or immersed themselves in struggles that might ameliorate their condition; to do so would have meant sacrificing a bohemian existence. When a Village rebel attempted to embrace a cause, he encountered the suspicions of those he wished to help. The bohemian had the burden of proving himself a committed radical rather than a sympathetic intruder. In his fictional autobiography, *More Miles,* Harry Kemp recounted what happened when he tried to join the I.W.W. At the local Wobbly office he was told: "An intellectual, huh. A writer titty-sucker to the Upper Classes." When Kemp replied that he was a poet, the I.W.W.

official retorted: "Pretty bad, unless you have guts like Joe [O'Carroll]."[28]
In demanding a courageous commitment, the Wobbly organizer
challenged Kemp's radicalism. This incident raised the question which
Villagers preferred not to ask of themselves: Did their political beliefs require total involvement and active participation? Feeling more comfortable with the style rather than the substance of rebellion, Villagers
believed that they could be radical without standing in picket lines.

The Village's contribution to the Paterson strike entailed a theatrical
pageant in Madison Square Garden to dramatize the suffering of the silk
workers. According to Mabel Dodge, a small group of Villagers hatched
the plan one night in the modest apartment of Bill Haywood's mistress,
Bee Shostac. Haywood complained to the gathering that the New York
newspapers were not informing workers in the city about the strike:

> Very few of them know what we've been through over there. . . .The police
> have turned into organized gunmen. God! I wish I could show them a pic-
> ture of the funeral of Modestino [Valentino], who was shot by a cop.
> Everyone of the silk mill hands followed his coffin to the grave and drop-
> ped a red flower into it. . . .As they marched they sang the 'International.'
> By God, if our people over here could have seen it, we could have raised
> a trunkful of money to help us go on. Our food is getting mighty scarce
> over there.[29]

When Mabel suggested a pageant to gain sympathy and funds for the
strikers, journalist John Reed volunteered to write a scenario and direct
the production. Enlisting the help of Mabel, Margaret Sanger, Ernest
Poole, John Sloan, and stage designer Robert Edmond Jones, the
Villagers erected a huge backdrop that depicted a dreary, six-story Paterson mill.

On Saturday night, June 7, 1913, the pageant was performed before a
crowd of some fifteen thousand spectators. Presented in the form of a
tableau, the production involved over a thousand immigrant men and
women in a moving re-enactment of the strike. The eight episodes showed the initial walkout and the singing of "La Marseillaise," the formation
of picket lines and the brutality of the police, Wobbly leader Carlo
Tresca's fiery speech to an assembly of workers, the funeral of Valentino,
the departure of strikers' children to New York homes, and finally a rally
with speeches by Bill Haywood, Elizabeth Gurley Flynn, and Carlo
Tresca. At the end the worker-actors pledged with upraised hands never
to return to the mills until the strike was won.[30]

By all accounts the Paterson pageant was a theatrical success.
Villagers became ecstatic about the prospects for a new, democratic art
form and the possibilities "for a real democracy." Hutchins Hapgood

thought that the presentation revealed the "creative and instinctive feelings of the mass," and writer George Cram Cook saw a union of "drama and real life." The pageant was, Cook reported, a "successful strike weapon" because it was "an imaginative success." Most importantly the performance demonstrated to him that art could have a "shaping influence" on "social life."[31] But the makeshift alliance of art and politics resulted in propaganda that could not determine the final outcome. The pageant had the effect of a pep rally; it generated a momentary sense of togetherness, but it could not produce a victory. The majority of spectators were members of the working class who contributed emotional, not monetary support. The pageant raised excessive expectations among the strikers. When these hopes were not fulfilled, the strikers suffered a disheartening letdown, which made it more difficult to maintain the picket lines.

Understandably the Villagers responded to the Paterson strike with a project that utilized their artistic skills. In concentrating their efforts on a pageant, Village rebels revealed their reluctance to involve themselves in day-to-day struggles; they hoped to sweep away difficult socioeconomic problems with a dramatic gesture. If the Village was sympathetic to the plight of the workers, it was animated by a mood of rebelliousness, symbolized by the defiant display of red lights that spelled out "I W W" on the Garden roof.[32] While the theatrical performance thrilled the Villagers, it brought no tangible benefits to the workers. The pageant lost money, depleted the strikers' emergency fund, and hastened the strike's defeat.[33]

Village involvement in the Armory Show and the Paterson strike required a minimal amount of time and energy, allowing Villagers to enjoy a rebellion that others had set in motion. The confrontation with respectability and the clamor of controversy exhilarated them. Partaking in these events dramatized their differences with conventional society and enhanced the notoriety of a bohemian style. The Village wanted to alarm polite circles by giving the impression that these revolts marked the beginning of a cultural explosion. To be in league with the forces of upheaval reassured Village rebels that they were the vanguard setting the values of a new society.

The adverse outcome at Paterson, which helped destroy the I. W. W. in the East, dampened Village enthusiasm for working-class disputes. Although *The Masses* continued to report on violent strikes and to damn capitalist magnates, Paterson was the high-water mark of Village participation in industrial strife. With the onset of war in Europe and the demise of international socialism, it became increasingly more difficult to anticipate a revolution. Accordingly, Villagers turned inward, focusing on group activities and each other.

In his historical sketch of Greenwich Village, Floyd Dell considered the establishment of a new club at 137 MacDougal Street crucial to the formation of a bohemian community.[34] Its founder was Henrietta Rodman, an English teacher and outspoken champion of equal rights for women. Henrietta belonged to the Liberal Club, an organization of genteel reformers, philanthropists, and middle-class progressives that met in a clubhouse on Nineteenth Street to discuss advanced issues of the day.[35] Henrietta herself became a topic of discussion when news of her marriage to blond-bearded Herman de Fremery, a former French medical student who worked at the American Museum of Natural History, appeared on the front page of the *New York Tribune*. Henrietta was a controversial figure because she had publicly urged female teachers to protect themselves from dismissal by concealing their marital status. Club members were not scandalized by her deception; they objected to her choice of de Fremery, who had been living out of wedlock with Village poet Grace Norton for eight years. Angered by their narrow-mindedness, Henrietta led her supporters (among them, Hutchins Hapgood, Mary Heaton Vorse, and Lincoln Steffens) out of chic Gramercy Park to a brownstone building south of Washington Square where she established a new Liberal Club, which became the center of bohemian life.

An ardent feminist of "compact figure" and "serious dark eyes," Henrietta took to wearing sack dresses, cropped hair, brown socks, and sandals. This costume became the fashion for those Village women who wished to flaunt their disdain for dress codes. Her sixth-floor apartment at 42 Bank Street became famous for spaghetti and wine dinners, which were served to curtail expenses and defy middle-class cuisine. That Henrietta became a notable figure in the community was emblematic of Village bohemianism, for the participants esteemed defiant gestures and emancipated women. Hutchins Hapgood maintained that "when the world began to change, the restlessness of women was the main cause of the development called Greenwich Village."[36]

In describing Henrietta's role in the formation of a bohemian community, Dell emphasized her ability to bring diverse groups together in Greenwich Village:

There had always been tiny cliques and groups of artists and writers, mutually indifferent or secretly suspicious of each other. Henrietta Rodman was in touch with the university crowd, and the social settlement crowd, and the Socialist crowd; and it was these, many of whom never actually lived in the Village, who, mixing with the literary and artistic crowds in the Liberal Club, gave the Village, a new character entirely.[37]

Henrietta Rodman was not alone in knowing individuals from various cliques. Artists, writers, social workers, and radicals met one another at socialist meetings, feminist rallies, anarchist balls, and local cafés. The Brevoort Hotel on the corner of Eighth Street and Fifth Avenue provided an Old World atmosphere for patrons who ate in the restaurant or drank at the basement bar. The game room of the Lafayette Hotel on University Place was "an after-dinner place for coffee and liqueurs and games and conversation."[38] Many preferred the less expensive, ethnic places: Enrico's, Baroni's, and Mama Bertelotti's, on Third Street under the Sixth Avenue Elevated, which served fifteen-cent lunches. Rebellious women accompanied men to the Golden Swan Saloon, commonly called the "Hell Hole" (at the intersection of Sixth Avenue and Fourth Street) or Luke O'Connor's bar, facetiously referred to as the "Working Girl's Home," where Villagers mingled with truck drivers, stevedores, prostitutes, and petty criminals.[39]

But the Liberal Club became the most important meeting place for fun-loving rebels who lived in the Village or elsewhere in the city. A private establishment for bohemians, the Club occupied two large parlors and a sunroom on the first floor of a former family residence. Below it was the Greenwich Village Inn, a homey basement café owned and operated by Paula (Polly) Holladay, a refugee from Evanston, Illinois. A quiet, slender blonde, Polly provided simple meals and easy credit for her bohemian customers. Polly was accepted in bohemian circles, Harry Kemp explained, because "in the creation of her unique little restaurant she had achieved art; she had hit upon her right form of expression."[40]

Polly's waiter and sometime lover was Hippolyte Havel, a mustachioed, bespectacled anarchist who once lived with Emma Goldman and contributed to her journal, *Mother Earth*. With a shock of disorderly black hair, Havel looked like a "gypsy from the real Bohemia of the old world," which he was. Having a violent tongue and a jealous temperament, Havel was generally in a state of vituperative excitement, alternately directing his hostility at the "God damned bourgeois," at competitors for Polly's affection, and at Polly herself. His immersion in Village activities reflected a loss of fervor for radical politics. "To drink much and often" had become his code of honor, a practice curtailed only by limited financial resources.[41]

The Liberal Club and Polly's Inn served as headquarters for writers, artists, and the "smattering of lawyers, newspapermen, and publishers who lived in the Village."[42] The Club was a focal point for Village coteries, and it provided a place where out-of-town artists and writers could go when they visited New York. On inviting H. L. Mencken to come up from Baltimore, poet Louis Untermeyer told him: "If you'd like to see New York's Latin quarter and O. Henry's abomination at its most devilish, we'll take you to the Liberal Club—the most energetically wicked freeloving den in Greenwich Village."[43] But the famous were more likely

Costume dance at Liberal Club in March, 1916. Left to right: Maurice Becker, Mary Davies, unidentified woman, K. R. Chamberlain, Rose Richmond, and Glenn Coleman in his favorite party costume. Private collection of K. R. Chamberlain.

to receive a warm reception than the unknown. When Randolph Bourne, a latecomer to the Village, ventured into the Club in January, 1915, he felt "lost in that wilderness of people . . . whose exterior appeal [was] certainly not excessive." There was, he told a friend, one young woman I warmed up to, but she froze me and began to run over a catalogue of her college friends with a neighboring man. Most of the people look as if life had knocked them around a bit, and they were trying to forget it; it took so much of their energy to be radical that they had no time left for the life of irony.[44]

There were also hazards for those who had acquaintances in the Village. Harry Kemp was reluctant to take a "new girl" to Polly's because he did not want to give "the gang food for gossip"; furthermore, if his escort was pretty, his male "friends were sure to linger about till they forced the introduction they sought."[45]

Villagers ate on Polly's "gayly-painted" tables and then everyone, except those who stayed behind to play poker around a high table in the kitchen, trooped upstairs to the Club. While poetry and one-act plays were read on occasion, bohemians gathered mainly to argue about socialism, Freud, and the relative merits of free verse, to meet friends, drink tea, and initiate romances. The Liberal Club advertised itself as a "meeting place for those interested in new ideas," but Lawrence Langner, a patent attorney with theatrical interests, remembered that few discussions "survived the onslaught of the electric piano," which hammered out "the popular music of the day." As Langner clutched his partner and swayed to syncopated rhythms on the crowded dance floor, he felt that he was "doing something for the progress of humanity."[46] Dancing to ragtime melodies was bold but not truly avant-garde, unless one drew the comparison (as Villagers did) with uptowners moving at arm's length to slow waltzes. By 1913, however, the turkey trot and the bunny hug had become so popular in dance halls and "tea trotteries" that New York City officials attempted (unsuccessfully) to curb dance steps respectable opinion considered immoral.[47] In the rebellion against social mores, celebrated as part of the bohemian revolution, Villagers were sometimes indistinguishable from other young people who affronted conventional sensibilities.

Late in 1912, Mabel Dodge, a thirty-four-year-old woman of wealth and leisure, arrived in New York City from Europe and rented a large, second-floor apartment at 23 Fifth Avenue. She immediately redecorated the rooms because she considered household interiors an embodiment of her aesthetic tastes and an extension of her personality. Determined to obliterate all traces of Victorian drabness, she painted the walls white, covered the windows with white linen drapes, and hung a venetian porcelain chandelier. To soften the overpowering brightness, she added "pale blue silk and velvet" couches, delicate French chairs, "chaises longues upholstered in gray-blues and pale yellows," colored glass, and two "turquoise-blue paintings."[48] Then she was satisfied with her effort to blot out the "ugly" city and its "grubby" inhabitants.

With the completion of the interior decorating, Mabel became listless and "quite definitely ill." These symptoms afflicted her whenever she was bored and unhappy. Having no special talents or interests, and spared the necessity of earning a livelihood, she occupied her time by collecting people. None were available until she met music critic Carl Van Vechten and journalist Hutchins Hapgood. They introduced her to journalists, artists, and radicals who began to animate her "lifeless rooms."[49]

In the third volume of her published autobiography, *Intimate Memories,* Mabel recalled that the rebels of New York were splintered into various factions whose contact with each other was irregular:

> It was very confusing to me that though they were all part of one picture, they were so jumbled and scattered that they never made a discernible pattern; they were in groups that did not meet, yet in each of these groups would be found one or more who had some contact with those in other groups.[50]

Eager to consolidate these rebels under "one roof," she decided to make her apartment the center of avant-garde life.

Born in 1879, Mabel was the only child of a loveless marriage between Charles and Sara Ganson. Her father, the idle son of a rich Buffalo banker, and her mother, an "obstinate, unloving" woman, lived together in a state of mutual hostility. Mabel was never certain if her father worked or what he did. After a morning visit to town, he invariably returned home and spent the afternoon locked in his room. Irascible and eccentric, he collected national flags as a hobby and had a personal flag with his monogram C.F.G. on it. With the arrival of a foreign dignitary in Buffalo, Charles would hoist the appropriate flag on a pole in the front yard. On those occasions when his wife stayed with her mother, he would run up his flag and keep it flying "all the time she was away." On the day of her return, he would lower it to half-mast.[51]

Growing up in a household that had few connections with public life, Mabel came to assume that existence revolved around interpersonal clashes. She witnessed numerous confrontations between her parents in which her father angrily vented his frustration. Whenever Charles flew into one of his rages, Sara ignored him with "cold, merciless, expressionless contempt behind her book or newspaper." Mabel recalled:

> My father would shout and fling his arms about and his face would seem to
> break up into fragments from the running passion in him, but my mother
> behaved as though she were not alive, and when he could shout no more
> he would stamp out of the room and mount the stairs and presently we
> would hear his door slam far away in the house. Sometimes, then she
> would raise her eyes from the pretense of reading and, . . . would glance
> at me sideways and . . . would grimace a little message of very thin re-
> assurance to me.[57]

Mabel "tried to imitate" that pose and model herself after her mother,
who kept busy "ordering" her household, "controlling the servants," and
subjugating the man of the house. It was a skill and a preoccupation that
became Mabel's forte.

As compensation for emotional deprivation, Mabel received anything
she desired from her parents. But material advantages did not offset the
emptiness of fashionable society. Mabel and her girl friends amused
themselves by gossiping and prying into one another's secrets. Because
of the silence which surrounded sex, it became their favorite topic of
conversation. In time, Mabel learned that sex could be used to conquer
others, women as well as men.

Soon after her "coming-out" ball, Mabel met Karl Evans, a frivolous
young man from a well-to-do family. Although Karl was already engaged
to someone else, she decided to capture him, even though he meant
nothing to her. Mabel admitted later that she had no qualms about this
selfish intrusion:

> I never had any feelings of the validity of personal claims and anything
> I wanted and could get seemed to be mine. Since I could get it, it became
> mine. This made people feel I was an outlaw of love and they started
> early enough to call me a pirate and a 'home breaker.' This never troubled
> me, for it only seemed to testify to my power, which I was forever feed-
> ing.[53]

An attractive woman with full figure, "pretty eyes," and a "lovely voice,"
Mabel persuaded Karl to break his engagement and pursue her, which he
did, "like a deer in rutting season." Once she had conquered him,
however, she "didn't need him any more."[54] Nevertheless, rebelling
against her father's explicit instructions, she married Karl in 1900.

The newlyweds were soon bored with each other. Mabel, who was
pregnant, remained at home while Karl was off motorboating or hunting.
Then, shortly after the birth of a child, Karl was killed in a hunting accident. When Mabel subsequently suffered a "nervous breakdown," her
mother sent her to Europe for a rest cure. On board the steamer she met

Edwin Dodge, a Boston architect of independent means and easy disposition. Dodge became enamoured with this widow and her young son, John. After a wedding in Paris, they honeymooned in Biarritz and then rented a villa on the French Riveria. But Mabel was not interested in the luxurious surroundings or in her new husband. Even though Edwin obeyed her explicit instructions, Mabel decided that she "really hated men."[55]

After a somewhat more pleasant stay in the Alps, the young couple moved to Florence and bought the Villa Curonia, a magnificent grey stone mansion surrounded by formal gardens and cypress trees. While Edwin applied his architectural training to structural renovations, Mabel spent lavish sums on antique furniture, paintings, and knickknacks. She wanted "*grandeur*" and "knew quite well the kind of queen [she] wanted to be" and the "type of royal residence" in which she would reside.[56] After exhausting her interest in artifacts, Mabel summoned visitors, particularly artists and writers who completed her aesthetic production. She was overjoyed when Gertrude Stein, one of her guests, wrote a piece entitled *Portrait of Mabel Dodge at Villa Curonia*.[57] Although it said nothing recognizable about herself or the villa, Mabel had three hundred copies printed and distributed them to her many acquaintances.

The "odd, uprooted" expatriates who lived on the hills around Florence provided another source of amusement. Mabel became entangled in the "bickering intrigues" and "secrets" that produced a "highly charged human atmosphere." She added to the tension by flirting with other men, a practice mainly intended to make Edwin jealous. Later she recounted:

> These different men who desired me and had never been able to overcome me, contributed to the feeling of life I enjoyed, . . . noting the magnetism that I exhaled like a perfume, something tangible like the musk of an animal, and irresistibly attractive to at least three of the men in my neighborhood. It seemed to me, as a substitute for love, the ascendancy over the desires of others was a good one. And, I thought, probably lasted longer.[58]

Except for a flirtation with a French girl, in whom she "lighted a little fire," Mabel was "faithful" to Edwin. She liked to stimulate others so as to feel the "strong draught of human fire blowing" upon her, but she wanted power, not sex.[59]

Mabel was an unhappy person. A lonely woman who hated to be alone, she was nonetheless unable to build lasting friendships because personal relations were always a struggle for supremacy. Whomever she yoked she used for her own purposes, all the while hating those who

Mabel Dodge in the blue bedroom of the Villa Curonia. Yale University Library.

yielded to her demands. She wanted to dominate and yet longed to be dominated. She praised spontaneity, but lived in environments she controlled. She longed for unusual experiences to relieve her ennui and yet was thwarted by a debilitating preoccupation with herself.

Late in 1912 Mabel returned to America in order to place John in a boarding school and rid herself of Edwin, who had become "only the figurehead on [her] ship."[60] Convinced that he stood between her and a "new fire of life," she engineered a separation. With Edwin out of the way, she acquired new admirers and launched her career as patroness of the avant-garde.

What began as a series of parties soon evolved into a salon where weekly "Evenings" brought "all sorts of people" together in Mabel's apartment. She assembled upper-class nonconformists, middle-class reformers, Villagers, journalists, critics, artists, editors, feminists, labor leaders, and political radicals for discussions about unconventional topics. The participants included Hutchins Hapgood, Carl Van Vechten, Lincoln Steffens, John Collier, Neith Boyce, Janet Scudder, Arthur Lee, Justus Sheffield, Avery Hopwood, Jack and Helen Westley, Walter Lippmann, Amos Pinchot, Mary Austin, Margaret Sanger, William English Walling, Max Eastman, Ida Rauh, Mary Heaton Vorse, Lee Simonson, Andrew Dasburg, Robert Edmond Jones, Hippolyte Havel, Donald Evans, Bayard Boyesen, Marsden Hartley, and Harry Kemp.[61] In addition, guests were invited to discuss controversial issues or introduce new ideas. In his fictional account, *Peter Whiffle,* Carl Van Vechten described the social diversity of the gatherings:

> All the chairs were filled; many were sitting on the floor or standing against the wall or in the doorways; ladies in black velvet, wearing diamonds, ladies with bobbed hair and mannish-cut garments, men in evening dress, men in workmen's clothes.[62]

The location of Mabel's apartment on the edge of the Village symbolized and facilitated the salon's function: to bring together rebels from various strata and create a vanguard.

Mabel remained mysteriously silent at the "Evenings." Dressed in a long, white gown, she assumed the role of a benign queen, giving each person her hand and "a very small smile." In choosing the topic of discussion or the "specialist" who expounded his views, she exercised control over the salon. Later she boasted that she "always decided more or less the *kind* of Evening we would have."[63] Directing the action behind the scenes, Mabel satisfied her will to power as she watched her "wonderful new game" unfold.[64] Animated by her success, she wrote to Gertrude Stein in Paris: "Life in New York is one long-protracted thrill. You must spend next winter here and be the fashion."[65]

The "Evenings" had no ideological uniformity or continuity; whatever was fashionably rebellious became the subject of discussion. Mabel would, Lincoln Steffens reported, seize a time when there was an I.W.W. strike to invite, say, Bill Haywood especially. He would sit or stand near her and strike out, in the hot, harsh spirit of his organization, some challenging idea, answer brutally a few questions, and—that evening everybody talked I.W.W.[66]

Mabel summoned Wobblies, psychiatrists, socialists, anarchists, feminists, and others with shocking notions to the salon. The opportunity to speak out on daring topics reinforced a belief that the participants were radicals. Intellectual discussion was, however, less important than stirring up passions and quarrels. Max Eastman noted that arousing emotions was habit forming and that Mabel was somehow responsible for the confrontations:

> She has neither wit nor beauty, nor is she vivacious or lively minded or entertaining. . . . [But] there is something going on, or going around, in Mabel's head or bosom, something that creates a magnetic field in which people become polarized and pulled in and made to behave very queerly. Their passions become exacerbated; they grow argumentative; they have quarrels, difficulties, entanglements, abrupt and violent detachments. And they like it—they come back for more.[67]

Eastman's remarks indicate that the salon was addicted to polemics. Mabel wanted it that way. She delighted in fomenting conflicts and the "Evenings" allowed her to manipulate people as artfully as she arranged her furniture. One night she juxtaposed anarchists Emma Goldman, Alexander Berkman, Hippolyte Havel, and Bill Haywood with William English Walling, a socialist intellectual and Walter Lippmann. But, Mabel recalled, the "Evening was not successful."[68] Haywood and Goldman failed to live up to form and there was "no quickening of vibration." At another gathering, however, Haywood produced the friction she wanted. He predicted that in the future there would only be proletarian art and everyone would become an artist. Nettled by his remarks, sculptress Janet Scudder told Haywood hotly that it took twenty years to become an artist. Mabel considered the "Scudder-Haywood Evening" a success:

> Bill [Haywood] was at his best, with [Andrew] Dasburg flashing and witty, and Arthur Lee, with terrific earnestness, trying to pound out his somewhat reluctant thoughts, and others cutting in, several talking at once, until in the end, we really had General Conversation and the air was vibrant . . . electrical.[69]

On another occasion Mabel invited Carl Hovey and Will Bradley, editors of the *Metropolitan Magazine,* to meet with free-lance artists who submitted drawings to them. Illustrator Maurice Becker, "hair on end, shook his trembling finger at the quaking" Bradley and accused him of exploiting poor artists. Mabel enjoyed watching Bradley grow "pale and cower" before this assault. Becker "let himself go," Mabel thought, because of her protection, and she "asked nothing better than the kind of reality he could provide." Although the salon was supposed to encourage an exchange of ideas and opinions, Mabel was more interested in having her guests tell "each other what they thought of *each other.*"[70] When they did, she relived the violent arguments she had witnessed as a child.

Mabel wanted to associate with radicals society considered dangerous. She assumed that she was "playing with dynamite" entertaining Haywood, Goldman, and their confederates. They plotted, she knew,

and planned and discussed times and places. Their obvious activity seemed to be publishing the anarchist magazine, *Mother Earth,* but beneath this there was a great busy humming complex of Planning; and many times they referred to the day when blood would flow in the streets of New York.[71]

Since the anarchists were actually a nonviolent group, Mabel was indulging in fantasies. Harboring a strong adversion for American society, she took pleasure in imagining the havoc conspirators would wreak someday.

If the participants sensed that Mabel manipulated them, they lodged no objections. Lincoln Steffens argued that Mabel "managed her evenings, and no one felt that they were managed."[72] When she left town late in 1913, the "Evenings" slumped, a sign that her machinations were indispensable. Van Vechten wrote to her that "the party at your house last Thursday . . . was a dull affair. Somewhere about the middle of it Hutch [ins Hapgood] arises and says, with authority, 'This will be the last of these meetings until Mrs. Dodge returns.' "[73] Although Steffens blamed the deterioration on "certain people" who came "not to listen to the talks but to eat and drink," he agreed with Hapgood that Mabel was essential for a successful "Evening."[74] Steffens wrote to her:

Neith [Boyce] and I and a few others decided during the last [session] that we'd hold no more till you returned. It was simply that we felt that we needed you to keep up the interest. We didn't care to risk it by ourselves.[75]

Mabel, was, Van Vechten observed, "the amalgam which held the incongruous group together."[76] She could provide a steady supply of outrageous visitors, unconventional ideas, and spirited arguments.

While Mabel's forum allowed socialities to mingle with radicals, the sessions were more social than intellectual. Although one topic was supposed to be discussed at each meeting, the participants simply aired their views without attempting to resolve their differences. Margaret Sanger, a proselytiser of free love and birth control, commented that "in the end, conversations were nil; all were convinced either for or against, and I never knew them to shift ground."[77] Not only were opinions unaltered and insights unassimilated, but talk sometimes revolved around incomprehensible subjects. Carl Van Vechten described the night when "a little school-marm type of person" asked those present if anyone could give an explanation of a cubist painting "that a mere lay woman could understand." Her request was greeted with "a ripple of amused laughter among the young artists and a rigid exchange of glances." After two participants attempted to enlighten her (one "massive lady" said she could only explain it in terms of music), the woman announced: "I don't think any one here knows anything, not a thing." She concluded that they were like the playing-card characters in Alice's Wonderland, only "a lot of flat plasterboards with kings, queens, aces and deuces painted" on their faces.[78]

Villagers uncritically accepted movements and activities that signified a rebellion against traditional standards. They thought that the Armory Show, the Paterson strike pageant, and Mabel's "Evenings" were events of cultural, if not revolutionary significance. Mabel compared her salon to Picasso's paintings and Gertrude Stein's writings, insisting that her guests were discovering new limits of experience and fresh perspectives on life. While ordinary people relaxed in "cozy" conservatism, salon votaries were, she argued, "*feeling* [their] way toward the truth of tomorrow."[79] Mabel and her friends assumed that emotional expression was the basis of achievement. They failed to realize the amount of work and discipline that went into a modern painting or a strike.

Although Villagers subscribed to the ill-defined idea of revolution, they mainly were interested in improving the quality of people's private lives. They proposed to free art and literature from outmoded standards, to free sexuality from puritanical practices, to liberate women from domesticity, and to liberate children from authoritarian teachers and rote learning. Abstract painter Max Weber told a group at Mabel's that raising the level of "art consciousness" would "sooner solve the great modern economic problem than any labour propaganda."[80] Hutchins Hapgood thought that Bee Shostac, who was a teacher by day and Bill Haywood's mistress by night, contributed to "the final disintegration of the community" by living a "double life." Ignoring social realities and the power of institutions, Villagers advanced cultural and sexual solutions to political and economic problems. Given their isolation and their lack of sustained involvement in radical groups or reformist organizations, Villagers proposed utopian suggestions, not practical programs. Mabel Dodge perhaps captured the spirit of bohemian radicalism in her characterization of Hutchins Hapgood. He was, she noted, "in revolt, but his acts were never very dangerous. . . . Talking was his principal outlet—so he talked and talked, always advocating resistance to authority."[81]

Mabel dabbled in revolutionary causes. She moved from one radical scheme to another with a deftness altogether flighty, though on that score she was not alone. From the time of her arrival in New York until the denouement of her love affair with John Reed, she became involved in numerous projects, but always to gratify personal needs. Alternating between manic and depressed moods, she only sought a "little bit" of people and causes, just "enough to color" her life.[82] She became involved in the Armory Show because she thought that the exhibition expressed her revolt against conventional society. Interest in John Reed caused her to assume an active role in the Paterson strike pageant. When she wrote Gertrude Stein about the strike, she commented unabashedly that there was "no news to speak of except [I am] in revolutionary circles here. Am working on the . . . pageant scheme, and see only red now."[83]

Mabel Dodge became famous in avant-garde circles although she was neither an artist nor a radical. Sculptor Jo Davidson recalled that when he read Gertrude Stein's *Portrait of Mabel Dodge* aloud at Mouquin's restaurant "the reactions were various." Some thought the work was "well-meaning nonsense. Others read into it esoteric significance." Regardless of their reaction to Stein's writing, "the name of Mabel Dodge was on everybody's lips."[84] Mabel had money, patronized the arts and radical causes, and established a successful salon. No one questioned the depth of her commitment to art or politics, and no one objected when she arrived at the pageant in a chauffeur-driven limousine. Carl Van Vechten wrote to her: "Greenwich Village stands aghast at your performance. Somebody who has really done something is too much for the villagers. Admiration mixed with awe describes them."[85] She was perhaps correct in concluding that her aloofness gave "people's imagination a chance to fabricate their own Mabel Dodge, . . . attributing to her all kinds of faculties and powers."[86] In valuing intuition over reason, she touched a responsive chord amongst those who acclaimed expressiveness as the most important trait. Her emancipated mode of living and the notoriety of the salon placed her among the avant-garde. Carl Van Vechten thought she was a pacesetter who could foretell, if not set, the coming fashions. He asked her: "The present question is WHAT is to dominate New York this Fall? It may be the [Leon] Bakst exhibition but how shall I know until you arrive and shed the searching light of your interest on what booms biggest?"[87]

Mabel's organizational ability impressed those who lacked such talents. When asking her assistance in assembling a finance committee, journalist Joe O'Brien told Mabel: "You have somehow the magic of making people come to committee meetings, which is a rare gift."[88] She also had, O'Brien knew, connections with wealthy benefactors. Moreover, she was a celebrity and *ad hoc* groups sought to link her name with their projects. Socialist Upton Sinclair pleaded with her to attend one of his political meetings: "You need only come for half an hour, and the reporters will print anything you say."[89]

The cynosure of rebellion, Mabel's role exceeded that of a famous patroness. A considerable number of Village men became attached to her. Carl Van Vechten, Max Weber, Robert E. Jones, Marsden Hartley, Bayard Boyesen, and Donald Evans sought her out as their confidante, and Hutchins Hapgood, John Reed, Arthur Lee, Andrew Dasburg, and Maurice Sterne fell in love with her. She cultivated friendships and encouraged intimate relationships because she liked to subdue men and include them in her entourage. Mabel had "learned very early to talk to people only of the things they knew about and liked," and she played the coquette with extraordinary skill.[90] She expressed interest in the work of artists, involved herself in personal difficulties, and conveyed a sense of enthusiasm. At lunch one day she overheard Van Vechten say to Hapgood: "That woman will drive me crazy, Hutch. She accelerates the tempo so." "Yes," Hapgood agreed, "it's her vibration."[91]

Mabel became the subject of works by male artists. John Reed composed an "Epitaph for Mabel"; Jo Davidson wrote a poem entitled "Portrait of Mabel Dodge"; Hutchins Hapgood described her as "A Promoter of Spirit" in the *New York Globe;* Maurice Sterne attempted to paint another *Mona Lisa* from Mabel; sculptor Arthur Lee used his wife, Freddie, to model the *Adoration of Mabel Dodge,* a figure on her knees with head bowed to the ground; and Donald Evans, a copyreader on the *New York Times* and a poet, composed a sonnet about her and contemplated ninety-nine more.[92] On discovering that Mabel had left the city, Andrew Dasburg poured out his disappointment by painting an abstract conception of *The Absence of Mabel Dodge.* It was, Mabel reported, "all a flare of thin flames with forked lightning in them and across the bottom of this holocaust, three narrow black, black, black bars." Mabel then asked Marsden Hartley to send a description of the painting to Reed. In this way she could maximize her pleasure by having three men thinking about her simultaneously. Finally, Mabel hung the painting in her apartment, and "there it burned in front of everyone" to her immense satisfaction.[93]

These works of art reflected a social narcissism in which Villagers wrote about, painted, or sculptured each other. In his long poem, *A Day in Bohemia* (or *Life among the Artists)*, John Reed described his friends and their antics in Greenwich Village. He penned "A Dedication" in *The Masses* to Max Eastman, who in turn wrote a novel, *Venture* (1926), in which the hero was a fictionalized Reed. Poet Harry Kemp extolled Reed's arrest in Paterson, and Mabel Dodge composed a poem, "My Beloved," for Hutchins Hapgood. Donald Evans's *Sonnets from the Patagonia* consisted of poetic portraits of his friends, and Carl Van Vechten characterized Mabel and salon participants in his book, *Peter Whiffle*. Max Eastman published a paean to feminist Inez Milholland while Floyd Dell wrote poems, plays, and short stories about himself and his loves.

Mabel's importance among Village rebels stemmed from her capacity to fulfill the needs of those who lived in the Village setting. She recalled how "everyone seemed to fumble and feel uncertain a good deal of the time, blind and unable to look ahead."[94] These struggling artists and uncertain rebels had chosen to step outside conventional institutions and socially-imposed roles. The difficulty in attaining self-definition in bohemia explains in part why mutual reinforcement, with its destructive and constructive consequences, was so important. To men who wondered about their talents and whose lives lacked stability, Mabel seemed to offer reassurance, sympathy, and security. Lincoln Steffens told her: "You attract, stimulate, and soothe people, and men like to sit with you and talk to *themselves*."[95] Maurice Sterne, a Latvian-born painter, was drawn to Mabel because she appeared so "fearless about life" and so decisive about what she wanted. He willingly delivered himself to her: "For the first time I could relax, rest my will, and do what someone else decided was best. It was a period when my own self-confidence had shrunk to zero."[96]

With her sexual lure, guile, and forcefulness, Mabel extracted secret anxieties and cultivated male dependencies, both financial and psychological. Those who leaned on her, however, paid a price and sometimes it was costly. Hapgood tried to warn Sterne about her:

She really is a witch. That woman has supernatural powers. She is insanely jealous. The only way she can be sure of a man is by castrating him. Since she must be the sole possessor and cannot make him impotent towards others only, she makes him impotent toward all.[97]

She demanded submission to her wishes. In Sterne's case she insisted that he give up painting, which he did for a while. She was, he came to realize later, bent on "first destroying completely, and then creating a new, synthetic being."[98]

The abortive end of Mabel's romance with John Reed, the only lover she never subjugated and therefore wanted, was a tremendous disappointment to her. She dropped her radical pose and moved to Croton-on-Hudson, a small village north of New York City, where she maintained a more tenuous connection with Greenwich Village. She surrounded herself with a small retinue and commenced an affair with Maurice Sterne. This romance proved no more satisfying than the others, and she alternately sent him away and brought him back. As always she tried to involve others in her private life, using Hapgood, Leo Stein, and Walter Lippmann as her advisors. Then she turned to psychoanalysts Smith Ely Jelliffe and Abraham A. Brill, whom she paid to listen to her misfortunes. For a while psychoanalysis was "an absorbing game to play with oneself, reading one's motives, and trying to understand the symbols by which the soul expressed itself." The sessions were entertaining, and like the salon, she introduced exciting topics "to keep the ball rolling."[99] While she did not learn much about herself, she did "get a very complete line" on Jelliffe, Bayard Boyesen, Leo Stein, and on Maurice Sterne, who, she believed, was caught "in the grip of his nervous fears and doubts."[100]

Despite her many objections to Sterne, Mabel married him in August, 1917, mainly because she had grown weary of hiding their illicit relationship. Immediately after the ceremony she became depressed and sent him off to honeymoon by himself in Taos, New Mexico. When Sterne told her of a need to "save the Indians" and their "art-culture," Mabel decided to join him.[101] Soon after her arrival, however, she became enamoured with just one Indian, a stolid Pueblo named Antonio Luhan, who awakened her "to a new impulse of sex and love."[102] Concluding that Maurice was "old and spent and tragic," she renounced him and the "sick old world of art and artists."[103] Although she married Luhan and proclaimed the superiority of primitive culture, she did not embrace Indian life. Instead she moved into a new adobe mansion and filled it with French furniture, Chinese paintings, and Venetian bronzes. She then commanded Robert E. Jones and Andrew Dasburg to move to Taos, for she intended to establish a new colony of artists and writers. Nothing had changed, and she and Tony lived out their lives together in a "strange, bleak separation from each other."[104]

Whereas the Liberal Club and Mabel Dodge's salon furnished the avant-garde with places to rendezvous, *The Masses* gave artists and writers the opportunity to express themselves and reach an audience beyond the boundaries of Greenwich Village. Owned collectively by twenty contributing editors, *The Masses* published political commentary, labor news, short stories, poetry, plays, book reviews, cartoons, and drawings. The range of its coverage, reflecting the breadth of Village interests, showed that the editors aspired to become the cultural vanguard in America. *The Masses* was to be, Inez Haynes Gillmore explained to Mary Heaton Vorse, an "experiment of turning out a magazine that should stand for socialism and yet be artistic, from every point of view."[105] Since everyone assumed that radical politics was compatible with artistic creativity, no one considered the possible conflict between an ideological commitment and an uninhibited imagination.

When Piet Vlag, a Dutch socialist and manager of the Rand School's cafeteria, launched *The Masses* in January, 1911, he enlisted the help of Art Young, John Sloan, writers Inez Haynes Gillmore and Eugene Wood, poet Louis Untermeyer, and artist Maurice Becker.[106] Originally a political journal dedicated to co-operative socialism, *The Masses* survived under Vlag's leadership until the summer of 1912 when Rufus Weeks, a vice-president of the New York Life Insurance Company, terminated his financial backing. Vlag proposed to move the journal to Chicago, but the contributing editors wanted to keep it in New York. They selected Max Eastman, a philosophy instructor at Columbia University and a campaigner for women's rights, as the new editor in chief. The successful completion of his first assignment, raising money from wealthy benefactors, insured Eastman's retention of the editorship.

Under Eastman's direction *The Masses* existed from December, 1912, until November, 1917, when the federal government suppressed it for criticizing American war policies. *The Masses* was a ten-cent, monthly magazine consisting of twenty-five large pages. (In June, 1916, its size was increased to roughly thirty-five pages and the price was raised to fifteen cents.) With its colorful, artistic covers, two-column format, cartoons, sketches, political commentary, poetry, and literary works, *The Masses* presented a striking, lively contrast to other "little magazines."

In December, 1912, Eastman reported in his first editorial that *The Masses* had five thousand regular subscribers and that between three and five thousand copies were sold at newsstands, particularly in metropolitan New York. Although the circulation eventually rose to an average of fourteen thousand copies per month,*The Masses* was not self-sufficient. It depended on various sources of income: patronage, earnings from Eastman's nationwide speaking tour in 1916, and the profits from costume balls held at Webster Hall on Eleventh Street just west of Third Avenue. These dances, which copied a practice begun by the Liberal Club, provided festive occasions when boldly costumed Villagers drank, danced, and romanced until dawn. In advertising Greenwich Village as a place of "pagan revelling," however, the balls attracted those who were mainly interested in greater social and sexual freedom for themselves.

Although there were nonresident contributors, *The Masses* was dominated by Villagers, particularly Eastman, Floyd Dell, John Reed, and John Sloan. Theoretically open to all artistic and political dissenters, entries (articles, poems, stories, cartoons, and drawings) were chosen at fortnightly meetings by democratic voting. Initially, when enthusiasm and interest were high, this practice was followed even though it generated friction, particularly between artists and writers who passed judgment on each other's work. Writer Mary Heaton Vorse remembered that the meetings, which were often held in her house, produced "clamor and strife." She recalled how "horrible" it was to have one's writings "torn to bits by the artists":

> Floyd Dell would read the contribution aloud without telling the author's name. It might be the work of an outsider, or it might come from one of the editors. As Floyd read along, Sloan would give a groan. Boardman Robinson would look bored behind his red beard. A voice would say, 'Oh, my God, Max, do we have to listen to this tripe?'
>
> Voices would clamor, 'Cut it out!' Floyd would go on. . . . The poor author would feel more and more like a worm. You could see him looking wildly around to see if there was any means of a swift exit.[107]

This practice was discontinued when Eastman and Dell came to exercise the greatest influence over standards and selection. The editors, therefore, could not prevent the appearance of "bourgeois" authoritarianism, a condition that they had intended to abolish.

In time, artists became incensed that Dell and Eastman placed captions under their drawings and used them for political purposes. The literary editors in turn were annoyed that the artists caused a "much greater stir than the writers." Eastman, who contributed political commentary and romantic poetry, felt that the reading public neglected the excellent work of the writers. On one occasion Eastman congratulated Louis Untermeyer for "Any City," a poem decrying the callousness of lustful men who used streetwalkers: "I've read your poem in the July *Masses* again and again. . . . If anybody now says that our graphic art excels the art of that poem he's a damned fool. That poem justifies our aim."[108] Eastman's "aim" was to reform society and he mainly wanted poetry, stories, and pictorial work that railed against social injustice and middle class hypocrisy. But the dissenting artists (John Sloan, Maurice

Becker, Stuart Davis, and Glenn Coleman) disliked the arbitrary manner in which Eastman relegated their work to the level of propaganda. Moreover, they resented the fact that Eastman and Dell received a salary (thirty-five and twenty-five dollars a week, respectively), whereas they earned nothing for their efforts.

The conflict finally broke into the open in March, 1916. John Sloan, the leader of the protesting artists, had increasingly become disillusioned with socialism and dissatisfied with Eastman's leadership. Although Sloan had contributed political drawings and cartoons, he wished to reassert his independence as an artist and create "human interest" pictures. He proposed that the positions of editor and managing editor be abolished and that artists choose the art work.[109] Eastman and Dell refused to comply with that request, and cartoonist Art Young attacked the dissenters for merely wanting to "run pictures of ash cans and girls hitching up their skirts in Horatio Street."[110] When Eastman collected enough proxy votes to defeat the proposal, Sloan, Davis, Coleman, and Becker resigned; their places were taken by cartoonists Boardman Robinson and Robert Minor who willingly produced political propaganda.[111]

In spite of their failure to maintain a democratic organization, the watchword of The Masses was freedom. The editors wanted to free the workers from economic exploitation, to free believers from hypocritical churches, to free prostitutes from ravenous men, to free women from second-class citizenship, to free society from Victorian prudery, and to free artists and writers from commercial journalism. Compiled and printed in the offices on Greenwich Avenue, The Masses afforded their contributors the opportunity to express themselves without catering to public tastes or publishers' pocketbooks. Joining the staff early in 1913, journalist John Reed proclaimed their outlook and intention:

> The broad purpose of The Masses is a social one: to everlastingly attack old systems, old morals, old prejudices—the whole weight of outworn thought that dead men have saddled upon us—and to set up new ones in their places. . . . We intend to be arrogant, impertinent, in bad taste, but not vulgar. We will be bound by no one creed or theory of social reform, but will express them all, providing they be radical.[112]

In articulating the many currents of the Village revolt, the editors combined feminism and socialism with nude drawings and Freudian psychology. No one analyzed these different interests to see if they were compatible because The Masses took pride in its ideological diversity. Although Eastman increasingly determined policy, and politics became more important than fiction or art, there was no single overriding purpose. Attitudes and concerns varied even while everyone agreed on the necessity and benfits of "revolutionary" changes.

One target of *The Masses* was the commercial press. The attack began in Eastman's first issue when Art Young portrayed newspapermen as whores being paid off by "big advertisers," a bloated, well-dressed figure with an enormous wallet of money. Subsequently, Eastman charged that the Associated Press had suppressed the story of a West Virginia miners' strike, and Young sketched Frank B. Noyes, the A. P. president, poisoning a reservoir of news with "lies" and "prejudice." The Associated Press responded with a criminal libel suit against Eastman and Young. Although Noyes eventually dropped the charge, *The Masses* editors reveled in the uproar they caused. Young drew caricatures of himself and Eastman, and a mass rally was held in Cooper Union for the defendants.[113] In this case arousing the ire of a commercial rival overshadowed the problems of the miners. The real issue was sidetracked when *The Masses* editors personalized the conflict and drew attention to themselves. The reaction of the Associated Press pleased the editors, for they were embroiled in a confrontation with an established institution. Similarly, when Columbia University library cancelled its subscription and the firm of Ward and Gow stopped selling *The Masses* at its New York subway newsstands, the editors exulted in knowing how repugnant they were to conventional opinion. It confirmed for the artists and writers that *The Masses* was too radical for conservative respectability.

Given its limited circulation and avant-garde readership, *The Masses* was not a powerful voice in the revolutionary struggle. Art Young recalled that newspaper editor Arthur Brisbane told him: "You *Masses* boys are talking to yourselves."[114] The realization that his cartoons reached only a select audience and the need for a regular source of income prompted Young to accept a position with the *Metropolitan* magazine. Others either presumed that *The Masses* had a greater impact or were content to achieve recognition in rebel circles. Floyd Dell explained that even though *The Masses* contributors were not paid, "it was felt to be a privilege to appear in its pages."[115] Since one was honored in having material published, *The Masses* could bestow prestige on the privileged, usually the editors or those who supported their views and conformed to their expectations.

In the first issue Eastman stated: "Our appeal will be to the masses, both Socialist and non-Socialist, with entertainment, education, and the livelier kinds of propaganda."[116] Despite this declaration and its name, *The Masses* was not directed to the masses. In providing a vehicle for artistic expression and in articulating the many currents of the Village revolt, *The Masses* primarily served and spoke to educated rebels. In ad-

"Oh, I think Mr. Morgan paints awfully well, don't you?" At the Metropolitan Museum of Art. Cartoon by Stuart Davis in *The Masses* (March 1913).

vocating modern dance, nudism, feminism, and free love, the editors promoted reforms that had little chance of reaching, let alone aiding, the
working poor. Bobby Edwards, a Village troubadour, satirically asked:

They draw nude women for *The Masses*
Thick, ungainly, ugly lasses.
How does that help the working classes?[117]

The Masses did not attempt to educate the unconverted, and thus much of its material served to reinforce shared assumptions about American society. The editors supported birth control, prison reform, and progressive education; they attacked capitalist exploitation, Christian churches, and American involvement in World War I. Except for the more violent strikes, the editors did not investigate social and economic conditions. While Eastman castigated black lynchings in the South and Reed reported on the Mexican Civil War, *The Masses* generally ignored New York's urban problems and local politics.

The Masses regarded prostitution as a social evil that needed to be eradicated. The prostitute fascinated the Village because she, like the bohemian, was an outsider without social standing. Artists and writers romanticized the streetwalker as a helpless victim sacrificed to preserve propriety. They assumed that prostitution thrived under capitalism. Discharged from their jobs by heartless employers, young girls were compelled to sell themselves in order to survive. Exploitation in the factory continued in the streets. The innocent factory girl was forced to the depths of degradation, yielding her body in intimate sexual acts that should be sanctified by love. The capitalist, therefore, personified all that was hypocritical and exploitive about American society. His prestige in conventional society only increased his disrepute in bohemia.

The Masses editors believed that the emancipation of women was bound up with the struggle of the working classes. Operating at the level of ideals and extrapolating from Village experiences, the editors supported movements that promised to enhance individual freedom and produce more "fully developed, active and intelligent" females. The editors saw birth control as a reform that provided a common link between the two movements; limiting pregnancies would give women control over their bodies and would reduce the size of working-class families. That conventional authorities were opposed to these changes proved to the editors that they were on the right track.

The Masses singled out Christian churches as institutions that impeded social progress and restricted individual freedom. The editors viewed priests and ministers as servants of capitalists, preaching submissiveness to the workers and deflecting attention away from existing social problems. According to the editors, ministers were hypocrites who refused to live by the teachings of Christ. When Frank Tannenbaum, a young Jewish radical, attempted to lead a group of unemployed men into several New

He hands over the fruit of his toil on a silver platter, and then gets about one eight of the juice. Cartoon by Arthur Young in *The Masses* (July 1913).

York churches, he was turned away by the pastors. The police then arrested Tannenbaum and he was sentenced to a year in prison at Blackwell's Island.[118] This incident, which became a cause célèbre in the Village, outraged the editors, and they lambasted the churches in cartoons, poems, and editorials. To them, it proved that the clergy lacked genuine concern for the poor.

Speaking of Anarchy. Cartoon by Arthur Young in *The Masses* (June 1913).

If the editors espoused socialism and rejected religion, they were more familiar with the teachings of Jesus Christ than the gospel according to Karl Marx. Idealists, they expected individuals and institutions to abide

The Masses

DECEMBER, 1913   10 CENTS

MASSES

COMING!

'HE STIRRETH UP THE PEOPLE'

JESUS CHRIST

THE WORKINGMAN OF NAZARETH
WILL SPEAK
AT BROTHERHOOD HALL
— SUBJECT —
— THE RIGHTS OF LABOR —

Drawn by Arthur Young.

SPECIAL CHRISTMAS NUMBER

Front cover of *The Masses* (December 1913).

by Christian precepts. At bottom the artists and writers were attracted to socialism because it promised a secular reformation based on Christian ethics. Art Young's cover drawing of Jesus Christ posing as the "Workingman of Nazareth" and advocate of the "Rights of Labor" revealed a socialism that shared the moral values of Christianity.[119]

Serene Onlooker: (To the Striker) "Very unfortunate situation, but whatever you do, don't use force." Back cover of *The Masses* (March 1913).

The Masses was the moral center of Greenwich Village. It repeatedly pointed out that American society did not operate on the basis of constitutional rights and democratic premises. This attack exploited the contradiction between existing institutions and their moral antecedents. A socialist perspective fixed responsibility for society's shortcomings on the capitalists, who were caricatured as fat, greedy men with top hats and diamond stick pins. Since the editors were bent on exposing evil men and their practices, they did not sufficiently analyze institutions and explain how the social order operated. Moral earnestness encouraged didactic writing; cartoons relied on grim humor and heavy-handed captions. Given Eastman's expectation that writings and drawings express socialist realism and moral judgments, The Masses missed an opportunity to become an important medium for experimental poetry and art.

The outbreak of World War I in August, 1914, shattered the confidence of those who prized Europe's cultural heritage. The collapse of international socialism left The Masses without a movement for social change. As the editors watched and reported on the slaughter in France, they found it increasingly difficult to believe in a socialist revolution. As the war dragged on without purpose, Eastman concluded that the fighting was simply a consequence of man's hereditary nature. Therefore, he abandoned the idea of a revolutionary class struggle and supported Woodrow Wilson and a League of Nations. Infatuated by Wilson's promise of peace and his intellectual credentials, Eastman and other editors were convinced that the President would keep America neutral and would mediate a cease-fire in Europe.

Even after the American declaration of war in April, 1917, The Masses argued against the use of American troops in Europe and protested the persecution of dissenters and political radicals. But its criticism of government policies angered administration officials and The Masses became a victim of repression in November, 1917. Before the end, the editors discovered a new reason to be hopeful. The revolution in Russia seemed to hold the promise of peace and a socialist society. In the Liberator, which was founded as the successor to The Masses, Eastman, Dell, and Reed hailed the Bolshevik revolution as the beginning of a new era with Nikolai Lenin as the "statesman of the new order."

The Masses was neither an instrument of political sectarianism nor an esoteric journal. It was primarily a gadfly that scorned the powerful, ridiculed the wealthy, derided the comfortable, and sympathized with the poor. It was cynical, irreverent, simplistic, and hortatory; it tried to be shocking and often succeeded. The editors challenged conventional institutions and respectable authorities to rearrange the social order according to a more equitable standard of justice. The Masses suggested that the good society would maximize individual freedom and social equality. From within the confines of Greenwich Village, The Masses raised a cry of protest against social injustice, sexual discrimination, political repression, moral hypocrisy, and war, even if it was not heard by those who held political and economic power.

In attempting to remake society, to create avant-garde culture, and to promote and pursue a bohemian style of life, the participants of the

Liberal Club, Mabel Dodge's salon, and *The Masses* squandered their energies and shortchanged their programs. In establishing a "community" outside traditional institutions and arrangements, Villagers created a bohemia that was subject to the shifting fortunes of local fashions and external events. The distractions of a romantic existence and the depressing course of external events—the outbreak of war, the disruption of international socialism, and the demise of domestic reform movements,—encouraged the development of a more self-regarding community. The achievements and limitations of Greenwich Village cannot, however, be fully explained by its ethos and "institutions." To understand why bohemians became so preoccupied with personal relationships, romance, and private life, it is helpful to examine the careers of rebels who chose to live in the Village.

NOTES

1. Milton Brown, *The Story of the Armory Show* (Greenwich, Conn.; 1963). pp. 25-63.
2. Barbara Rose, *American Art Since 1900: A Critical History* (New York, 1967), pp. 71-75.
3. *Ibid.,* p. 75.
4. *New York Tribune,* February 17, 1913, p.7.
5. "Bedlam in Art," *Current Opinion,* Vol. 54 (April 1913), p. 316.
6. Frank Mather, Jr.; "Newest Tendencies in Art," *The Independent,* Vol. 74 (March 6,1913), p. 512.
7. Theodore Roosevelt, "A Layman's Views of the Art Exhibition," *The Outlook,* Vol. 103 (March 29, 1913), p. 719.
8. Jo Davidson, *Between Sittings: An Informal Autobiography* (New York, 1951), p. 85.
9. William Zorach, *Art is My Life: The Autobiography of William Zorach* (New York, 1967), p. 34, pp. 73-74.
10. William Glackens, "The American Section: The National Art," *Arts and Decoration,* Vol. 3 (March 1913), p.159.
11. Rose, *Art Since 1900,* pp. 80-89.
12. Mabel Dodge Luhan, *Movers and Shakers* (New York, 1936), p. 36.
13. *Ibid.,* p. 39.
14. John Sloan, *John Sloan's New York Scene: From the Diaries, Notes, and Correspondence, 1906-1913,* ed. Bruce St. John (New York, 1965), p. 633.
15. Hutchins Hapgood, "The Insurgents in Art," *New York Globe* (October 24, 1911), p. 8; "Art and Unrest," *New York Globe* (January 27, 1913), p. 10; "Life at the Armory," *New York Globe* (February 17, 1913), p. 8; "An Impression of Bergson," *New York Globe* (February 19, 1913), p. 10.
16. Roosevelt, "Layman's Views," p. 719.
17. *New York Times* (March 16, 1913), 4, p. 6.
18. Letter, Mabel Dodge to Gertrude Stein, in *The Flowers of Friendship: Letters Written to Gertrude Stein,* ed. Donald Gallup (New York, 1953), pp. 70-71.
19. Philip S. Foner, *History of the Labor Movement in the United States,* Vol. 4 (New York, 1965), pp. 306-350.

20. Max Eastman, "Knowledge and Revolution," *The Masses,* Vol. 4 (December 1912), p. 5.

21. Foner, *History of Labor Movement,* Vol. 4, pp. 351-364.

22. Harry Kemp, *More Miles: An Autobiographical Novel* (New York, 1926), pp. 357-358.

23. Hutchins Hapgood, "Haywood at Henri's, "*New York Globe* (April 22, 1912), p. 10.

24. Hutchins Hapgood, "A Day at Paterson," *New York Globe* (April 22, 1913), p. 8.

25. Letter, Wilbur D. Steele to Mary H. Vorse (1913?) Vorse Papers, Wayne State University.

26. Max Eastman, "Knowledge and Revolution," *The Masses* Vol. 4 (August 1913), p. 6.

27. Quoted by George Cram Cook, "New York Letter" (*Friday Literary Review*) *Chicago Evening Post* (June 13, 1913), p. 9.

28. Kemp, *More Miles,* p. 352.

29. Quoted in Mabel Dodge Luhan, *Movers and Shakers,* p. 188.

30. Foner, *History of Labor Movement,* Vol. 4, pp. 364-367; Luhan, *Movers and Shakers,* pp. 186-212. *New York Times* (June 8, 1913), Sec. 2, p.2; *New York Times* (June 9, 1913), p. 8, p. 18; Rose Watson, "The Paterson Strike From Workers' Point of View," *New York Tribune* (June 8, 1913), Sec. 6, p. 3; *New York Tribune* (June 8, 1913, p. 1; "Pageant as a Form of Propaganda," *Current Opinion,* Vol. 55 (July 1913), p. 32; "Paterson Strike Pageant," *The Independent,* Vol. 74 (June 19, 1913), pp. 1406-7.

31. Hutchins Hapgood, "The Strikers' Pageant," *New York Globe* (June 9, 1913), p. 6; George C. Cook, "New York Letter" (*Friday Literary Review*) *Chicago Evening Post* (June 6, 1913), p. 9.

32. Luhan, *Movers and Shakers,* p. 203.

33. Foner, *History of Labor Movement,* Vol. 4, pp. 367-372. Elizabeth Gurley Flynn, *The Rebel Girl: An Autobiography* (New York, 1973), pp. 152-173.

34. Floyd Dell, "The Rise of Greenwich Village," *Love In Greenwich Village* (New York, 1926), pp. 17-20.

35. George C. Cook, "New York Letter" (*Friday Literary Review*) *Chicago Evening Post* (February 7, 1913), p.6.

36. Letter, Kenneth Chamberlain to Robert Humphrey (October 30, 1975). Hapgood, *A Victorian in the Modern World* (New York, 1939), p. 152.

37. Floyd Dell, *Homecoming: An Autobiography* (New York, 1933), pp. 246-247.

38. Harold E. Stearns, *The Street I Know* (New York, 1935), p. 128.

39. Louis Sheaffer, *O'Neill: Son and Playwright* (Boston, 1968), pp. 332-334.

40. Kemp, *More Miles,* p. 364.

41. Hutchins Hapgood, *A Victorian in the Modern World,* pp. 198-199, p. 328.

42. Lawrence Langner, *The Magic Curtain* (New York, 1951), p. 71.

43. Letter, Louis Untermeyer to H.L. Mencken (November 5, 1914), Mencken Papers, New York Public Library.

44. Letter, Randolph Bourne to Alyse Gregory (January 13, 1915), Bourne Papers, Columbia University Library.

45. Harry Kemp, *More Miles,* p. 373.

46. Lawrence Langner, *Magic Curtain,* p. 72, p. 68.

47. *New International Year Book* (New York, 1914), p. 667.

48. Luhan, *Movers and Shakers,* p. 5, p. 10.

49. *Ibid.,* p. 10, p. 16.

50. *Ibid.,* p. 23.

51. Mabel Dodge Luhan, *Background* (New York, 1933), pp. 116-117.

52. *Ibid.,* pp. 25-26.

53. Mabel Dodge Luhan, *European Experiences* (New York, 1935), p. 28.
54. *Ibid., p. 30.*
55. *Ibid.,* pp. 34-92.
56. *Ibid.,* pp.95-135.
57. *Ibid., pp. 328-333.*
58. *Ibid., p. 236.*
59. *Ibid., p. 221, p. 259.*
60. *Ibid., p. 445.*
61. Luhan, *Movers and Shakers,* pp. 74-95.
62. Carl Van Vechten, *Peter Whiffle: His Life and Works* (New York, 1922), p. 134.
63. Luhan, *Movers and Shakers,* p. 90.
64. *Ibid.,* p. 84.
65. Letter, Mabel Dodge to Gertrude Stein (1913), Stein Papers, Beinecke Library, Yale University.
66. Lincoln Steffens, *The Autobiography of Lincoln Steffens* (New York, 1931), p. 655.
67. Max Eastman, *Enjoyment of Living* (New York, 1948), p. 523. Eastman commented: "Salons exaggerate three things that I don't like: literariness passing as wisdom, opinions passed around like confections, organization of what ought to be spontaneous."
68. Luhan, *Movers and Shakers,* p. 90.
69. *Ibid.,* p. 91.
70. *Ibid.,* p. 86.
71. *Ibid.,* p. 59.
72. Steffens, *Autobiography,* p. 655.
73. Letter, Carl Van Vechten to Mabel Dodge (December 24, 1913), Van Vechten Papers, Beinecke Library, Yale University.
74. *Ibid.*
75. Letter, Lincoln Steffens to Mabel Dodge (December 24, 1913), quoted in Luhan, *Movers and Shakers,* p. 248.
76. Van Vechten, *Peter Whiffle,* p. 125.
77. Interview with Andrew Dasburg, July 30, 1972. Margaret Sanger, *Margaret Sanger: An Autobiography* (New York, 1938), p. 73.
78. Van Vechten, *Peter Whiffle,* pp. 139-141.
79. Luhan, *Movers and Shakers,* p. 94. Emphasis added.
80. Quoted in Van Vechten, *Peter Whiffle,* pp. 137-138.
81. Luhan, *Movers and Shakers,* p. 187, p. 47.
82. *Ibid., p. 17.*
83. Letter, Mabel Dodge to Gertrude Stein (1913), Stein Papers.
84. Davidson, *Between Sittings,* p. 85.
85. Letter, Carl Van Vechten to Mabel Dodge (December 24, 1913), Van Vechten Papers.
86. Luhan, *Movers and Shakers,* p. 140.
87. Letter, Carl Van Vechten to Mabel Dodge (September 14, 1913), Van Vechten Papers.
88. Letter (April 1913), quoted in Luhan, *Movers and Shakers,* p. 199.
89. Letter, quoted in Luhan, *Movers and Shakers,* p. 153.
90. Luhan, *European Experiences,* p. 27.
91. Luhan, *Movers and Shakers,* p. 44.
92. *Ibid.,* pp. 253-254.
93. *Ibid.,* pp.249-250.
94. *Ibid.,* p. 150.
95. *Ibid.,* p. 80. Emphasis added.

96. Maurice Sterne, *Shadow and Light: The Life, Friends and Opinions of Maurice Sterne,* ed. Charlotte L. Mayerson (New York, 1952), p. 111.
97. *Ibid.,* p. 126.
98. *Ibid.,* p. 118.
99. Luhan, *Movers and Shakers,* p. 439, p. 445.
100. *Ibid.,* p. 454, p. 439.
101. Letter quoted in *Ibid.,* pp. 534-535.
102. Mabel Dodge Luhan, *Edge of Taos Desert* (New York, 1937), p. 273.
103. *Ibid.,* p. 193; Mabel Dodge Luhan, *Lorenzo in Taos* (New York, 1932), p. 52.
104. Mabel Dodge Luhan, "The Statue of Liberty: An Old Fashioned Story of Taboos" (1947), p. 6, Luhan Papers, Beinecke Library, Yale University.
105. Letter, Inez H. Gillmore to M.H. Vorse (January 19, 1912), Vorse Papers.
106. Louis Untermeyer, *From Another World: The Autobiography of Louis Untermeyer* (New York, 1939), pp. 37-45. Art Young, *Art Young: His Life and Times,* ed. John N. Beffel (New York, 1939), pp. 270-275.
107. Mary Heaton Vorse, *A Footnote to Folly: Reminiscences of Mary H. Vorse* (New York, 1935), p. 42.
108. Untermeyer, *From Another World,* pp. 46-47.
109. Van Wyck Brooks, *John Sloan: A Painter's Life* (New York, 1955), pp. 1-199. "Transcript of Masses Meeting" (March 27, 1916), Vorse Papers.
110. Art Young, *New York Sun* (April 6, 1916), quoted in Arthur Wertheim, "The Fiddles Are Tuning: The Little Renaissance in New York City, 1908-1917," unpublished dessertation, New York University, 1970, p. 153.
111. Eastman, *Enjoyment of Living,* pp. 548-559.
112. Quoted in Granville Hicks, *John Reed: The Making of a Revolutionary* (New York, 1936), p. 94.
113. Young, *His Life and Times,* pp. 295-300. Eastman, *Enjoyment of Living,* pp. 464-482.
114. Young, *His Life and Times,* p. 232.
115. Dell, "Rise of Greenwich Village," p. 26.
116. Max Eastman, "Editorial," *The Masses,* Vol. 4 (December 1912), p. 3.
117. Untermeyer, *From Another World,* p. 46.
118. Luhan, *Movers and Shakers,* pp. 96-116.
119. Art Young, *The Masses,* Vol. 5 (December, 1913), front cover.
120. Frederick J. Hoffman et. al., *The Little Magazine: A History and a Bibliography* (Princeton, 1947), pp. 35-51.

CHAPTER TWO

Hutchins Hapgood and the Art of Personal Relations

Among the bohemians in Greenwich Village were men and women who dabbled in avant-garde art and radical politics. Ill-adapted to society and hostile to conventional restraints, these rebels sought friends who shared a disdain for competition, regular employment, social advancement, traditional monogamy, and familial responsibilities. With few plans for the future but ample time at their disposal, these Villagers became intensely involved with one another. In cafés, apartments, and taverns, men and women troubled over their private lives. One of the most ardent devotees of Village entanglements was Hutchins Hapgood.

After enjoying the luxuries of a sheltered upbringing and a genteel education, Hapgood became a connoisseur of conversation, good food, women, and pleasure. Working as a part-time journalist and mingling with outcasts, he remained on the fringes of respectable society. When a bohemian community formed in Greenwich Village, Hapgood quit journalism and limited his contacts with the lower classes. The concentration

Hutchins Hapgood at graduation from Harvard College. Yale University Library.

of unhappy nonconformists and aspiring artists drew him into a web of friendships. Hapgood, already forty-four years old in 1913, expended his time and energy in cultivating personal relationships.

Charles Hapgood, Hutch's father, was a product of "Puritan New England." After graduating from Brown University and Harvard Law School, Charles left the East to seek his fortune in Chicago. The Great Fire of 1871, however, destroyed his commercial investments, forcing a retreat to Alton, Illinois, a small town on the Mississippi. There he established a plow factory and, after considerable effort, managed to recover his losses and establish a genteel existence for his wife and three sons.[1]

Born in 1869, Hutchins looked to his successful father for moral and practical guidance. Hutchins remarked in his autobiography: "I was extremely sensitive to my father's sense of values, because of what I truthfully felt was his pure, intense, and superior character." But Hutchins, the second son, was unable to measure up to his father's example or expectations. In comparison to his older brother, Norman, Hutch was visibly inadequate. When the elder Hapgood attempted to teach "typewriting and other office work" to the boys, Hutchins failed while Norman "learned easily." Consequently, Charles came to demand less of Hutchins and more of Norman on whom he bestowed his attention and praise. Lacking the skills his father valued, Hutchins concluded that he "did not amount to much." But that painful judgment and his family's tolerance allowed him to enjoy the pleasures of irresponsibility and self-indulgence.[2]

In reviewing his life Hutchins decided that the relationship with his parents stunted his emotional and creative development. He blamed his father for denying him the opportunity to express artistic and religious emotions. Although "often overcome by a poignant sense of sin," he was never given religious instruction. Charles, an atheist, discouraged "Church, fairy-tales, and dancing" because he thought that they "held forth futile dreams from which there must be a severe awakening." Hutchins felt a need for these dreams, but his father offered him moral codes that one obeyed without question or transgressed with a sense of "wickedness." Having no outlet for his "religious and imaginative impulses," Hutchins withdrew into himself and doubted his own worth. He was only able to express himself "with the village epileptic and a half-crazed gardener" because they were "not ashamed" of his emotional temperament. When Hapgood finally escaped his family, he sought out social outcasts who provided fellowship and stimulated his imagination.[3]

A lack of encouragement was only part of a deeper grievance. Hutchins thought that his parents denied him warmth and compassion. He perceived that Norman received Charles's attention and his mother doted on William, his younger, sickly brother. Later he wrote: "I remember well how deeply I wanted intimacy as a child, and yet how deeply I feared it and how little I was able to receive or preserve it." Because each parent had a favorite son, Hutchins was left alone. "I was a stranger to everything around me. I seem . . . to have been struggling always for contacts, but in vain." To mitigate his feeling of abandonment, Hutchins developed an imagination that entertained him for hours. He recalled that "as a boy, hardly a day passed without a dream" at school or at home. He also discovered masturbation early and practiced it frequently, but with "horror and remorse." Self-absorption and "self-abuse" added to his sense of being a "cripple," a permanent affliction of his personality.[4]

Although Hapgood enjoyed a big yard, dogs, ponies, a tennis court, a baseball field, and a billiard table, he did not like Alton, which was "ugly, arid, and sterile." Negative attitudes were reinforced by his parents who considered themselves exiles living amongst the unsophisticated; "there was only one other family in Alton" who had what the Hapgoods considered to be a "civilized attitude toward eating." His parents never accepted the town; their friends lived in Chicago, and talk about that city caused him to think "that Alton was not home."[5] He recalled:

> Indeed the town had no temperament, though it had a physiognomy. Its look was ugly. . . . Civic life never called attention to itself. There was a town hall, we never knew why, a theatre to which no one ever went, two newspapers which never had any news. There was a cigar-store where the young dull bloods of the town gathered to look at the baseball scores; there were the usual colorless haunts of vice.[6]

Spiritually and culturally moribund, Alton corrupted those who remained there. The young people who showed a spark of originality were "weighted down by the sodden environment" of respectability and small-town cupidity. He remembered trapped young women, hungry for experience and doomed to a prosaic existence.

In 1889, after an unhappy year of "nervous prostration" at home, Hapgood escaped from Alton to Harvard College, where Norman was already a student. It was at Harvard, the most distinguished school in the country, that his depression lifted. He no longer had to wage a "futile attempt at self control" and keep his thoughts "away from the forbidden subject" of sex. In the "spiritual elevation" of college his emotional life found outlets in poetry, philosophy, and other genteel pleasures, including conversation, quiet walks, rowing on the Charles River, and visits to the Boston Museum Theater. He met young men and distinguished professors who shared his interests, and he learned that "the seemingly peculiar qualities of [his] temperament harmonized with the world of real culture." Since "gentlemanly indifference" prevailed among the undergraduates, those students with an aptitude for art and philosophy were valued by a faculty which included William James, Josiah Royce, George Santayana, and Barrett Wendell. Consequently, Hapgood exchanged views with his professors in the classroom and at social functions in Cambridge. "It was," he recalled, "an indescribable cool pleasure to come in contact with . . . men of real culture and power who were not burdened by themselves but who moved about freely in the world of intuition and thought."[7]

At the end of the nineteenth century American colleges and universities were the guardians of high culture. Gentlemen-scholars reputedly pursued learning for its own sake, preserving the standards of scholarship and virtue in a nation dominated by businessmen and their brand of materialism. Colleges were expected to counteract the commercial spirit by cultivating and imparting an appreciation of the best art and literature. Given Hapgood's hostility to practical training and monetary concerns, it is understandable that he felt "the exhilarating sense of being in an environment of mental and moral freedom."[8]

In his commencement address, "The Student as Child," Hapgood characterized the years spent in college as an interlude between a carefree youth and the calculating careers of mature men. The end of childhood usually entailed the "suppression" of "artistic tendencies" that children developed naturally. But college extended the period of "contemplative life" and strengthened the "child element" in developing adults. While Hapgood conceded that most men had to become practical, he hoped that they would retain an "interest in the world" and "in things unconnected with ends." As for himself, he had no intention of giving up a "delight in beauty" and a "belief in the unreal" for the mundane world of competition and advancement.[9]

After receiving a B.A. in 1892, Hapgood remained at Harvard for a year of postgraduate work. He accomplished very little, however, because he was "generally incapable of activity." His father then advised and financed a continuation of his studies in Europe. Formal education, however, lost its appeal after his first sexual experience in France, and thereafter sexual images flooded his mind.[10] He told a friend:

> The Woman has been bothering me again—not in body— . . . but in Vorstellung [imagination]. I work all I can to keep her down. But I can't work enough, somehow, to tire myself out every day [as] I should really like to do, and the passion to investigate the town comes upon me at night very frequently. I am [more] uncomfortable in that way at present than I have been for four or five years, and I attribute it to the general sensuous over-development which paintings, statuary, music, and life have caused. My nervous force is not enough to balance my sensuous material, and I feel now that with me it is a question of a long and doubtful fight with myself or a permanent arrangement with a woman. . . . Any light which you might have on this point is most welcome. I wish I were thoroughly grounded in Physiology and Pathology and I could then act more consequently.[11]

When he arrived in Berlin to attend the university, he had little zeal for academic studies. Freed from the restrictions of gentility, he drank in beerhalls and delighted in prostitutes.

Hapgood's lifelong association with prostitutes did not quite fit the "victorian" pattern of sexual exploitation in which gentlemen used lower-class girls to break the inhibitions of upper-class respectability. He believed that his affairs were neither trivial nor casual; he approached them with "an excited stirring of [his] whole nature, mental and imaginative as well as physical, so that experience, although in a sense impersonal, . . . was full of beauty." Hapgood granted himself dispensation to violate "victorian" codes by ascribing to sex the power of perceiving "higher truths." He also sought "love and friendship . . . not so much for their own sake, but as a means of escape" from solitude and loneliness.[12]

After returning to America, Hapgood decided that he was not ready to begin a career. He felt "moody, maladjusted, . . . and in a worldly sense, unambitious, keen only about sensual and spiritual experience." In 1895, he sailed to Japan and there pursued "sensuous" living on the scale of a nobleman; he and Leo Stein (Gertrude Stein's brother) lived in Kyoto with a cook, rickshaw men, maids, and a "wife" apiece.[13]

Finally ending his long rest-cure, Hapgood went back to Harvard where he studied for a Master's degree and taught English. But academia had lost its glow. In comparison to his unregulated experiences in Europe and in Japan, university life seemed dull and regimented. His brother Norman, a drama critic for the *New York Commercial Advertiser,* soon presented a route of escape, obtaining for him a position on the paper, which Hutchins held from 1897 to 1902.

Edited by Lincoln Steffens, the *New York Commercial Advertiser,* an old paper of limited circulation, encouraged its Harvard-educated journalists to display their literary talents when gathering and reporting the news. Reporters like Hapgood were allowed to work without deadlines or editorial mandates. Later, when Steffens left and the new editor requested more conventional news coverage, Hapgood resigned.[14]

In an era when daring journalists exposed corruption in politics and filth in tenements, young men and women of sheltered background ventured into immigrant ghettoes to experience reality and to reform the ignorant. Hapgood, however, was neither muckraker nor reformer. A voyeur, he was excited by excursions among the unfortunate, and being a reporter legitimized his pursuit of the illegitimate.

In the bowels of the city Hapgood searched for "expressive" characters who had those "temperamental qualities," fostered by a "certain amount of unnervous ease and agreeable companionship," which escaped "the ordinary nervous, moral and busy American."[15] On the

Bowery he met the discredited and the disabled—bums, thieves, Tammany Hall politicians, "dance-hall" girls, and common laborers—who had no security. They were "so near the line" that he "came against what is called the real thing."[16] Colorful Bowery characters provided picturesque material and "vitality," for the poor lived "intensely," suffered "keenly," and vented their feelings "with the utmost frankness."[17] Ill at ease among the socially ambitious, he was consoled by the company of social outsiders with whom he shared a sense of fellowship.

If Hapgood fraternized with the lower classes, he retained a sense of his superior standing. He referred to himself and his kind as "intellectual aristocrats"—men distinguished from the "bourgeois classes by the precision and simplicity of their feeling and expression."[18] Like other gentlemen he deplored the cultural decline that accompanied the triumph of the middle class. He longed for a conservative revolution that would re-establish "more definite classes" and resurrect refined upperclass culture. His sentiments echoed the complaints of Henry Adams, E.L. Godkin (editor of *The Nation*), and other disgruntled heirs of gentility who lamented their displacement.[19] While Adams and Godkin held tightly to the past, refusing to identify with anything outside genteel sanctuaries, Hapgood found solace and hope among the downtrodden and the poor.

Hapgood argued that those at the top and the bottom of the social system, the "aristocrats" and the "toughs," were "spiritually" affiliated. In accepting their station in society, the "aristocrat" and the "tough" acted with dignity and self-assurance. By contrast, the middle-class person, striving constantly to rise, was "vulgar, graceless and unformed." Social ambition made the middle classes secretive, nervous, hypocritical, and anxious for they feared the loss of face or position. Despite their efforts at emulation, the *nouveaux riches* could not acquire the "calmness, independence, and self-confidence" of the "Bowery tough" and the "aristocrat."[20] In comparison to the middle-class woman, who was "filled with a cheap desire for comfort and social progress," the Bowery "dance-hall girl" was attractive, dignified, interesting, and exotic. Purity and innocence flourished where one expected lewdness and cynicism, and Bowery girls exhibited virtues only respectable women were supposed to have.[21]

Hapgood was favorably disposed toward the lower classes because they were generally unassuming and unaffected by any social pretense. He objected strongly to the lowly who tried to imitate "genuine refinement." In particular, he scorned pretentious "department-store girls" who dissociated themselves from "roughly drest [sic] brothers, fathers, and mothers" to elevate their status.[22] Nonetheless, he expected lower-class women to observe traditional morality. He warned, for example, that the waltz was an activity fraught with potential evil because it brought working class girls together with "undesirable men." He believed that "when danced excessively" the waltz was "as bad as drink or gambling."[23]

While Hapgood suggested there was a link between gentlemen and outcasts, he maintained that "toughs" exuded a sturdiness delicate "men of culture" lacked. While "toughs" were self-sufficient, gentlemen went "down and out . . . early in the hard struggle" of life.[24] In proposing that gentlemen live "close to life," Hapgood did not intend to prepare them for political and economic competition. He wished to merge genteel refinement with lower-class exuberance and create a bohemian mode of existence.

Bohemianism combined "loafing" and "agreeable companionship" to form a philosophic and "artistic habit of mind." Bohemianism was foreign to the American experience because in New York, "a very 'swift' town," contemplation was "shut out of the life" of its residents. In choosing bohemianism, and few men did, one endured social reprobation, "for when a man is not busy in America, he is generally a bum or a foreigner."[25] To Hapgood's way of thinking, civilization should esteem good wine, relaxation, sensual experiences, and the art of conversation.

Hapgood's curiosity about disreputable characters was shared by Alfred Hodder, a Harvard alumnus who also liked to roam the Tenderloin. Hapgood, Hodder, and Josiah Flynt, a man who had written about lawbreakers and tramps, met regularly at the Griffou, a little French hotel on Tenth Avenue, to drink whiskey and discuss criminals. Flynt introduced Hapgood to Jim Caulfield, an Irish pickpocket, who had been released from the state penitentiary. With Hapgood posing as "a confidence man from Chicago," Caulfield guided him through underworld haunts.[26] Hapgood then decided to record and publish Caulfield's life story. For three months they met every afternoon, and often in the evening, at a German café on the East Side where Hapgood listened and took notes.

Although Hapgood defended his book as an inquiry into the "manners, customs, and mental habits of the professional criminal," he made no attempt to analyze his material or generalize from his findings. The deficiencies of this study suggest that its primary function was to provide Hapgood with more experiences. But Caulfield and the underworld disappointed Hapgood, for he discovered that criminals were "vain and frivolous" and not at all dangerous.[27]

Hapgood's search for social misfits was temporarily interrupted by his meeting Neith Boyce, a slim, pale, red-haired editorial assistant for the

New York Commercial Advertiser. Born in 1872, Neith grew up in Illinois, Milwaukee, and Los Angeles. The disturbances of a rootless childhood were overshadowed by a major family tragedy; her four brothers were killed by an outbreak of diphtheria. This disaster removed her closest companions and left the lingering fear that an unforeseen force might strike again without warning or reason.[28]

Her father's unsuccessful economic ventures strengthened her pessimism. In 1882, Henry Harrison Boyce, who had been wounded and partly crippled during the Civil War, acquired a half interest in the *Los Angeles Times.* The partnership with Harrison Gray Otis proved to be a profitable investment, and the family's standard of living greatly improved. But four years later, Boyce, disgusted by his partner's antilabor views, decided to sell out to Otis and establish a new paper, the *Los Angeles Tribune.* The paper prospered until Henry Chandler, an unscrupulous controller of circulation routes in the city, induced *Los Angeles Tribune* subscribers to switch to the *Los Angeles Times.* Boyce was forced to sell out to Chandler at a tremendous loss, and, Neith recalled: "The big house went, the horses and carriages, the furniture, the silver, [mother's] diamonds, and most of the pictures. They could keep only a few things to furnish the tiny house to which they moved, far out on the cableline."[29]

Economic reverses deepened the gloom in a family where, Neith recalled, "caresses were not familiar" and "kisses almost unknown." Growing up in a household without warmth or playmates, Neith developed into an aloof young woman who preferred to dwell in "the untrammeled world of the imagination." Writing became the chief means of expressing herself and communicating with others.[30]

After her father moved the family to Mt. Vernon, New York, Neith decided to live in Manhattan and support herself. When Steffens hired her as a reporter and copy editor, she rented rooms in the Judson Hotel on the south side of Washington Square. There she lived quietly and devoted her spare hours to writing.

Hutchins entered her spinsterish existence and disturbed its quietude. Short and broadshouldered, he exuded, she thought, "physical vigor" and "fire." In contrast to herself, Hutch was "enthusiastic about life" and "open to experience." He "loved pleasure, he was good company, he was charming. He wanted to make every little dinner that they had together a festival. He was unreasonable, unexpected, surprising; he insisted that life should be, and was, pleasant, varied, rich."[31]

While they shared an aesthetic appreciation of books and art, Neith was serious about writing, while Hutch "didn't think much about" it; he wrote, she realized, "as a by-product of his life." Differences in outlook and temperament provoked numerous conflicts during their long courtship. She was not sociable, and he upbraided her whenever she was "rude" or "acted bored" in the company of others. Whereas he believed that "good literary work" required full participation in life, she wanted to "observe and reproduce life at a safe distance from those physical involvements." She feared the "demands of physical and family life," and it was clear that Hutch "would be a demanding person; nothing halfway could satisfy him."[32]

Neith Boyce's wedding picture. Yale University Library.

Despite numerous quarrels, "warring passions," and "bitter reproaches," they were married in June, 1899. The newlyweds rented a fourth-floor apartment on the corner of Sixth Avenue and Twenty-Third Street, and hired an Irish servant girl to do the housework. Although they frequented hotels and restaurants in Greenwich Village, they did not limit their social life to this section of New York. Artists were buying old houses west of Washington Square, and single women held "miniature salons, with tea or coffee and cake, for people who had things published in the small new magazines," but the Village still lacked a bohemian community. Genteel families lived on the north side of the Square and kept their horses and barouches in stables on Washington Mews. While Italians had moved into tenements to the south, Washington Square and the immediate environs retained their traditional dignity.[33]

In this period bohemianism consisted of informal "parties" where emancipated women smoked and drank with male escorts. On Saturday nights "newspapermen, artists, and women" gathered at Maria's restaurant for lively conversation and romance. For the Hapgoods bohemianism also involved safaris to disreputable saloons or foreign restaurants; they drank at Chuck Connor's or Barney Flynn's on the Bowery and dined at the Café Boulevard on Second Avenue or the Café Liberty on Houston Street. Wherever they went, talk remained the most important activity.[34]

Marriage did not halt Hapgood's visits to the Jewish ghetto on the Lower East Side. To him it was an enclave that had not been completely infected by the "American spirit" of enterprise. The genteel intruder found the Jewish quarter an agreeable field of operations, and its cultural traditions appealed to his aesthetic sensibilities. Hapgood began his explorations by reviewing plays at the "submerged" Yiddish theaters. He liked the "realistic pieces" portraying "contemporary manners" and ghetto conditions; they were a refreshing improvement over the "inane cheerfulness of the uptown theaters." But if he took "comfort in generalized misfortune" on the stage, he avoided overcrowded tenements and sweatshops on his wanderings. Hapgood wanted melodrama, not realism; he longed for a dramatic world that was more expressive than life in the streets.[35]

Hapgood was attracted to the "melancholic" inhabitants of the Lower East Side. Every face in the ghetto was "picturesquely serious." Some Jews showed the "solemnity of religion," and some "the melancholy of fatigue or longing"; most displayed "a religious passion for business," and Jewish intellectuals endeavored "to further their almost religious ideas in society or literature."[36] Hapgood viewed this "seriousness of nature" as a manifestation of religious impulses developed by Judaic and Hebraic traditions. He hoped that Jewish culture and "moral earnestness" would be shielded from the corrupting influences of American civilization. He believed that America needed "something similar to the spirit underlying the national and religious unity of the orthodox Jewish culture."[37] He did not explain where this spiritual force would come from nor how it would transform American society, and he rejected socialism, an important movement in the ghetto, as being destructive to "both American and Hebraic ideals." Hapgood doubted that the Lower East Side could generate a moral revival, for Jewish immigrants, intoxicated by freedom, had "thrown off their orthodox religion" without seeking a "religious and ethical substitute." This rebellion had generated "an atheistic and disillusioned frame of mind," anarchism "in theory and practice," and "uncommon vice."[38]

Although Hapgood called himself a "philosophical anarchist," his political identity had no connection with concrete proposals or organized groups. He had little practical interest in politics. With a reformist vocabulary that included "spirituality," "intensity," "national ideals," "religion," "morality," "soul," "self-expression," and "brotherhood," he sounded like a secular puritan in the Emersonian tradition. Social reform would occur outside the political system by arousing the moral idealism and religious fervor of each individual. As a religious enthusiast who apprehended reality emotionally, he could only hope that a spiritual brotherhood would replace America's "uncivilized individualism." In advocating moral and cultural reform without assessing the importance of political and economic power, Hapgood proved to be a cultural evangelist, not an effective social critic.

Late in 1902, Hapgood quit the New York Commercial Advertiser under criticism from the managing editor who accused him of "thinking aloud" instead of reporting the news. In May, he, Neith, and Boyce, their two-year-old son, left for Florence where they prepared manuscripts for publication, quarreled with one another, and whiled away their time in the company of sophisticated American and English expatriates. Their stay came to an end with word that Neith's father had been killed in a streetcar accident, and they returned to New York in November.[39]

With the help of humorist Finley Peter Dunn, Hapgood found work with the New York Morning Telegraph, which catered to mass consumption. Unlike the New York Commercial Advertiser, the New York Morning Telegraph had no interest in serious matters. Except for Frank Butler, a talented but alcoholic reporter, Hapgood found no one of redeeming value on the staff. A pariah amongst his colleagues, Butler associated with saloon-keepers, racetrack touts, prizefighters, and chorus girls. When Butler died unexpectedly, Hapgood quit the *Telegraph*.[40]

In 1904, Hapgood moved his family to Chicago where a friend secured him a position as columnist and drama critic for the respectable *Chicago Evening Post*. As in the past, however, "strained relations" with the editor forced him into unemployment. Neith and their two small boys returned to New York while he remained behind to investigate another subculture, the "riotous" working class.

Characteristically Hapgood was more interested in "expressive" workers than in the labor movement. In Chicago's saloons he hunted for an exuberant labor leader who philosophized about labor problems. But he had difficulty overcoming the distrust of laborers who considered him "a parasite" because he did not work with his hands. They became "stiff, inexpressive and conventional" when Hapgood asked them to talk "about their lives and their personal opinions."[41]

Finally, after searching for eight months and receiving a beating from three steelworkers, Hapgood met Anton Johannsen, the president of a local union and a woodworker who was "alive in every way." "Pleasurably excited" by Anton's "free, anarchistic habit of mind" and the "rough, sweet health of his personality," Hapgood moved into a boarding house near Johannsen's house and saw him as often as possible.[42]

A former hobo and tavern owner, Johannsen was a man who had "lived roughly" and knew how "to get into life." According to Hapgood, he was both a trade unionist and an anarchist, a rebel and a family man. His rise within the union, an organization which improved "his moral hygiene," had not corrupted him. Unlike the "Russian-Jewish idealists of New York," whom Hapgood denounced, Johannsen had not attempted to further "practical and personal" ambitions. With the "flowing energy" of the "practical idealist and of the forming artist," Johannsen was both a worker and a poet. In contrast to the "anaemic" radicals of Chicago (anarchists, free-lovers, anthropologists, and "long-haired cranks") Johannsen was "stormy, aggressive, varied, complex, sometimes vulgar, more often fine and truly delicate, often above their heads though his language [was] ungrammatical."[43]

Hapgood's association with Anton and other "vigorous personalities" persuaded him that he was in the midst of a "renaissance of labor." It was not Jewish immigrants but the workers of the "democratic" Middle West who would inject America with moral idealism. In contrast to the "crushed" workers of Europe, the American "proletariat" displayed "hopefulness," "mental joyousness," and "vitality." Although the skilled union members whom Hapgood met hardly represented the proletariat, he designated them the working class and maintained they had achieved the "solidarity" of a religious movement. Ignoring political ideology, worker demands, and economic exploitation while arguing for "individuality" and the "rights of the soul," he turned the labor movement into a spiritual awakening without political or economic dimensions.[44]

The ease with which Hapgood traded Jews for workers suggests that he was primarily interested in his own emotions. He used alienated individuals and groups to support his fantasies. They expressed what he felt, not what existed in the real world. Chronically bored, Hapgood sought excitement without involvement in order to dispel a sense of personal isolation and emptiness. Unable to participate in any practical or meaningful activity, he was drawn to individuals who had vitality and energy. While Hapgood's appreciation of social outsiders countered conventional prejudices, he did not understand the reform movements he celebrated.

Hapgood originally intended to write about "the spirit of labor," but became intrigued with a group of anarchists. At an anarchist ball he encountered a gathering of men and women who "seemed so much at home together." The beer flowed freely, speeches were given about liberty and love, "everybody kissed everybody else's girl, and all were happy." By discarding the "ordinary conventions of conservative society," the anarchists created "a natural and intimate social life" that attracted "gentle and intelligent" women who esteemed "ideas, temperament, and poetry." Men and women accepted each other's company gracefully, and their free love code granted sexual freedom to lovers.[45]

Hapgood's interest in anarchism subsequently narrowed to a "free union" involving Terry Carlin (aged forty-six), who later was a fixture in Greenwich Village, and Marie (aged twenty-three), a "dark-haired, interestingly temperamental girl." A former tanner, Terry had become an anarchist and refused to work. He had converted Marie to his political philosophy, and she had joined him in a "slum garret." Supported by Kate, who worked as a cook, Terry and Marie spent their days and nights reading, smoking, drinking, and talking. Terry encouraged Marie to be a "free-lover," and she carried out his "ideas" without "hardship." Hapgood attributed this and other instances of sexual rebelliousness and "unbalanced license" to the "prudishness, hypocrisy, and stupid conventionality" of American society.[46]

For weeks Hapgood was a regular visitor at the apartment where they lived "with as little social restraint as possible." Their candid confessions about themselves provided the kind of intimacy that he wanted. Although Terry had never been formally educated, and had "a career of unusual deprivation and toughness," Hapgood discovered that he was an independent thinker of "excellent manners" who could discuss poetry, literature, and "abstract conceptions of justice."[47]

While it pleased Hapgood to associate "with people who at least were civilized, and not overcivilized," he was dismayed that Terry "seemed perversely to love whatever was rejected by organized society." Although Hapgood thought that anarchism offered "spiritual improvement and moral comfort" to the proletariat and that free love fostered "love and interest" by increasing marital insecurity, he considered Terry and Marie to be "an extremely harmless eddy in the current of social life."[48] Existing without work, children, or social involvement, they engaged in "strenuous personal relations with one another," which resulted in physical and emotional "anaemia."[49] He did not, however, apply such judgments to his own life.

Leaving Chicago, Hapgood rejoined his family in order to write up his experiences. After he and Neith confessed their infidelities and reconciled their difficulties, they sailed to Europe, where they remained for two years, living on a stipend from his father. In Italy, villas were inexpensive and companions plentiful. Hapgood assembled a book on Marie, began a literary portrait of a "neurotic" Swede, took long walks to appease "a profound nervous disquiet," had sexual encounters, and enjoyed conversations that were "free, sophisticated, and balanced."[50]

When Neith became intimately involved with his old college friend, Arthur Bentley, Hapgood decided that they should return to America. Initially Hapgood tried to work as a salesman for his younger brother, but went back to journalism—four months on the New York Evening Post, a shorter period for the New York Press, and finally, from 1911 to 1913, on the New York Globe, which had been combined with the old New York Commercial Advertiser. Since his duties on the Globe entailed just three columns a week, he was able to pursue a bohemian life in Greenwich Village. Living outside New York City, eventually at Dobbs Ferry (twenty miles north of Manhattan) in a large brick mansion purchased by his father, Hapgood commuted to bohemia.[51]

Reviving his favorite technique of interviewing "expressive" personalities, Hapgood again focused on the labor movement. In his eyes the fight for higher wages and shorter hours was a "divine impulse toward human solidarity that would enhance the spiritualization of American life," and he viewed the Industrial Workers of the World as a religious movement that aroused the "spirit of independence" among workers. Although he perceived that industrialization relegated work to a form of slavery, he advised each worker to "understand his work [and] become an artist in it."[52]

Insisting that the differences between management and labor resulted from ignorance and prejudice, Hapgood suggested that conflict could be eliminated by bringing groups together in clubs or social centers. Opposed to social repression because it damned up ideals and impulses, he would direct lower-class energies into civilized activities.[53] The Paterson strike pageant showed that the working classes were capable of appropriate behavior, for the immigrants acted with "gentleness, with a fine mass—not a mob—feeling." He told his readers:

> People interested in the possibilities of a vital and popular art, and in constructive pageantry, would learn much from it. . . . Think of . . . combining this mass initiative and this phalanx of life into a spectacle. . . . This kind of thing makes us hope for a real democracy, where self-expression in industry and art among the masses may become a rich reality, spreading a human glow over the whole of Humanity.[54]

He proposed that Americans celebrate the Fourth of July with a national, historical pageant instead of igniting firecrackers, which were "bad for the nerves and character of the young and harmful to the taste of the entire nation." Hapgood envisioned that saloons might be freed of "universally recognized evils" by converting them into European cafés. Adding tables, chairs, and "lighter" drinks, and inviting wives to join their spouses, would upgrade the saloon and "rehabilitate the industrial outcast." America could establish a creative and refined society by emulating the "balance and proportion" of classical Greece.[55]

Just as Hapgood viewed "aristocrats" and "toughs" as natural allies, he thought that rebellious artists and striking workers exuded the same impulse "for more life." A working-class leader who expressed "the turbulent reaching out and reaching up for a new life of submerged masses of men" was "esthetically and emotionally similar to an artist" who sought "to express feelings and works hitherto unexpressed in art forms."[56] "Real art" told the "people about their lives," and the artist could not cut himself off from the labor movement and "remain vital." Similarly, Hapgood viewed Big Bill Haywood as a labor leader who "spoke for the poetry of work." The "real workers," in art or in the labor movement, wanted "to loosen up the old forms and traditions, to dynamite the baked and hardened earth so that fresh flowers" could grow.[57]

Since Hapgood viewed strikes as essentially aesthetic and religious movements, he assumed that labor "insurgents" and avant-garde artists were allies. While artists and workers confronted entrenched authority and conventional opinion, simple identifications and cultural remedies did not help the poor. But then Hapgood believed that political reform would come only after "an advance in culture and civilization," and "real democracy" would be led by cultural elites. He wanted to aid forces that established the "ideals" of his "privileged class." He explained:

> When I write sympathetically about a radical labor movement, it is not so much because I want the laborers to be better off—though I do—as because I want me and my class . . . to be better off spiritually and morally, to have greater life and more real pleasures than they have in this organized misconception of true values that we call our society. I want to assist . . . all developing forces in the community . . . which seem to me calculated . . . to increase the self-controlling, self-determining democracy of the majority.[58]

Hapgood's imaginative interpretations of external events and other people often resulted in implausible, but poetic visions of reality. He believed, for example, that the sinking of the Titanic had "deepened the psychology" of the survivors. Having been "brought face to face with the terror and beauty of eternity," the surviving passengers realized the triviality of "practical ends and ambitions." He considered the "spectacle of the band playing on" as the ship plunged into the sea an "inspiring" event. That these musicians could detach themselves "from the pressing and dread reality" and have "freedom of imagination necessary to render music" was "absolute grandeur."[59]

While Hapgood exhorted his readers to contemplate the "highest and the best," his attention increasingly turned from avant-garde art and labor radicalism to personal relations and "restless" women. "Neurasthenic," middle-class wives, especially those educated "more broadly" than their "hard-working" husbands, were excited "emotionally about art, literature, [and] human relations of an expressive kind." These women sought men who could satisfy their emotional needs. This situation threatened the "unity of marriage" and civilization. To solve the problem he recommended that husbands and wives violate conventional strictures and have friends of the opposite sex; "wives ought to have many friends among men, and husbands many friends among women." "Intimate sociability" would break down the "anti-social exclusiveness" of each family and end the "brutal and unkind things" men do to the "whole community" for their families. While there were "obvious dangers" in creating a more natural society, "resourceful and well-intentioned men and women" could stand "the test of true civilization."[60]

Hapgood's interest in promoting extramarital friendships also reflected his activities in Greenwich Village. The growing concentration of rebels and independent-minded women expanded the possibilities of friendships, especially since Neith usually remained in Dobbs Ferry with their four children. According to Hapgood, marriage required "resourcefulness" and a "creative imagination," and the husband who did not give "his wife some occasion for jealousy" was "deficient in the art of life." Extramarital friendships increased the excitement of marriage, for the "jealous wife" had "great attractiveness." But this self-serving recommendation obviously could create more problems than solutions. Given his unstable relationship with Neith, Hapgood might well believe that marriage involved "a constant work of art." He erred, however, in thinking that emotional conflicts were a sign of artistic creativity. He justified the continuation of marriage by maintaining that his "deep, subconscious self" preferred what his "small, civilized, logical or subconscious self" rejected. Unable to break away or accept divorce, Hapgood praised his marriage as a revolt against organized society.[61]

Neith was independent, strong-willed, and emotionally withdrawn. "She was," he commented, "no self-conscious neurasthenic, as I was. She was cool, unconscious, possibly cold, the ignorant would call her."[62] She refused to take his mystical flights seriously or support his interest in social misfits. Mabel Dodge recalled:

> Neith let him think he was pursuing God, but she held the end of the leash in her enigmatic white hand and smiled a secret smile. . . . She seemed to feel that Hutch was at play in the city among the anarchists and radicals and that his ideas were no more important to real life than a bunch of red and blue ballons. She was as sweetly half-attentive, half-*distrait*, when he talked, as when one of the children told of his exploits.[63]

In serving as a remote mother-wife and in tolerating his bohemian escapades, Neith recreated the relationship Hapgood had first formed with his parents.

Failing to penetrate Neith's reserve or reshape her personality, Hapgood sought out women who appreciated his volatility. Early in 1913, he became involved with Mabel Dodge who confided her unhappiness to him. She recalled: "I told him all about myself—everything—and oh! how he sympathized. Tears stood in his eyes and he passed his hand tenderly over my head."[64] Hapgood had discovered a disconsolate soul who shared his misery. Thereafter, they saw each other daily. Mabel remembered:

> We sorrowed over each other and felt our mutual woe. We both felt like failures from the angle of worldly success and we were proud of it, and and we considered each other to be failures—and this drew us together into

a luxurious, rich companionship. We thought we were the only ones in the world who longed for perfection.[65]

They had much in common: aesthetic interests, free time, minimal responsibilities, and a mystical view of reality. Believing Mabel to be a "promoter of spirit," Hapgood introduced her to notorious radicals and brought interesting men to her apartment.[66] Together they tried to alleviate their discontent and boredom.

Their relationship waned when Mabel went off to Europe with John Reed. After her departure Hapgood languished in depression and alcohol. He wrote to her:

> I suppose you are having a gay and beautiful time in Villa Curonia. And that I seem very far away. But, I hope, still attractive? I think of you quietly and peacefully, and if I saw you walk into the room, it would seem as if you had never gone away. But the whole world is misty to me, at present . . . . I feel keen about nothing just now. I don't want to read, or drink, or exercise, or think, and am good only to do what I must and not very intensely. . . . I think I never had quite the mood before—a distant, unreal, unintense quality about everything. . . . Am I alive, I wonder? I don't seem to have any personality. . . . I wonder if I never drank again if I would always be like this.[67]

He retired to Provincetown, stopped writing for the *New York Globe,* and confessed that he no longer wanted to agitate for "the unbuilding or improvement of conditions," but would let "the world as it is to come fully to him."[68] But "the world" had shrunk to a small colony of dissatisfied bohemians.

In the summer of 1913, the vacationers at Provincetown included the Hapgoods, writer Mary Heaton Vorse, George Cram Cook and his wife, Susan Glaspell, and writer Wilbur Steele and his wife, Margaret. The "caressing mood" of the sleepy fishing village "soothed" their "fevered brows to the point" where writing anything became a "Sisyphus-like task."[69] In his autobiography Hapgood maintained that this group of writers, in contrast to the Villagers who appeared the following summer, lived in friendship and tranquility. But even his memoirs seem to contradict this nostalgia, for he recalled:

> Sometimes we struck a deeper note, as when Wilbur, humorously or pathetically oppressed by his passionate love for Margaret, or his economic burden, or under the influence of Aeschylus, or Haig and Haig, drew an expressive picture of a female spider devouring a male after the latter's duty was performed.[70]

The analogy with a spider was not whimsical; Wilbur was very much at the mercy of his devouring wife.[71] Moreover, the troubles of the Hapgood and Steele marriages apparently overlappped, for he and Wilbur traded overt gestures toward each other's wives. Wilbur "paid many a pretty compliment to Neith, as I did to Margaret, who was a racy girl with a strong sense of humor, like Neith."[72] Dominated by idleness, gossip, liquor, and tension, life at Provincetown was less than idyllic.

Hapgood argued that the community only degenerated in the summer of 1914 with the arrival of the Village's "more theologically minded revolutionists"—"the Anarchists, the I.W.W.'s, the extreme left wing of the Socialists, the females militantly revolutionary about sex-freedom, and the Cubists and Post-Impressionists in art." Steered to their Provincetown sanctuary by anarchist Hippolyte Havel and his lover, Polly Holladay, these newcomers engaged in "extreme outbreaks" and "nude bathing-parties." Although the original settlers frequented Polly's new Provincetown restaurant, Hapgood maintained that they always retired "to their own homes where relative peace was secured." By contrast, the new arrivals "huddled together in the restaurant all the time" and initiated "jealousies, nerves, drunkenness as a relief, and physical enormities."[73] Mary Heaton Vorse's description of Lucy Huffaker's party suggests, however, that the original settlers neither behaved differently nor segregated themselves from the newcomers. She reported:

> Hutch thought that Eastman's attitude [was] critical [of him]—he was with them for not drinking—and fought bitterly with Ida—calling her a prostitute in the course of hostilities and Hippolyte called Lucy the most loathsome and horrible person in all the world since she had taught free love to Polly. So you see with Lucy's arrival we're at it again.[74]

Hapgood had reason to remember an unhappy summer because in June he and Neith separated once more. Remaining in Provincetown while Neith journeyed to Florence with Mabel Dodge, Hapgood reviewed their marriage, which was published anonymously as *The Story of a Lover*. Perceiving the "loneliness" of their lives and the "complete isolation in which [Neith's] spirit dwelled," he brooded over his failure to achieve a deep and untroubled relationship. He maintained that "the most difficult art in the world" was "the art of human relations" and what others called art was "mere child's play in comparison."[75] Since this observation was based upon a marriage of "constant nervous friction," his claim was fairly accurate.

Hutchins Hapgood. Yale University Library.

Unlike most men, who could only create a "sketch" in the "difficult" art of love, Hapgood called himself the exceptional "artist-lover" who had the "patience to build a work of art," even if it took "an eternity" to finish. He admitted that a "beautiful love relationship" was impossible without "a delicate sexual adjustment," and that it was difficult "for a civilized man and woman to have an adequate sensual relation." But

Hapgood blamed himself for their marital incompatibility; Neith was cold and unresponsive because he "lacked something." Hapgood attempted to arouse her by having "adventures with other women" and telling her about them. He encouraged her to "know other men intimately" because it would enhance the "social relations" of their marriage and would provide "richer material for conversation."[76] When she showed any interest in someone else, he thought it "an exciting sign of imaginative vitality" and "life-spirit in her." He wrote to her: "Tell me you love me and also tell me about the flirtations you are having. Have you been unfaithful? Have you sinned? Did you like it? Come and hug me and confess it all."[77] When she had intimate relations with other men, he demanded that she recount all that happened. Although his interest in her quickened, he also felt miserable. Mostly, however, she remained uninterested in his schemes and unruffled by his attempts to break through her reserve. Therefore, he "hated" and "loved" her "never-failing egotism" and the "unconscious completeness with which she remained herself."[78]

Hapgood's book, which he distributed to friends before its publication, was an elaborate defense of his behavior. Although Villagers applauded his candor, Hapgood did not probe deeply or gain a perspective on himself. In writing an abstract account of his relationship with Neith, he avoided a realistic appraisal of their conflicts and any criticism of the free-love theories that rationalized his behavior. In maintaining that the "purpose and destiny" of civilization was a society "where the architecture of human relations may tower to its fullest and most lovely height," he justified his preoccupation with personal relations. Although he admitted to "a restless reaching out, a striving to connect" himself with "something foreign," in a "vain, unconscious hope of finding the rich peace" that did not exist in his "soul," he did not connect his sense of emptiness and loneliness to his narcissism.[79] Unwilling to abandon his floating existence or sacrifice his unrealistic desires for a commitment to a cause or a lover, Hapgood remained unhappy.

The war in Europe, which began late that summer, deepened Hapgood's despondency, for "all Nature," it seemed, was "at war with man."[80] The Provincetown bohemians responded to news of the war with an alcoholic binge. Fred Boyd, an unbalanced political extremist, called a conference of Villagers on the beach in order to draw up a resolution to stop the fighting, which would be cabled to the belligerent governments. Boyd announced:

> By a fortunate accident we happen to have here assembled the brains of America. We must draw up a statement of the working class in this and

Frolicking at Provincetown, Mass. in September, 1914. Left to right: K. R. Chamberlain, Maurice Becker, Robert Parker, and Polly Holladay. Courtesy of K. R. Chamberlain.

all other countries, stating the real economic cause of the War and so nipping this inhuman affair at its very inception. For the working class of every country at war will revolt when they understand the capitalistic cause . . . . The time has gone by when a few unscrupulous men can lead the masses to ruin. Socialist principles and the revolutionary philosophy of the proletariat is too widespread for that.[81]

But the participants, who included Bayard Boyesen, Max F. Eastman, Mary Heaton Vorse, Joe O'Carroll, Hippolyete Harvel, George Cram Cook and his mother, could not agree on a statement, especially after everyone became intoxicated. Then Joe O'Carroll took off his clothes and headed for the sea, apparently bent on committing suicide. Hapgood and the other men hauled him out of the water and, after beating "him into relative insensibility," put him to bed. Next Polly, who was being pursued romantically by O'Carroll, Charles Demuth, Stuart Davis, and Hippolyte Havel, decided to drown herself. But she changed her mind when she discovered that the water was too cold. Hippolyete, wounded by her flirtations with other men, attacked Polly with the intention of giving her, as was customary, a sound thrashing. But Hapgood intervened, much to the consternation of the lovers, and peace was temporarily restored.[82] The sincere but pathetic plan to end hostilities was forgotten in the ensuing turmoil. While the war dampened spirits, it was not responsible for unhappiness and social disharmony. The "external explosion" in Europe,

Hapgood admitted later, "corresponded to the latent possibility of explosion in our own souls."[83]

The summer of 1915 in Provincetown continued much like its predecessor, and the war remained an unfortunate event but a distant concern. No one wanted to discuss the war because, Mary Heaton Vorse recalled, no one wanted "to think about disagreeable things."[84] The Hapgoods were reunited, and Mabel arrived with an entourage headed by painter Maurice Sterne, her latest lover. Since she was no longer involved with Reed, Mabel had abandoned the "revolution" for "aesthetics" and surrounded herself with artists. She kept her brood together by impregnating them with a suspicion of Mary Heaton Vorse and others who were not of her group.[85] But Hapgood remembered that the conflict between Mary and Mabel was "only one instance" of what happened that summer:

> Mabel was a symbol rather than a cause. She was far from being the only poison-distributing center. We were all of us, so in some degree. . . . Suspicion, bitterness, disappointment, and a certain instinct to destroy each other's personalities were revealed.[86]

Hapgood went around "analyzing" his friends to the "point of their ultimate discomfiture." These destructive tendencies ruined his dream of "a superior race of men and women capable of maintaining beautiful and intense relations."[87]

If, as Hapgood maintained, the atmosphere that summer was vicious, depressing, and "anaemic," then the establishment of a theatrical group, which subsequently became the Provincetown Players, bordered on the miraculous. But this enterprise, launched by amateurs who wished to express "the simple truth of their lives" and "to recover from discouragement and disappointment," largely continued their fascination with personal relations.[88]

The Hapgoods participated in the early dramatic experiments. Together they wrote and acted in *Enemies,* a devastating portrayal of their unhappy marriage. George Cram Cook, who conceded that they had written the play "to get it off their chests," approved of its subject-matter because the theater was a "laboratory of human emotions."[89] Hapgood maintained, however, that they were attempting to answer certain questions: "How are we really living [and] what are the relations actually existing between us?" The solution to "bigger social problems" lay in knowing "their own intimacies," for "without self-knowledge and honest reconsideration our political and economic effort is useless."[90] There

On the beach in front of Max Eastman's cottage. Provincetown, summer, 1914. Left to right: K. R. Chamberlain, Maurice Becker, and Harry Kemp.

was, however, no understanding or resolution of personal problems. Ill-equipped to see emotional conflicts within a larger context, the Hapgoods offered no insights into American society, the Village, or themselves. They magnified personal problems almost as if they hoped the theater would dramatize and justify their lives. Under the aegis of artistic expression, the Hapgoods moved marital conflict to center stage.

Hutchins's ineptitude as an actor and Neith's limitations as a playwright disposed them to forsake the theater. Hapgood then began an affair with John Collier's wife, Lucy, who was "interested exclusively in the human and in the sensuous values of life."[91] Since Neith and John learned of the romance, all became emotionally involved, and the drama continued offstage.

Hutchins selected Mabel Dodge as arbiter in the dispute, a choice which maximized dramatic possibilities. Naturally Mabel jumped at the opportunity to intervene, supplying information and her own interpretations to Neith and John. Next she visited Lucy and argued against the continuation of the affair. At that point Hapgood complained to Mabel about her machinations:

Hutchins and Neith in *Enemies*. Provincetown, 1916. Yale University Library.

You have a need, under your present fad of 'analysis' to immolate yourself—and others, on the altar of self-sacrifice. . . .

I never said to you or any living soul that 'Lucy needs to have her body loved.' That is a coarse and untrue report of anything I said and I *forbid* you ever to repeat that statement to anybody. If you do, I'll never speak to you again. You are simply an abominable reporter and you ought never to trust yourself to quote anybody—not even their meaning.

I am willing always to have you or any friend tell me what you think

about me. . . . Or, if you had gone to my friends and 'analyzed' me unfav-
orably, I should not have thought it unfriendly, but to do so in a practical
and important situation is unfriendly.

You have put your 'heavy hand' on more things than me in the course of
your life, and you are still keeping it up. . . .

You are not, at this moment, frank enough to admit that what love you
had for me is gone.[92]

Neith did not object to Mabel's intrusion but to her report of the facts,
namely that she and Lucy were "fighting over Hutch's body." She did not
"care so much about the sexual act" and had no objection to Lucy's sexual activities with her husband. Neith accused Mabel of taking a "very
primitive" view "of what started out to be a very civilized arrangement."
She and Hutch "could swing such an arrangement, if the third person
were all right for it." Unhappily, Neith decided, Lucy was not the right
person; she was simply a tragic figure whose eight-year marriage had
come to an end.[93] By contrast, she and Hutch, "a couple of hard nuts,"
were inured to separations and infidelities; unfortunately, the "young
and tender" were injured by "associating too intimately," with them.
Finally, Neith concluded that Villagers did not know "their own minds"
or what they wanted from intimate relationships. The result was turmoil
and instability. The "longer" she lived, the more she was "struck with the
uprooted character of most people in their human relations."[94]

Hutch concurred with Neith's view that an intimate relationship with
Lucy was possible without destroying his marriage. He criticized Mabel
for demanding "a well-defined relation in love," and explained to her:

I am in a really *social* situation with several persons—and you understand *only individual* situations and clashing wills. There are clashing wills
here, too, but there is also an unusually beautiful social desire, in the
small group involved.[95]

Although he and Neith had endured "a very emotional time," perfect
"frankness" had brought them "nearer together."[96] Both felt better for
the experience, and Neith thought that "for the first time" they had
achieved "a completely happy and satisfying relation together."
Hapgood learned that his wife did want him "completely and absolutely," and Neith realized that she had "some impersonal" and yet
"very deep personal" feeling for him. Neith hoped that Lucy, "who
wasn't in [their] class as regards experience," would not break with
Hutch. Lucy could enjoy "intimacy of all kinds" but not "passion," which
he had never "felt for her." Neith and Hutch were "free to love other

people" because nothing could "break or even touch the deep vital passionate bond" between them.[97]

After the affair languished, Hapgood told Mabel that he no longer could "stand as much as [he] used to." "Things" that touched on "human relations" bothered him "as they never did before." At least he "now" realized that he was "altogether ridiculously sensitive to emotional disturbances."[98] But this knowledge did not deter him from subsequently pursuing other women and intense relationships. Although Hapgood continued to visit Greenwich Village, his connection became more remote as he and Neith weathered the remaining years in quieter backwaters.

NOTES

1. Hutchins Hapgood, *A Victorian in the Modern World* (New York, 1939), p. 55.
2. *Ibid.,* p. 53, p.20, p.46.
3. *Ibid.,* 16, p. 11.
4. *Ibid.,* p. 30, p. 10, p. 19.
5. *Ibid.,*p. 42, p. 48.
6. *Ibid.,*p. 49.
7. *Ibid.,* pp. 65-66, p. 68.
8. *Ibid.,*p. 66.
9. Hutchins Hapgood, "The Student As Child," *Harvard Monthly,* Vol. 15 (1892-1893), pp. 11-13.
10. *Ibid.,* pp. 82-83, pp. 86-91.
11. H. Hapgood to Arthur F. Bentley (May 12, 1894), Hapgood Papers, Beinecke Library, Yale University.
12. Hapgood, *A Victorian,* p. 100, p. 18.
13. *Ibid., p. 128, pp. 117-123.*
14. *Ibid., pp. 138-139.*
15. Hapgood, "The Bohemian," *Types From City Streets* (New York, 1910), p. 118.
16. Hapgood, *A Victorian,* pp. 111-112.
17. Hapgood, "Literature in Low Life," *City Streets,* p. 22, p. 17.
18. *Ibid., p. 16.*
19. Robert E. Humphrey, "E. L. Godkin: Genteel Critic of Mass Society," unpublished M.A. thesis, University of Iowa, 1966.
20. Hapgood, "Literature in Low LIfe," *City Streets,* pp. 14-22.
21. Hapgood, "The Real Bowery," *City Streets,* pp. 28-29.
22. Hapgood, "The Shop-Girl," *City Streets,* p. 127.
23. *Ibid.,* p. 135.
24. *Ibid.,* pp.140-141. Hapgood, "The Pathos of Low Life," *City Streets,* pp. 165-166.
25. Hapgood, "The Bohemian," *City Streets,* pp. 113-124.
26. Hapgood, *A Victorian,* pp. 162-171.
27. Hutchins Hapgood, *Autobiography of A Thief* (New York, 1903), pp. 9-13. Hapgood *A Victorian,* p. 171.
28. Neith Boyce, "Autobiography," unpublished manuscript, Boyce Papers, Beinecke Library, Yale University, pp. 1-9.

29. William G. Bonelli, *Billion Dollar Blackjack* (Beverly Hills, Calif., 1954) pp. 25-29; Neith Boyce, "Autobiography," p. 65, pp. 68-69, p. 72.
30. Neith Boyce, "Autobiography," p. 36.
31. *Ibid.,* pp. 136-139, p. 152.
32. *Ibid.,* pp. 153-154.
33. *Ibid.,* pp. 167-168, pp. 101-106, pp. 126-130.
34. Hapgood, *A Victorian,* pp. 153-156.
35. Hapgood, "The Picturesque Ghetto," *Century Magazine,* Vol. 94 (July 1917), p. 471. This article was written fifteen years before publication date. Hapgood, *The Spirit of the Ghetto* (New York, 1969), pp. 113-176. The book is a collection of articles that were written for the *Commercial Advertiser.*
36. Hapgood, "The Picturesque Ghetto," pp. 469-470; "The Earnestness that Wins Wealth," *World's Work* (May 1903), p. 3459.
37. Hapgood, *Spirit of the Ghetto,* p. 34, p. 37.
38. Hapgood, "Earnestness that Wins Wealth," pp. 3458-3465.
39. Hapgood, *A Victorian,* pp. 172-177.
40. *Ibid.,* pp. 178-182.
41. Hutchins Hapgood, *The Spirit of Labor* (New York, 1911), pp. 13-15.
42. *Ibid.,* p. 200, p. 17.
43. *Ibid.,* p. 25, p. 280, p. 96, pp. 200-201.
44. *Ibid.,* p. 324, p. 11, p. 109, p. 398.
45. *Ibid.,* pp. 276-277.
46. *Ibid.,* pp. 266-268, p. 271; *An Anarchist Woman* (New York, 1909), p. 154.
47. *Spirit of Labor,* p. 264, p. 269.
48. *Ibid.,* p. 390, p. 326, p. 398, p. 264.
49. Hapgood, *An Anarchist Woman,* p. 224.
50. Hapgood, *A Victorian,* pp. 211-251.
51. *Ibid.,* pp. 255-275, p. 283.
52. H. Hapgood, "A Day at Paterson," *New York Globe* (April 22, 1913), p. 8; "Trend of the Time," *New York Globe* (March 28, 1912), p. 8; "What we Overlook," *New York Globe* (December 13, 1912), p. 10. "The Limitation of Production." *New York Globe* (September 26, 1912), p. 6.
53. H. Hapgood, "The McNamaras and the News," *New York Globe* (December 14, 1911), p. 12; "Ben the Bum," *New York Globe* (November 23, 1911), p. 10; "Fire and Revolution," *New York Globe* (July 11, 1915), p. 5
54. Hapgood, "The Strikers' Pageant," *New York Globe* (June 9, 1913), p. 6.
55. Hapgood, "Reforming the Fourth," *The Nation* (July 15, 1909), pp. 48-49; "Prohibition," *Forum* (March 1916), p. 263, p. 257.
56. Hapgood, "Haywood at Henri's," *New York Globe* (June 5, 1912), p 10.
57. Hapgood, "The Pennsylvania Station," *New York Globe* (November 27, 1911), p. 12; "The Trend of the Time," *New York Globe* (March 12, 1912), p. 4; "Labor and Poetry," *New York Globe* (November 27, 1917), p. 6; "Art and Unrest," *New York Globe* (January 27, 1913), p. 10; "To My Readers," *New York Globe* (May 1, 1913), p. 8
58. Hapgood, "To My Readers," *New York Globe* (May 1, 1913), p. 8.
59. Hapgood, "The Titanic and Human Nature," *New York Globe* (April 22, 1912), p. 10.
60. Hapgood, "Will She Break Into Life?" *New York Globe* (June 6, 1912), p. 10; "Women in Society," *New York Globe* (December 9, 1912), p. 12; "Husbands and Wives," *New York Globe* (December 20, 1911), p. 7.
61. Hapgood, *A Victorian,* p. 318; "The Jealous Wife," *New York Globe* (December 28, 1912), p. 6; "Husbands and Wives," *New York Globe* (December 20, 1911), p. 6; "Two Women and a Ghost," *New York Globe* (April 11, 1913), p. 10.

62. H. Hapgood, The Story of a Lover (New York, 1919), p. 13.
63. Mabel Dodge Luhan, *Movers and Shakers,* p. 45, p. 48.
64. *Ibid.,* p. 47.
65. *Ibid.,* pp. 54-55.
66. H. Hapgood, "A Promoter of Spirit," *New York Globe* (June 12,1913), p. 8.
67. Quoted in Mabel Dodge Luhan, *Movers and Shakers,* pp. 230-231.
68. H. Hapgood, "Cripples and Passivity," *New York Glove* (July 18, 1913), p. 8.
69. H. Hapgood, "The Cares," *New York Globe* (July 23, 1913), p. 6.
70. Hapgood, *A Victorian,* p. 373.
71. Mary H. Vorse told Joe O'Brien: "I would hate more than anything else to dominate another human soul the way Margaret does Wilbur." Letter (October, 1915), Mary Heaton Vorse Papers, Wayne State University Library.
72. Hapgood, *A Victorian,* p. 373.
73. *Ibid.,* pp. 379-380.
74. Mary H. Vorse to Joe O'Brien (June 1, 1914), Vorse Papers.
75. H. Hapgood, *Story of a Lover,* p. 54, p. 45.
76. *Ibid.,* pp. 46-47, pp. 65-66, p. 112.
77. Hutchins to Neith, undated letter, "Saturday Night," Hapgood Papers.
78. Hapgood, *Story of a Lover,* p. 92. Mabel observed what Hutchins called "the savage joys of family life." "The [Hapgood] children listened to Hutch delivering philo-sophical paradoxes to Neith across the table—half-veiled innuendoes that were trying to lay her out and failing, sliding off her guarded front, unable to find an opening [sic]." Luhan, *Movers and Shakers,* pp. 315-316.
79. Hapgood, *Story of a Lover,* pp. 184-185, p. 40.
80. *Ibid.,* p. 55.
81. Hapgood, *A Victorian,* pp. 385-386.
82. *Ibid.,* pp. 386-388.
83. *Ibid.,* p. 385.
84. Mary H. Vorse, *A Footnote to Folly,* pp. 9-10.
85. Luhan, *Movers and Shakers,* pp. 376-379, pp. 386-399.
86. Hapgood, *A Victorian,* p. 394.
87. *Ibid., The Story of a Lover,* p. 108.
88. Hapgood, *A Victorian,* p. 394.
89. Quoted in Helen Deutsch and Stella Hanan, *The Provincetown: A Story of the Theatre* (New York, 1931), p. 26.
90. Hapgood, *A Victorian,* p. 393.
91. *Ibid.,* p. 413.
92. H. Hapgood to Mabel Dodge, undated letter, Hapgood Papers.
93. Neith to Mabel, undated letter, Hapgood Papers.
94. *Ibid.;* Neith to Mabel, another undated letter, Hapgood Papers.
95. Hapgood to Mabel (January 27, 1916), Hapgood Papers.
96. Hapgood to Mabel (December 29, 1915), undated letter, Hapgood Papers.
97. Neith to Mabel (January); Neith to Mabel, undated letter, Hapgood Papers.
98. Hutch to Mabel (November 6, 1916), Hapgood Papers.

CHAPTER THREE

George Cram Cook: A Bohemian in Search of Classical Greece

George Cram Cook's claim to recognition rests on his establishment of the Provincetown Players, an amateur theatrical group that flourished in New York City between 1916 and 1922. Composed initially of men and women from Greenwich Village, the Players were the first group to stage the plays of Eugene O'Neill, probably the most important playwright in the history of American drama. While the Villagers were short on experience and money, they provided a theater, actors, set designers, directors, a rebellious spirit, and a receptive audience for O'Neill and amateur playwrights. With O'Neill's plays at their disposal the Players were able to challenge the commercial theaters of Broadway, which relied upon lavish sets and melodramatic productions. In striving to replace artificiality and standardization with realism and experimentation, the Provincetown Players inaugurated a revolt comparable to contemporary innovations in painting, fiction, and poetry.

The organizing force behind the enterprise was Cook, who in many respects epitomized the Players' strengths and weaknesses. Mercurial

George Cram Cook in Greenwich Village. New York Public Library.

and undisciplined, alternately imperious and lackadaisical, he intended
to develop creativity and stage plays without regard for monetary gain or
critical acclaim. He believed that idealism and freedom would nurture

artistic talent and that the Provincetown Players would confirm his genius and produce a community of artists. A dreamer who rejected contemporary society, Cook wished to recreate the glories of Periclean Greece. He imagined that the rebels of Greenwich Village could reclaim the past and begin a renaissance in America.

George Cram Cook was born (1873) into one of Davenport, Iowa's first and most distinguished families. Arriving in Iowa in 1836, John P. Cook (George's grandfather) became involved in railroad development, real estate, banking, the practice of law and was elected to the House of Representatives in the Thirty-Third Congress. But he retired from politics and lost much of his wealth while acquiring a fondness for whiskey.[1]

When Edward Cook joined the family law firm in 1863, he had to work hard to restore its clientele. Perhaps in reaction to his father's example, Edward developed an addiction to work instead of alcohol. A strait-laced, taciturn man of considerable self-discipline, he achieved a statewide reputation for honesty and industry. He established a successful corporate law practice and served as general counsel for the Iowa Telephone Company, the Rock Island Railroad, and the Tri-City Railway.[2]

In 1866, Edward married Ellen Dodge, a small lively girl whose father owned and captained steamboats on the Mississippi River. Ellen's mother died when she was very young, and her father, LeRoy Dodge, subsequently married twice more. Possibly this succession of mothers and her father's absences accounted for the independence of a woman who embraced vegetarianism, the arts, and theosophy, a religious philosophy with mystical overtones.[3]

Although Edward and Ellen had divergent interests, they liked each other's company. Equally energetic and active, they rose early each morning and walked for an hour together. Having overcome difficult childhoods and developed into self-reliant individuals, they shared a belief in puritan virtues and a preference for solitude. Although they qualified as members of Davenport's upper crust, they did not participate in its social functions.[4]

On a large section of land fronting the Mississippi River near Buffalo, a village nine miles south of Davenport, Ellen converted a pioneer cabin into the family's summer home. "The Cabin," or the "Vale of Bohemia" as it was known, became a gathering place for artists and writers, including such notable out-of-town visitors as Elbert Hubbard and Mark Twain. Here Ellen pursued her artistic interests without fear of social disapproval.

Although the sons, Reuel and George, grew up in a comfortable, middle class home with "colored" servants, their situation was not easy. The

Ellen and Edward Cook as newlyweds. Courtesy of Edmond Cook.

parents expected them to excel, either professionally or artistically, and yet they coddled the boys. Consequently, Reuel and George remained dependent on their parents. Reuel, the oldest, became a lawyer and joined the family firm, but he was not particularly happy with his situation. Throughout his life he, like George, struggled against alcoholism.

Ellen was particularly attached to George, whom she nicknamed "Jig." She hoped that he would pursue an artistic career as if to compensate for a community that had little appreciation for such matters. Later she confessed to him: "I have also longed for the art of the world, and wondered sometimes why I was held here [Davenport], but that very fact has forced my spirit to find its own beauty."[5] Convinced that her son was unusually gifted, she wanted to provide him with an opportunity to develop his creativity. Her pampering and extravagant claims, however, left him ill-prepared for steady effort or modest achievements.

Ellen's instruction in theosophy and life at the Cabin cut George off from conventional influences and encouraged mystical speculations. This tendency became so pronounced that even Ellen worried about his development. She told him:

> I wish you had some of Reuel's audacity and happy careless confidence in himself. . . . You two are so nearly complements to each other you ought to work together. Each one of you could supply what the other lacks. . . . You were born to be a solitary soul to some extent—to climb heights undreamed of by the real sociable people, those who go in crowds. I have tried to keep you surrounded by a circle of jolly young friends so that you might not yield too much to such an inclination.[6]

Her efforts to counteract his isolation and reveries proved unsuccessful. Ultimately he became an outsider unable to achieve happiness in his fantasy world or to derive satisfaction from reality.

For a time Jig participated in ordinary activities. He was attracted to sports, particularly baseball, and the military. Interest in military life began during his school days at Griswold Military Academy in Davenport when he learned the spartan pleasures of drilling.[7] Unlike violin lessons, baseball and martial activities allowed him to develop his masculinity and assert his physical strength.

In 1889, sixteen-year-old George Cook entered the State University of Iowa where he majored in classical literature, played on the school baseball team, and belonged to the Phi Kappa Psi fraternity. Despite his involvement in social activities, Cook's interest in poetry and theosophy set him apart from other students. Later he recalled: "I used to sound people as to their capacity to understand theosophical ideas and when they failed I set them down as people of no inner light, which was usually the case."[8] Although he did not finish in the upper third of his class, the Collegiate faculty appreciated his literary interests, for he was one of

Literary Society at University of Iowa, 1891. Cook is fifth from left.

three students chosen to "proctor" the Advanced Rhetoric Class. Some schoolmates were, however, critical of his appointment; the school year book commented: "George C. Cook—Poet, Philosopher, Pessimist, Prohibitionist, Proctor, and Professor's Pet."[9]

After graduating in 1892, Cook transferred to Harvard College for one year in order to "make life glorious for myself and others before I die."[10] Ellen assured him that in the East people appreciated culture; a short trip to Minneapolis convinced him that "in the city great Art is in one's daily life, and people of beautiful culture and experiences are found on every block."[11] In some respects his hopes were realized, for he concluded, some months after his arrival in Cambridge, that Harvard was "worth a hundred thousand State University of Iowas" because one could "think of more than corn and hogs without being visionary or crazy."[12]

Life in the East was, however, far from ideal; he suffered from loneliness and a sense of cultural inadequacy. Near the end of the school year he complained to his mother about feeling out of place. Ellen offered little consolation:

> That sense of being an outsider you are bound to have in New England. The sense, of change from your comrades here, to the disciples of 'good form' in Massachusetts [sic]. I warned you against it at first. If you desire to harden yourself, to rub against granite until the worst of your sensitiveness is removed by harsh contact and heavy bumps, you are in the right place.[13]

If Harvard valued culture, it did not build self-confidence. When he made friends with students who shared his interests, the result was a mixed blessing because Cook felt "profoundly ashamed of [his] shallow scholarship." He thereupon resolved "to learn something about old English, Gothic, Old Saxon," history, and literature.[14] To become more refined he devised a program of cultural self-improvement. "It will," he wrote in his diary, "be a good plan each day to play *some* on my violin, to look for five or ten minutes at some one of my art photos, to read *creatively* some piece of good style, and to make my dailies [assignments] the very best I can write."[15]

When John Alden, a fellow student, escorted him to the Boston Museum of Fine Arts, Cook was transfixed by the artifacts of classical civilization. Assyrian art conjured up "sculpture palaces soaring from flat Mesopotamia," and he forgot about college and himself.[16] Fantasies about preindustrial societies stimulated his imagination and screened out the ugliness of modern America. Such daydreams, however, provided only temporary relief. The "few hours in the Art Museum" could "not prevail against the hideous lines and colours" produced by "machinery and unloving labor." He wondered: "Is beauty only an impossible dream? Will it ever be real with us as it has been in the far-off sunlands?"[17]

Cook's exposure to classical culture at Harvard reinforced attitudes learned from his mother, for she despised the "rawness and raspiness of modern life with its feverish haste" and yearned for the "golden days of Greece" when there was time "to consider beauty in all things." If, she told him, "we had time in America, we could" teach young people "harmony of dress and movement, give them fitting surroundings and make beautiful pageants."[18] These influences intensified an interest in antiquity and removed him even further from the contemporary world. He would face the future with his eyes directed toward the past, dreaming about a community that produced and valued beauty.

Cook's plan to improve his education and write poetry required discipline, which became more difficult to acquire, particularly after he began to drink. In notes for an autobiographical novel Cook admitted that he and a classmate saw "things in Greek sculpture that nobody else had seen." They would celebrate their vision by drinking "a couple of quarts of champagne apiece." Then, their "discoveries grew more gleamingly beautiful to them, the long-dead chiselers of stone acquired more and more distinctness as living men, their qualities became more valuably related to the opening minds of ardent investigators."[19] The assumption that alcohol heightened his sensitivity justified its use then and later, when drinking played a more important role in sustaining Cook's imagination. Periodically he felt guilty about his dissipation, and on one occasion he boldly announced in his diary: "I am willing that father should know just how bad I am even if he loses faith in me for it."[20] The internalization of paternal values and expectations generated self-reproach but seldom checked his excesses. Moreover, he exaggerated Edward's reaction to his shortcomings; the elder Cook tolerated his son's lapses and subsequently supported him through years of unemployment.

Cook was conscious of "the opportunities that [had] been showered" upon him, and he resolved to live for "poetical work" and to "purify" his "soul and let its light shine forth."[21] But extraordinary resolutions were undermined by inactivity and windy monologues in which he tried to impress "the bright, witty, well-read crowd of fellows." Although he pledged "not to cheapen [his] deepest thoughts by senseless talking of them," he invariably found fellowship more pleasant than solitary work.[22] Alternately excited by aesthetic experiences or depressed by a lack of creativity, Cook did not achieve a sense of well-being at Harvard.[23]

At the end of the term Alden invited Cook to accompany him to Greece. In requesting travel funds from his father, Cook acknowledged a reluctance to engage in everyday concerns, but argued that after the trip, "with the intimate knowledge of the most stirring life the world has known," he would be ready "to unfold the powers of [his] soul in the Homeric West—perhaps in Chicago" and "be a power making for the ennobling of life in America." He could then "deal with things" with a "Homeric unconsciousness of self."[24] His mother, who yearned for "art, travel, and intellectual companionship," was wildly enthusiastic about the projected journey.[25] Viewing it as an opportunity to escape "the Moderns, whose ideas of beauty are mostly so crude," she told him: "If only we could do without a kitchen, live as they did in Greece, mostly on fruits and nuts, cultivating trees and vines rather than corn and pork, life with us might regain and surpass the beauty of Greece."[26] Sensing her need to share his adventure, he confessed in his diary:

> She has set her heart on my going to Greece. . . . My words about my longing to play a noble part in the history of the West—she feels that longing with me, she believes that the longing is not in vain. For her sake it must not be in vain.[27]

He had a mandate from Ellen to visit Arcadia and find his future there.

When his father's mine investment failed to realize a profit, there was no money for the trip. Cook returned home to an uncertain future. At the age of twenty-one he was very much a divided individual. He wished to remove himself from society and yet believed that self-respect depended on economic success. He thought of himself as a poet but wrote few poems. When he could admit to being "a man of average talents and character," he became depressed and intoxicated.[28] He wanted to stop drinking, but feared that "without stimulants I might miss a certain brilliancy of performance that I might otherwise attain in writing, in conversation, or in music."[29] He contemplated a program of moral regeneration so that "the finer powers of [his] soul would unfold themselves and grow"; at the same time he sought the approval of Davenport's social elite. If he could not, he told himself, become a "Messiah or a saint," he would at least "be a merry, whole-souled gentleman with good sense and good manners."[30] Having grown up in a household that shunned fashionable society, he was not adequately prepared for interaction with "the best people." To overcome this handicap he tried to emulate Robert Finch, the son of a wealthy family and a friend from Harvard, in matters of "perfect cleanliness."[31] By December, however, he was ready to accept defeat. Dejectedly he commented: "What hope have I of ever being graceful in mind and manners when I must strive against the stream of twenty years of absorption of Davenport and Iowa City life? Even in Cambridge the thing clung to me like a nightmare."[32]

To cope with social ineptitude Cook emphasized his poetic gifts and ennobled his actions. He believed that his behavior remained above the vulgar and the immoral. He felt the "fearful fascination of physical love," but assured himself that he would never satisfy sexual desires wantonly. He yearned for "that not impossible she" who would become his wife, and presumed that as a lover he would "rank spiritually among the great ones of the earth."[33] But inflated assessments of his conduct and talent ultimately would mislead him.

In April, Cook left for Europe protectively accompanied by his mother who, he complained, was "not brave enough to trust me in any hardship or danger."[34] On board the steamer he befriended George DeForest Brush, an American painter, whose socialist ideas "helped to free" him "from the fear of worldly failure." Socialism warranted a "trust in [himself]" and a "new disregard of the world's standards."[35] In addition, Brush's nonacademic pursuit of art persuaded Cook to follow a "Bohemian bachelor life . . . of work and simple pleasure" for the next two years. Bohemianism, which meant being free "to read, write, play, draw, [and] *live* without the wretched necessity of earning money," would become his ideal.[36]

Cook enrolled at the University of Heidelberg with the intention of "work[ing] in master thoughts," but a lack of discipline sabotaged his plans. Although he realized "the emptiness . . . of all people who do not work," he frittered away his time, especially with an English-American colony in Geneva. One member of the group, "a cultured, noble" woman, "held out her hand . . . to help [him] upwards in the world," and he "rose from the society of a middle and commonplace class to that of the best class." Thereafter, he decided to emulate the "worldly" Greeks, who "got all they could out of life," because the "best people of today do the same."[37]

In the fall of 1895, Cook returned to America and became an instructor in English at the State University of Iowa. Naturally he was predisposed to be unhappy, for after Harvard and Europe, Iowa epitomized provincialism. The streets of Iowa City "were always either muddy or dusty [and] ashes and refuse were dumped by the wooden sidewalks. . . . The older men talked shop; the women, babies and cake. The younger men were unattractively wicked."[38] Even the University failed his "test of civilization," which was the "production and appreciation of noble beauty." The students, sons and daughters of farmers and retail tradespeople or the children of country lawyers and physicians, wanted education to be "practical—that is, worth money."[39] Since they were infected with a "Puritanic distrust of pleasure and beauty," his task, "to clean and freshen" their minds with culture, was seemingly an impossible one. In a letter to his friend in Geneva he expressed a dissatisfaction that echoed his mother's sentiments:

I live in a flat island; I wish to live where the mountains meet the sea. I live in an ugly land devoid of beautiful faculties. . . . I want to live with beauty-loving, expressive people, here they are heavy and honest as oxen, fed on corn and ham and water (or whiskey) instead of fish and fruit and wine. Do you know what it is to talk about poetry to these dolts? It is like taking a beautiful, black-figured, brown Greek vase and trying to pound a hole in a stone wall with it.[40]

Exiled to a land of boors, Cook dreamed of escaping to Greece where he would live like Thoreau. "I'll do it as soon as I can. I'll get out of this Anglo-Saxon contagion once for all [sic], and change my character so I can't live among these busy people."

The small-town environment of Iowa City placed severe restrictions upon social behavior. In his first year Cook encountered trouble over reports of his drinking and he was forced to deny the charges in a letter to Dr. Charles Schaeffer, the president of the University:

Dr. Wauchope [chairman of the English department] writes me that all kinds of 'scandalous rumours' about me came to the ears of the Board of

Regents. He says that but for these I might have been made assistant
professor. . . . I do not believe I need tell you that I was not drunk last
year, for I was not.[41]

Given the stultifying atmosphere and the apparent lack of female company, drinking and conversation were the chief forms of entertainment
for young instructors like himself. Since teaching was not sufficiently
rewarding, and allegedly kept him from creative work, Cook wanted to
abandon academic life.

His chance came in the spring of 1898 when the conflict with Spain offered a patriotic way out and the promise of adventure. Two days before
the American declaration of war, Cook volunteered for "national service" and left in the middle of the semester. He apologized to President
Schaeffer for the confusion caused by his sudden departure, but excused
his rashness by declaring that he had "no heart for anything that does not
bear upon the coming struggle."[42]

Company B of Davenport, as Cook recorded in a subsequent history,
departed zestfully for Camp Cuba Libre in Jacksonville, Florida.[43] At
Camp no one was more infected with war fever than Cook. In his diary he
wrote: "Every one of us volunteer soldiers must thoroughly make up his
mind to die in battle or disease [sic]."[44] When it became apparent,
however, that Company B was not going to Cuba, Cook asked his father
to arrange a transfer. The elder Cook refused his request, replying with
wry humor: "I appreciate your anxiety to begin shooting Spaniards, and
get into the front line where you can be shot yourself, but I decline to be
a party to sentencing you to the life of a private in a regular regiment."[45]

Returning home without having fired a shot, Cook acknowledged to
President Schaeffer, in a letter accepting his old teaching position, that "I
should never have enlisted last spring had I forseen the unglorious [sic]
part in the war which it became my duty to perform.[46] But even in the
aftermath of uneventful army service the University was no more attractive. In October, he complained in his diary that he was already twenty-
five and had accomplished "nothing." A sense of futility, he concluded,
could be overcome by "the joy of imaginative creation."[47] Despite the
promise of a hundred-dollar raise, he resigned at the end of the year, and
headed for the family Cabin at Buffalo to begin a writing career.

When he and Charles Banks, a Davenport newspaperman, published *In
Hampton Roads,* a Civil War romance, the future seemed promising.[48]
Cook then set to work on a novel, *Roderick Taliaferro: A Story of Maxmilian's Empire* (1903), another tale of love, war, and bravery.[49] Taliaferro,
a former cavalry officer in the Confederate army, exiles himself to Mex-

ico after the South's defeat. As a soldier of fortune he joins Emperor Maxmilian's army in a losing effort against the Republican forces. This character, who fights for an unpopular cause and becomes involved in a forbidden love affair, could have inhabited Cook's daydreams.

In May, 1902, Cook married twenty-two-year-old Sara Swain of Chicago, and accepted a position at Stanford University for the 1902-1903 term. He was, however, not happy there. By contrast, he claimed later, his "superficial" wife enjoyed the "bourgeois" academic world where she was a social success.[50]

Cook's year at Stanford revived his desire for the simple life at Buffalo. Having read that Leo Tolstoy, the Russian novelist, combined farming with writing, Cook decided to imitate him.[51] But after completing the draft of a novel, he set literary ambitions aside, and fitfully raised chickens, muskmelons, and peas while depending on his father's subsidies. Truck farming provided a pastime, but it could not elevate Cook's spirits. Unable to accept his lack of literary accomplishment Cook, at the age of thirty-two, greatly regretted the loss of his youth.[52]

Idleness and drinking strained Cook's marriage to the breaking point, and Sara left him in the fall of 1905. Overwhelmed by self-pity and depression, he brooded over his miserable fate. Since no publisher wanted his latest manuscript, "A Balm of Life" (a "bitter and truthful" novel about drinking and marriage), he had little incentive to write.[53] He tried to dispel his gloom by having an affair with a bohemian friend, but she resisted his advances.[54]

In this moment of despair, Cook turned to the writings of Friedrich Nietzsche, a lonely outsider who, he thought, had reaped neither praise nor profit exploring truth and madness. Like Nietzsche, Cook "entered regions more desolate and more unadapted to life than the high arctic" and endured "a terror beside which freezing to death" was peace.[55] Cook elevated his suffering and flattered himself by comparing his life and talent with Nietzsche's. "Lazy minds, tired minds, and minds made up," Cook wrote, were "not for Nietzsche nor he for them." Nietzsche was "only for the energetic, the playful, and the free."[56] At a time when despair and loneliness seemed overwhelming, Nietzsche's exhortations about self-mastery inspired him to gain control of his emotions.[57]

If Cook felt isolated, he enjoyed the company of rebellious friends, attended meetings of "The Contemporary Club" (a group which discussed current topics) with his father, and played baseball for a local team.[58] The pending divorce did, however, limit his opportunities to meet women. Since local girls avoided him, Cook was forced to seek someone outside the community. He found one when the Chicago Press Club en-

Interior and exterior of the Cabin. Courtesy of Edmond Cook.

joyed an outing in Moline, Illinois. Among the group was Charles Banks, who introduced him to Mollie Price, a vivacious, young anarchist. Cook soon visited her in Chicago, and they made love on a deserted beach.

Mollie Price at the age of 18. Newberry Library.

Cook returned to Davenport and for the next year and a half managed to keep their romance going with letters. Needless to say, its survival at long distance required more than an ordinary talent for arousing the imagination. He wrote Mollie:

To be in you, making you know that the bodily bliss is one same thing with my soul's delightedness. . . . To lie in you, loving you infinitely, without desire—it will feel like the fulfillment of the great end for which we have our being. . . .

You gave me the beautiful beauty to touch, to clasp to mingle with. You opened to me its more than velvet softness, laid bare the entrance to your sacred womb—the inmost vessel of life where sex and sex finally accomplish their marvelous fusion. . . . I . . . felt delight in being able to penetrate such loveliness. To be provided with an organ just made to penetrate—when penetration is an urgent spiritual necessity—oh nature is good to man. . . . Thanks for the ivory thighs, thanks for making her want to open them for me—and thanks for the hidden nest I found. It was really too good to be true—that it should be there. . . . There I was with you on that lake shore, the spray flying, . . . the masculine coiter[sic] swollen stiff, its little yearning mouth watering—it and I alike full of firm faith that over there in you was orifice capable of containing the pink six and half inch circumference [sic?]. . . . What makes the slipping squeeze and clasp of luscious flesh an affair of the spirit is that one's whole being is in it. The energy we call spiritual—it is all fused and glowing there. Soul touches soul in that fierce joy—that torture of delight. . . . [T]he pretty fine lips of your sex orifice—they are too good to be true—and the sweet little tunnel slippery smooth to glide in—that is much too good to be true—and yet it is. . . . I make the pink lips and the little tunnel true for you. They are as nothing to you till my love-tool gets to them. Your sex is not sex at all till mine touches it. I make it sweet to you—I make you lovely to yourself. . . . [P]raise for my phallus—the key that unlocks for her her secret treasures of sensation. Why those old savages who worshipped the phallus were righter [sic] than the modern degraders of it. . . . Oh little pink door, oh tender tunnel—don't you wish you could get hold of the man-stuff now seething in my living stones? Deep within you you'd feel the tragic spurt and pour of me—my life convulsively seeking your life. . . . And you will be made for it—your whole body, using your vagina as a mouth, will suck at me. . . . I want you here—to slake the infinite thirst of my sex passion—so white hot that it is pure as man's love of gold—I want you here as my chum . . . my playfellow. . . .[58]

To rekindle Mollie's interest, Cook skillfully recalled their ecstasy in this and other letters, and suggested that her happiness depended on his sexual prowess. Given his uninhibited celebration of sexuality, Cook might well believe that he belonged to the sexually liberated. In glorifying the reproductive organs and sexual intercourse, Cook saw himself in the tradition of Walt Whitman.[59] But where Whitman's view was comprehensive, expanding to encompass everything in life, Cook's was limited to himself and sensual pleasures, where sex was mainly an act of physical and "spiritual" gratification.

Despite his desire for Mollie, Cook would not leave home. He wanted to live with her in Davenport, but, he explained, his father, "a great-hearted man" yet "a provincial lawyer," would expect them to marry.[60] That was not possible because the waiting period after his divorce had not expired. But Mollie did not pine away in Chicago. Since adolescence she had been eager for new experiences and was prone, like her eccentric father, to follow almost any whim including vegetarianism, nature cults, anarchism, and nude modeling. Unfortunately her impulsiveness and "her sympathy for everyone and anyone's troubles" led to misadventures.[61]

Mollie joined a road company as a dancer and traveled about the country, much to George's displeasure. He was particularly irritated at her visit to a disreputable tavern in New Orleans, and warned: "I find it best to keep away from those places . . . because of their effect on me. If they are not good for me who am tough and have seen a good deal of nastiness . . . why how can they *not* be bad for a *girl?*"[62] Soon thereafter, perhaps to appease Cook, Mollie left the show and joined the staff of Emma Goldman's *Mother Earth* in New York.

Mollie viewed Cook as a virile genius and he welcomed the flattery. He told her without modesty: "You idealize me into supermanhood and that you do it just tickles me to death. I fear I'm inclined to accept your version of me as true."[63] He explained that his "uncanny powers" had been attained by realizing "what life is—what death is—what infinite space is—[and] . . . the immense process of development from amoebae to man." That was "genius—to see so [and] to feel so."[64] Since, however, he had "no record of value," he was "extrinsically" a "failure." With her help, he asserted something significant would be produced.

Cook's mood soared as he imagined pleasures with Mollie and developed a friendship with Floyd Dell, a twenty-year-old newspaperman interested in poetry and socialism. Despite Dell's youthfulness, Cook considered him to be his only friend. Cook wrote Mollie: "I would be in New York now were it not for Floyd Dell. I couldn't live alone here now. I couldn't hold myself to any literary work however fascinating."[65] Dell remembered a similar dependency in their relationship: "I felt for George . . . the impulse of protectiveness which the worldly, calloused, hard-boiled person feels for the too fine-natured to endure the hard knocks of life."[66] But Dell was no better prepared to endure the demands of ordinary existence; they both preferred to live outside society and dream about writing books and making love.

Expansively Dell and Cook began a novel based on themselves and their rebel friends. Dell planned to write the first chapter, and then they would decide who would finish it. Despite this haphazard approach, Cook told Mollie that "an intellectual egg and seed leaped together that night." The sexual metaphor reflected their fantasies, for they became excited at the prospect of including Mollie in the novel. Cook told her "how the ideas seethed" when "Mollie-girl" became the focus of their attention: "We chased her through woods and over hills. She laughed at us and lured us and escaped us, and let herself be caught an instant and then broke away free again and fled like wind in the tree-tops."[67] Not only did Mollie serve as an elusive nymph, she was asked to report on the bohemians in New York. He instructed her:

> You bottle up some New York scenery and atmosphere for seasoning in the life of the bunch there. How about the 'Mother Earth' Ball for which you were going to cut cake? Golly. Nail down a description of that Ball, Mollie. . . . Jump on some of those cafe scenes with wine and music and an after theatre crowd. A little swelldom in the background maybe, but mainly the haunts of the Bohemians — their pet places.[68]

The manner in which Dell and Cook concocted this story testified to their limited perspective. Their subject was themselves (they also began novels about each other) or rather a romanticized view of themselves as radical bohemians. Narcissistic productions would be repeated in New York when Cook and Dell became Village playwrights.

Cook's spirits sagged, however, when Mollie admitted that she had gone to bed with someone else. According to the anarchist's code, she had every right to sleep with anyone she chose, for restrictions on sexual freedom were thought immoral. But Cook refused to extend her the freedom he demanded for himself. Assuming the role of a wronged lover, he told her: "I have nothing to do but be lonely and long in vain."[69] He had not tried "to woo" her from New York because "he didn't want to impregnate her." He had remained continent while she had not, suppressing the fact that his celibacy was not self-imposed. When he accused her of lessening their chances for an "enduring natural marriage," he invoked conventional guilt feelings to influence her behavior.[70]

In February, 1908, the waiting period was over, and Jig and Mollie were married. Floyd Dell, who was living at the Cabin and working for Cook, remembered that Mollie "was a little girl with dark hair and a round face, twenty-two years old, happy and sparkingly and delightfully talkative, much in awe of her god-like husband."[71] Dell fell in love with this "emancipated" girl who boldly went about bare-footed in overalls. To Cook and

Dell she seemed to exemplify the wonderful potential of the liberated woman.

Marriage to Mollie provided a measure of stability in Cook's life, and he became more sociable. Under Dell's influence his interest in socialism revived, and soon he held socialist picnics at the Cabin. In addition, Cook and other Davenport "free-thinkers" formed the "Monist Society" for those who were "ready to reject conventional beliefs" and to accept the "scientific truths" of evolution. The group included "fearless club-women" who wanted a broader education, free-thinking Germans, "the town atheist," the "young people always to be seen at the Public Library," and "various lonely souls."[72] The club provided a measure of security for outsiders and independent thinkers, encouraging them to be rebels. "The beauty of the Monist Society," Susan Glaspell explained,

> was that you could wreck it if you wanted to. The Socialist Party had to be treated a little too respectfully. The Society had a stirring Statement of Belief, and attracted to itself all of us who were out of sorts with what we were supposed to believe. Declining to go to church with my parents in the morning, I would ostentatiously set out for the Monist Society in the afternoon.[73]

Taking their name from the evolutionary philosophy of biologist Ernest Haeckel, the Monists supported a melange of socialist and bohemian positions. Cook led the attack against Christianity because the churches taught "that sex is corrupt." According to him, that idea was responsible "for the evil of divorce, and the more pernicious evil of miserable marriage."[74] Typically Cook did not develop this argument in any systematic fashion. By damning Christian churches for their obscurantism and repression, he counted himself among the liberated, and held society responsible for the failure of his first marriage.

Cook thought that monism and socialism were mutually supportive because they rejected conventional standards and promised a freer society in the future. He envisioned that these "scientific doctrines" would produce a bohemian utopia for artists and writers. He wanted to "live in a prosperous healthy community in which all men and women who so desire" would have "time to think, to read, to study science, to love nature, to cultivate artistic tastes, to develop strong, sympathetic, beautiful personalities, to live interesting lives, and give birth to interesting literature and art."[75] Despite his socialist sympathies, Cook did not identify with the poor. He was an elitist who perceived that "the mass of mankind moves on, ignorant of the achievements of its master minds, ignorant and hostile to the new Knowledge" that scientific investigators discovered. Since the masses repudiated "reason," the enlightened few "must let the majority go its way, and they themselves must go their way."[76]

In 1910, Susan Glaspell, thirty-four years old and unmarried, returned to Davenport after a two-year absence and became Cook's newest lover. Born into a middle-class Davenport family, she attended Drake University where she wrote for the school newspaper and served as assistant editor to Lucy Huffaker, who became a lifelong friend and a fellow Villager. "A delicate woman with sad eyes and a sweet smile," she seemed to Lawrence Langner, as "fragile as old lace."[77] Beset by numerous physical ailments, including a weak heart, she was attracted to Cook partly because he was physically robust. An incurable romantic, she idealized him as an heroic figure and a "tormented" poet.

The revival of Cook's literary aspirations enhanced his interest in Susan, whom he courted even though Mollie was pregnant with their second child. In March, he finished *The Chasm,* a melodramatic novel about Nietzschean aristocrats and socialist revolutionaries in Russia. When he and Susan made plans to collaborate on a novel, he dreamed about two lover-writers "who study, think things out together, sow seed in each other's minds, keep them warm and growing," and establish "intimate and intense relationships" with other "living minds." They would "radiate hitherto unformulated ideals of art and love."[78]

Since their families and friends opposed the abandonment of Mollie and the children, Susan and Jig could not remain together in Davenport. Susan returned to New York in order to finish a second novel and to see her publisher about Jig's manuscript. Cook went to Chicago and became Dell's assistant on the *Friday Literary Review*, a weekly supplement of the *Chicago Evening Post.* His decision to leave Davenport at the age of thirty-eight was primarily motivated by a desire to escape the past. Behind him lay failure—two broken marriages, two novels without literary merit, an unprofitable venture in farming, unemployment, depression, and drinking. Ahead of him lay perhaps a brighter future: literary creativity, marriage to Susan, and life in a community of artists.

Once in Chicago and among like-minded rebels, Cook leveled a blast at his hometown. In a letter to the local newspaper he attacked Davenport for having neglected its writers, presumably himself and his friends. Only the "European exiles of 1848," he maintained, had nourished the growth of a literary coterie in the city. The immigrants had brought a "liberalizing stream of continental culture" to the "edge of the Puritan state of Iowa." Thanks to the Germans, "men could sit up all night drink-

ing beer at a table—conceiving and planning novels in a blaze of talk."
But, he warned, the enforcement of a new 10 P.M. tavern curfew would
result in "a pitiful end of [Davenport's] vaunted literary supremacy."[79]
While Cook and his friends may have discussed writing over beer, their
creativity was hardly dependent upon all-night sessions in local taverns.
If anti-drink ordinances epitomized provincial Davenport for Cook, his
preoccupation with the saloon issue reflected a greater concern for
bohemian freedom than literary achievement.

Since Cook's duties as assistant editor only required him to write a few
book reviews each week, there was time for socializing with other staff
members. Cook, Dell, Charles Hallinan, and Lucian Cary often met to
discuss books and plan novels. But Cook's social life was not restricted to
his colleagues on the newspaper. Through Dell he met the writers,
painters, sculptors, and poets, who congregated in cafés, studios, and the
Fine Arts Building. Liberated women with artistic interests were a part of
this group, and Cook had love affairs with poet Eunice Tietjens and
photographer Marjorie Jones.[80]

In the years before the war, Chicago became a literary and artistic
center, attracting men and women from small towns throughout the
Midwest. The galaxy of writers and poets included Carl Sandburg, Vachel
Lindsay, Sherwood Anderson, Edgar Lee Masters, Ben Hecht, and Maxwell Bodenheim. Harriet Monroe founded *Poetry,* a magazine for modern
poets, and Margaret Anderson established *The Little Review,* which endorsed Nietzsche, Henri Bergson, anarchism, feminism, psychoanalysis,
and avant-garde writing. In addition, Maurice Brown, an English poet,
and his wife, Ellen Van Volkenburg, started "the Little Theatre," an
amateur group which staged plays by Euripides, W. B. Yeats, August
Strindberg, Henrik Ibsen, and George B. Shaw.[81]

The outburst of literary and artistic activity convinced many of the
participants, especially Cook, that America was on the verge of a cultural
Renaissance. This cultural awakening, he predicted, would be carried out
by a mere hundred artists and writers. He considered himself among the
chosen who would "reach out to find each other" and kindle a "communal intellectual passion." Cook called on the "vital writers of
America" to develop "more depth and fire" and "to make themselves
strong as caryatides, prepared to bear together each the hundredth part
of our Renaissance."[82] In exhorting Americans to emulate Richard
Wagner, Gabriele D'Annunzio, and Rudyard Kipling and create a "national art," Cook identified with the spirit of cultural nationalism that
distinguished the prewar revolt against genteel culture.

In the fall of 1912, Cook left for Greenwich Village. While he continued with the *Friday Literary Review,* contributing a weekly "New York

Letter" of news and gossip, he planned to do serious writing. On his third wedding day, April 13, 1913, he was optimistic about his prospects in bohemia. He wrote Dell: "There's going to be a bully atmosphere for work there or I miss my guess."[83]

The change in wives did not improve Cook's discipline, and writing came no easier in the artistic milieu of Greenwich Village and Provincetown. While Susan earned money turning out popular stories, Cook amused himself at the Liberal Club, drank in the cellar of the Brevoort Hotel, and chased women. When they purchased a two-story house in Provincetown, he kept busy with household improvements: installing an elevator for Susan, constructing new furniture, and cultivating a vegetable garden. He played chess with Hutchins Hapgood, discussed

Susan Glaspell in Greenwich Village. New York Public Library.

Greek poets with Harry Kemp, built a boat with Joe O'Brien, played baseball with Wilbur Steele, and drank with friends.[84] Sober, painter William Zorach recalled, Cook was "dull and commonplace and plodding"; drunk, he became "dynamic and intelligent." Fortunately, Zorach added, Jig was "more often drunk than sober."[85] After drinking several glasses of wine, Cook would entertain his companions, Hapgood recounted, with "picturable ideas" that flowed from "his laughing mouth."

"His eyes danced with the joy of ideas becoming poetic realities. The fact that he never paused an instant in quick transitions, from one flashing thought or impulse to the next, made his talk a living reality."[86]

In the winter of 1914 some members of the Liberal Club experimented with amateur theatrical productions. As an art form, drama suited bohemia—one could be creative and yet enjoy the company of others. Informal readings led to the formation of the Washington Square Players in February, 1915. The Players intended to present realistic plays, particularly the works of European playwrights neglected by American theaters, and they rented the Bandbox Theater on 57th Street for their productions.

A fervent admirer of the ancient Greek dramatists, Cook became excited about the new theater. He and Susan became involved in the new project, and they wrote *Suppressed Desires,* a satirical play debunking the Villagers' indiscriminate use of Freudian theories and psychoanalysis. But the leaders of the Washington Square Players, who had some theatrical experience and were more conventional in outlook, rejected Cook's contribution. Since the play was Cook's first creative effort in some time, the rejection was difficult to accept. That summer in Provincetown he gave up his part-time position with the *Friday Literary Review* and organized his own theatrical group. Cook was joined by other Villagers, particularly Ida Rauh and Floyd Dell who also thought that the Washington Square Players had slighted their talents, and by his mother who was freed from Davenport by the death of her husband. Using an abandoned fish house as a theater, the group presented *Suppressed Desires* and *Change Your Style,* a light satire by Cook on the competing art schools in Provincetown.[87]

What began as an informal endeavor subsequently developed into a new Village "institution" with Cook as its founder and leader. Bursting with enthusiasm and energy, he returned to Provincetown in the summer of 1916, converted the fish house into the "wharf theatre," and optimistically announced a season of four bills with three one-act plays for each bill.[88] Susan, who had orders to use her skills to write plays, remembered that no one had a chance of escaping from Jig. "Purpose had grown in him," she remembered, "he was going to take whom he wanted and use them for the creation of his Beloved Community."[89] Floyd Dell recalled that Cook's "life was . . . hardly within his own control; it was as if he were being driven on by a demon to some unknown goal."[90] Determined to atone for years of inactivity and unfulfilled promise, Cook intended to achieve the dream of his adolescence. He conceived of his theater as an experimental stage for undiscovered talent, and envisioned that it would produce a creative community rivalling classical Athens. For him it was a last, desperate chance to fulfill an enduring ambition. Cook wagered everything on the outcome; it became his greatest triumph and his final defeat.

The immediate and lasting problem for the group was to find more plays. In the process of asking everyone and anyone for scripts the Villagers met Eugene O'Neill, who was spending the summer across the harbor at Truro. When O'Neill offered *Bound East for Cardiff,* he was invited to join them. While most Villagers recognized (and some resented) O'Neill's talents, they did not like to think of their theater as simply a stage for O'Neill's plays. Nevertheless the acquisition of his plays and professional guidance convinced them to become a semipublic enterprise. Cook told Edna Kenton: "You don't know Gene yet. You don't know his plays. But you will. All the world will know Gene's plays some day. . . . Some day this little theatre will be famous."[91] In September,

Scene from Eugene O'Neill's *Bound East for Cardiff* in Provincetown, 1916. John Reed second from left. George C. Cook lying on bottom bunk, extreme right. Yale University Library.

Cook went to New York, rented three rooms at 139 MacDougal Street and converted them into a tiny, crude playhouse. Adopting the name, the Provincetown Players, the group made preparations for a fall season, and announced that their experimental theater would "encourage the writing of American plays of real artistic, literary and dramatic—as opposed to Broadway—merit."[92]

In New York as elsewhere in America the theater was monopolized by a few commercial-minded producers who served lavish musicals, domestic comedies, silly farces, exaggerated melodramas, and the Ziegfeld Follies to the public. Serious-minded playwrights and intellectuals seldom had the opportunity to see or offer social criticism and psychological drama. By contrast, in London, Paris, Berlin, Moscow, and Dublin there had existed "free theaters," organized on a subscription basis, that presented uncensored, realistic drama and ironic comedy.[93] These independent theaters had introduced simple, authentic sets and natural lighting techniques. The Provincetown Players hoped to bring this tradition to America as the "ill wind of war" blew in Europe.[94]

Although O'Neill remained on the fringe of Village social circles and was hostile to its fashions, he had much in common with the rebels. He too was engaged in a war against Broadway, which was personified by his father, James O'Neill, a matinee idol who squandered his talents in four thousand performances of *The Count of Monte Cristo*. Unlike the excessive melodrama of *Monte Cristo*, O'Neill wanted realism and tragedy. Lust, incest, infanticide, atavism, and insanity—taboo subjects in commercial playhouses—were essential for O'Neill's plays. No character, regardless of origins or station in society, escaped his attention. He preferred the lowliest, those who lived beyond the pale of society (and of the theater) because he empathized with their alienation and pain. Prostitutes, ordinary seamen, criminals, and blacks, creatures moved by instinct and illusion, vividly portrayed man's fate in a universe indifferent to his dreams and needs. While materialism, industrialization, and sexual repression were inimical to human happiness, social conditions were the circumstances, not the final cause of man's dilemma. Ultimately O'Neill was concerned with human psychology or how men confronted, overcame, or succumbed to personal weaknesses and the tragedy of human existence.

Although most Villagers had a rudimentary understanding of Freudian and Jungian psychology, their plays did not explore the deeper springs of human motivation. They wanted to stage realistic drama, but they never analyzed the impact of economic conditions or social conventions. Cook told poet Edgar Lee Masters:

> What you did in *Spoon River [Anthology]*—a direct, first hand, new version of our new life, is what we are seeking to do on our little amateur stage . . . . No one has brought to the stage so much straight truth of life as you brought to the pages of *Spoon River*. That truth would be immeasurably powerful on the stage—it would transform the stage.[95]

But if Cook urged Masters to stage *Spoon River Anthology,* a series of confessional monologues revealing the frustration, hypocrisy, and tragedy of life in an Illinois town, he did not insist that his associates create a similar realism. While Masters's revelations coincided with the attitudes of Cook and his friends, the Village playwrights limited their attention to more esoteric subjects.

From the beginning the group wrote and staged plays that concerned themselves or Greenwich Village. In *Constancy,* Neith Boyce described the Mabel Dodge-John Reed romance while mocking the proponents of free love. Wilbur Steele based *Contemporaries* on Village hero, Frank Tannenbaum, who had been arrested for leading unemployed men into a church. John Reed's *Freedom* poked fun at idealistic Village poets, and Susan Glaspell satirized and honored *The Masses* in a play about a radical journal that inspires idealists throughout the country.

The content of these and other plays was either daily events or mere gossip, and the Players' horizons seldom extended beyond their community. Village drama, consisting of one-act plays that were easy to write and cheap to produce, neglected the larger world and its satires presented mock critiques of bohemia. Suggestions of confusion and unhappiness were usually transformed into comedy. In poet Pendleton King's *Cocaine,* two drug addicts decide to commit suicide, but their attempt fails because neither has money for the gas meter. (This play evidently masked King's deeper feelings, for he subsequently committed suicide.) In producing a reflection of Village life, the participants gained no perspective on themselves, either individually or collectively. The theater, therefore, was almost a private affair, an acting out of social and individual narcissism. Had the Villagers not stumbled upon Eugene O'Neill, who retained his detachment and independence, the enterprise would have remained insignificant. But in giving O'Neill the chance to present his plays and in allowing Robert Edmond Jones the opportunity to design sets, the Players made an important contribution to the development of the theater in America.

The inferiority of the Villagers' writing was matched by the inexperience of their acting and directing. When Nina Moise, who had experience in stock companies, arrived, she was shocked by the level of incompetency. "They didn't know anything about blocking, staging, any of the fundamentals; they were bumping into themselves and stepping on one another's toes."[96] Moreover, many of the actors lacked dedication. Susan Glaspell recalled that they would "cut rehearsals, be late—things professionals would not dream of doing."[97] The Players' problems were compounded by the inevitable personality clashes, which became more acute when the theater became more successful. Cook reported to Susan:

Nord [painter B. J. O. Nordfelt] is to do sets occasionally, but not be on the committee. Mary [Vorse] O'Brien asked him yesterday why he was so fierce around the place and told him that he ought . . . to have had his spleen removed. Today he said he had decided that he was fitted to work only individually not with a crowd. Perhaps with him in the background the theatre will become fun again.[98]

While the author was supposed to have the final word in the staging of his work, this rule did not deter others from challenging that authority, especially when the playwright turned the directing over to someone else. When Ida Rauh decided to eliminate the "ghosts" in O'Neill's *Where the Cross Is Made,* Cook objected to her alterations and asked O'Neill to come to New York and support him.[99] Louise Bryant reported to Reed about another of these conflicts: "There is a terrible struggle over the MacDougals. Jig came over and told me this morning. . . . Anyway it seems that Nord[feldt] has always hated [Duncan] MacDougal ever since he first saw him and Teddy [Edward J. Ballatine] has a great contempt for him and Ida [Rauh] doesn't like him and they won't have him in the group but more than that they want to kick him out altogether. Jig was awfully worried and said Nord was perfectly childish about it. When some one asked what MacDougal had done, Teddy said sarcastically, 'Oh played in country towns in Scotland!' You see Floyd [Dell] gave his play 'A Long Time Ago' to MacDougal unconditionally to produce and he insists on having a chance to do it his way, *not* Ida's way or Teddy's way. Jig says even Susan [Glaspell] wants to put him out. I think she has a complex over it, really. She has loathed Floyd and everyone connected with him ever since he put her out of his play."[100] Rivalries and competition increased particularly as talented newcomers replaced the original members. Dell, one of the dispossessed, commented bitterly that "it was all that one had ever heard about Broadway, in miniature; but nobody seemed to mind." Unsympathetic to Cook's sense of purpose, Dell claimed harshly that "over this crew of artistic ruffians, seething with jealously, hatred, and self-glorification, George ruled, with the aid of a punch-bowl, like one of the Titans."[101] But Cook's seriousness, as Dell cynically reported, was tempered by alcohol and conversation. Susan conceded that when Jig found someone "to play with him—nothing else was so important. A solemn business appointment waited while he and Joe O'Brien and Hutchins Hapgood 'recreated religion' at the bar" of the Brevoort Hotel. Although he could be zealous at times, Cook was susceptible to depression and lassitude, especially when personality clashes threatened to undermine the whole experiment. Susan admitted that they needed parties, particularly after "first night" performances, because "it was important we drink together, for thus were wounds healed, and we became one again."[102] Actor James Light recalled that the opening night parties at Christine Ell's restaurant, located on the second floor above the playhouse, provided "a way of working off steam; things got pretty tense, you know, backstage, and this was our outlet."[103] The Provincetown Players pulled the Villagers together and also set them at odds with one another.

The enterprise survived because O'Neill kept supplying new plays and because Cook believed in the theater. Cook thought that he understood O'Neill and that they shared a common sensitivity. He mistakenly concluded that O'Neill needed his companionship. He told Susan:

> O'Neil[l] isn't seeing Louise [Bryant] now and is nearing the snapping point of suspense and tension. . . . O'Neil[l]'s nervous tension is a thing I feel instantly when I see him. I mean that I instantly catch it from him—feel it myself in myself, [a] sort of anxiety complex. He likes to be with me since he discovered that I feel what he feels. But it isn't good for me.[104]

While Cook also harbored a melancholic view of life, he lacked the ability to move outside himself or universalize his experiences. Cook failed to understand that O'Neill did not share his emotional attachment to the Provincetown Players. Whereas O'Neill wanted a vehicle of artistic expression, Cook viewed their theater as an extension of himself. He wanted a monopoly on O'Neill's talents and convinced himself that they were a creative team. When he finally realized that O'Neill had no intention of subordinating his talents to the Players, Cook became disenchanted with him.

Limited as a thinker and a writer, Cook functioned well in roles which required manual skills. When the Players arrived in New York, and two years later when they moved to larger quarters at 133 MacDougal Street, Cook shouldered the responsibility of constructing a theater. He would not and for a long time could not restrict himself to carpentry. He also wanted to be actor, director, and playwright. In the early stages when the theater was a sectarian affair run by Villagers for themselves, there were no serious conflicts and no questioning of his abilities. As the theater grew in importance and O'Neill demanded professional standards, Cook was gradually pushed into the background.

In April, 1918, Cook forced the Players to perform *The Athenian Women,* an ambitious undertaking involving three acts, six scenes, and a cast of thirty characters crowded together on a tiny stage.[105] Inspired by Aristophanes's *Lysistrata* and a cyclical view of history, it represented Cook's protest against war. His play recalled how the women of Athens had forestalled the Peloponnesian War and channeled the city's energies into artistic creativity. The action centers around Aspasia, a strong-willed woman who convinces the women of Athens to refuse sex with their men until they sue for peace. Their determination succeeds in convincing Pericles and his warriors to lay down their arms. In the end, however, the women (like the Villagers) cannot prevent the outbreak of hostilities. Pericles, speaking for Cook who played the part, consoles himself with the observation that for a time "they had been able to subject one city to the generous will of its artists, thinkers, and lovers." *The Athenian Women* suggested an historical analogy with the rebels of Greenwich Village. Having failed to keep America out of World War I, the Players would "keep alive in the world the light of imagination."[106] Cook and the Players articulated the myth that Greenwich Village was an island of creativity and enlightenment in America.

Cook's production was not well-received; it seemed ludicrous to some, for the actors, who were dressed in cheese cloth robes and sandals, shivered through their lines in the unheated theater. A few Players felt that they had been "commandeered" for their roles, and they resented Cook's squandering of the treasury on an inferior play. Consequently, Cook's attempt to reassert his authority failed. Offended by the criticism, and sensing that others "undervalued him," he and Susan took a leave of absence from the Players in 1919 and retired to Provincetown. Ostensibly he wanted time to write new plays; once in seclusion, however, he busied himself with clay modeling, map making, and the construction of a sun-dial.[107]

In the fall of 1920, Cook and Susan trudged three miles through sand dunes to O'Neill's isolated beachhouse and read a draft of *The Emperor Jones,* a haunting study of the downfall of Brutus Jones, an ex-Pullman porter who installs himself as dictator over ignorant natives. Cook became excited by the "challenge" of staging the play, which he considered simply as an exposition of "the rich emotional and imaginative temperament of the negro people." On the return trip, he told Susan: "This means the success of the Provincetown Players. Gene knew there was a place where such a play would be produced. He wrote it to *compel* us to the untried, to the 'impossible.' "[108] Cook also saw it as an opportunity to regain his position as head of the Provincetown Players and "recreate in a group of modern individuals a spiritual oneness . . . resembling the primitive oneness of a tribe."[109]

Cook left for New York and threw himself into the work of staging and directing the play. On the insistence of Ida Rauh, the Players hired an unknown black actor, Charles Gilpin, for the role of Brutus Jones, and thereby broke a long-standing tradition of excluding blacks from white companies. Overriding the opposition of the other members, Cook spent the Players' funds on materials for a plaster sky dome, which he constructed. This cyclorama, the first used in America, successfully produced an illusion of spaciousness on the tiny stage. Nevertheless, there were other set problems that Cook could not solve. It was only through the efforts of Cleon Throckmorton, who came to the rescue at the last moment, that a smooth-running performance was assured.[110]

The Emperor Jones, which opened November 1, 1920, was a tremendous success. Instead of the usual two-week performance, the play ran two months, and then received offers to move to Broadway. Although Cook later maintained that he had been opposed to the uptown production, he put up money for the venture and allowed Tickless Time (a play written by himself and Susan) to be coupled with The Emperor Jones at the Princess Theatre where they lasted for the entire season.[111]

But financial success, bringing salaries for the actors and money for the playhouse, caused more dissension. When plans were discussed about taking The Emperor Jones and Suppressed Desires to London, the Players divided into two factions—one headed by Cook, Ida Rauh, and Edna Kenton and the other led by actors James Light and Charles Ellis—who "bickered" over the casting of roles. Although the overseas presentation was finally cancelled, the bitterness remained.

Cook did not participate in the commercial production of The Emperor Jones, and O'Neill asked Charles O'Brien Kennedy, a Broadway veteran, to direct his next play, Diff'rent, at the Provincetown Playhouse. This affront, and jealousy of O'Neill, prompted Cook to leave for Provincetown. On arriving, however, he decided, perhaps to avoid painful reminders of early successes, to live across the bay in Truro. Vaguely he flirted with the idea of forming a new group, the Truro Players, and sketched a theater of "domes," which would be erected in Washington Square. But plans to supplant the Provincetowners with a fresh group never materialized.

Cook's condition had become desperate. He had lost control of the Provincetown Players and had little confidence that he could equal or surpass O'Neill's accomplishments. Always susceptible to theories about the unseen, he turned to the occult for inspiration and renewal of his waning creativity. He studied "automatic writing," supposedly an unconscious process by which an individual recalls past events and develops his talents. He then began a play about Madame Curie's discovery of radium. He intended to show that she had been guided by her husband's unconscious, a theme which may have reflected a need to take credit for Susan's plays. Next he became engrossed in Paracelsus, the sixteenth-century Swiss alchemist, who was driven "to the point of madness" by "the religion and the government and the scholarship of his age." Unlike the persecuted materialist, however, Cook dreamed of discovering "the oneness of all men's minds."[112] Murky sentiments about the spiritual unity of mankind revealed his preoccupation with irrationality.

Speculation about mysterious forces, the past, and death, gave birth to *The Spring,* a play which takes place in Iowa.[113] A fantastic melodrama, *The Spring* involves the Indian Chief Blackhawk, love, insanity, hypnosis, and extrasensory perceptions of the past. Notwithstanding its bizarre and obscure intentions, Cook forced the Players to present it in January, 1921. Then, despite an unenthusiastic reception, Cook moved it uptown with his own money, a decision that contradicted previous criticism of O'Neill and the Players. On the third night the Princess Theatre sold four tickets and *The Spring's* run was over.[114] The attempt to outdo O'Neill ended in failure.

In November, Cook directed *The Verge,* one of Susan's weaker plays, which the Players performed listlessly. Despite an unfavorable response in the Village, it was then presented at the Garrick Theatre, where it followed the disastrous fate of *The Spring.* Hoping to repeat his success with *The Emperor Jones,* Cook implored O'Neill to let him direct his new play, *The Hairy Ape.* But after rehearsals began, O'Neill felt that Cook was unequal to the task and took command of the production himself.[115]

Unwilling to acknowledge O'Neill's talent and unable to accept a subordinate position, Cook began to drink more heavily. Convinced that O'Neill had usurped his position and corrupted the Players, he asked that the Provincetown Playhouse suspend operations. As far as he was concerned the attempt to recreate Athens had failed and the particiants were to blame. He told them:

> I am forced to confess that our attempt to build up, . . . in this alien sea, a coral island of our own, has failed. The failure seems to be more our own than America's. Lacking the instinct of the coral-builders, . . . we have developed little willingness to die for the thing we are building.
>
> Our individual gifts and talents have sought their private perfection. We have not, as we hoped, created the beloved community of life-givers . . . . As a group we are not more but less than the great chaotic, unhappy community in whose dry heart I have vainly tried to create an oasis of beauty.[116]

It was time, he told Susan, to leave the "New York hog-trough" and "withdraw into ourselves."

Early in 1922, Cook left with his wife for Greece. This trip, once a youthful dream, signaled defeat and retreat. Cook's inability to appraise himself and others realistically or accept a pedestrian world made it necessary for him to seek refuge from the present. Unwilling to give up his illusions, he went to Greece in order to preserve them. Even in Greece, however, he needed alcohol to sustain his enchanted vision of antiquity. He drank continually and bitterly contemplated his failures. He grew a beard, put on the traditional costume of a Greek shepherd, and lived with peasants on Mount Parnassus. Pathetically he attempted to recapture the past by rebuilding and reviving the ancient theater at Delphi. Cook wrote to Edna Kenton that he needed Cleon Throckmorton for this project because he had "formulated mathematically and straight to the face my shortcomings as a theatrical director." But Cook was broken, shattered by envy, self-contempt, and a sense of betrayal. He no longer had the energy or the enthusiasm to begin anew and he could not forget the loss of the Provincetown Players. He complained to Edna that O'Neill had forced him to leave. "The thing that finally drove me out of the Provincetown Players was that Gene, coming in from the outside. . . broke up my league with Throck[morton]."[117] Then he directed his vengeance at Harry Weinberger, a lawyer with an interest in the theater, even though Weinberger had contributed a thousand dollars to Cook's abortive commercial venture. Cook demanded that Weinberger withdraw from the Players or he would "kill him — that or be killed." He warned Edna that he was carrying a revolver and "now that youth is gone I am keen for a good cause to die in."[118] Furthermore, he thought shooting "certain men" would "purify" America; President Warren Harding, he added, "should be shot for his English."[119] He decided, after a fight with Susan, that Ida Rauh, his former mistress, was the "only friend and lover" that believed in his "prophetic gift." He wrote to Ida:

> I think of myself as a prophet, because for many years I made estimate of what the now defunct Provincetown Players would spend of money in a year, what income would be, and what the balance [would be].
> If only Pen[dleton] King hadn't died, and Hutch[inson] Collins [an alcoholic actor]. They never could have become so mean and little if Hutch Collins had been around.[120]

In assessing his value to the Players, he conceived of his role solely as a business manager. Having spent years of effort in establishing an experimental theater, he pathetically underestimated his real contribution to the Players. His identification with two self-destructive figures was significant; it revealed a desire to destroy himself. He soon got his wish, for he contracted glanders from his pet dog and died in January, 1924.

Appropriately, the peasants buried him in a graveyard near the Temple of Apollo.

NOTES

1. *History of Scott County, Iowa* (Chicago, 1882), p. 610, p. 614. *History of Davenport and Scott County, Iowa,* Vol. 2 (Chicago, 1910), p. 187-188. Susan Glaspell, *The Road to the Temple* (New York, 1927), pp. 1-12. E. E. Cook, "Early Iowa," in *Contemporary Club Papers* (Davenport, Iowa, 1909), pp. 133-138.
2. *History of Scott County, Iowa,* p. 358. Glaspell, *Road to Temple,* 13-14. Davenport *Daily Times* (June 16, 1914), p. 1. Edward E. Cook, Diary (1892, 1900-1912), Cook Family Papers, University of Iowa Library. Interview with Edmond Cook, grandson of Edward Cook (June 26, 1973), Moline, Illinois.
3. *History of Scott County, Iowa,* p. 624, p. 975. Glaspell, *Road to the Temple,* pp. 15, 19.
4. Interview with Edmond Cook. Edward E. Cook's Diary (1892, 1900-1912).
5. Quoted in Glaspell, *Road to the Temple,* p. 62.
6. Ellen Cook to George C. Cook (May 18, 1893), Cook Papers, New York Public Library. Interview with Edmond Cook.
7. Glaspell, *Road to the Temple, pp. 28-32.*
8. Quoted in *Ibid.,* p. 37.
9. *The Hawkeye* (Iowa City, 1892), p. 199.
10. George Cook Diary (October 20, 1892), Cook Papers.
11. George Cook Diary (September 6, 1892), Cook Papers.
12. George Cook Diary (November 20, 1892; December 11, 1892), Cook Papers.
13. Ellen Cook to George Cook (May 18, 1893), Cook papers.
14. George Cook Diary (November 20, 1892), Cook Papers.
15. George Cook Diary (October 28, 1892), Cook Papers.
16. Quoted in Glaspell, *Road to the Temple,* pp. 50-51.
17. Quoted in *Ibid.,* pp. 53-54.
18. Ellen Cook to George Cook (January 8, 1893), Cook Papers.
19. Quoted in Glaspell, *Road to the Temple,* p. 60.
20. George Cook Diary (June 23, 1893), Cook Papers
21. George Cook Diary (October 25, 1893; June 15, 1893), Cook Papers.
22. George Cook Diary (October 27, 1892; May 17, 1893), Cook Papers.
23. George Cook Diary (May 16, 1893), Cook Papers.
24. George Cook Diary (June 13, 1893), Cook Papers. Glaspell quotes this passage as a letter to Edward Cook, *Road to the Temple,* p. 62.
25. Ellen Cook to George Cook (November 17, 1892), Cook Papers.
26. Quoted in Glaspell, *Road to the Temple,* p. 62.
27. George Cook Diary (June 23, 1893), Cook Papers.
28. *Ibid.,* August 8, 1893.
29. *Ibid.,* August 20, 1893
30. *Ibid.,* September 12, 1893.
31. *Ibid.,* August 24, 1893, November 16, 1893.
32. *Ibid.,* February 7, 1894.
33. *Ibid.,* November 17, 1893.

34. *Ibid.,* February 6, 1894.
35. *Ibid.,* May 2, 1894.
36. *Ibid.,* May 12, 1894; June 10, 1894.
37. *Ibid.,* October 14, 1894; October 16, 1894.
38. Glaspell, *Road to Temple,* p. 80.
39. *Ibid.,* p. 80.
40. Letter, April 14, 1896, Cook Papers.
41. Cook to Charles Schaeffer (June 13, 1896), President's Office Files, Special Collections, University of Iowa Library.
42. Cook to Charles Schaeffer (April 23, 1898), President's Office Files.
43. George Cook, *Company B of Davenport* (Davenport, Iowa, 1899).
44. George Cook Diary (July 14, 1898), Cook Papers.
45. Quoted in Glaspell, *Road to Temple,* p. 98.
46. Cook to Schaeffer (September 4, 1898), President's Office Files.
47. George Cook Diary (October, 1898), Cook Papers.
48. Charles Banks and George C. Cook, *In Hampton Roads: A Dramatic Romance* (Chicago, 1899).
49. Cook, *Roderick Taliaferro* (New York, 1903).
50. George Cook, "Loose Pages" (January 3, 1911), Cook Papers.
51. George Cook Diary (January 14, 1900), Cook Papers.
52. George Cook Diary (May 8, 1905), Cook Papers. Quoted in Glaspell, *Road to Temple,* p. 136.
53. *Ibid.,* pp. 142-143.
54. *Ibid.,* pp. 144-164.
55. Cook to Mollie Price (August 5, 1906), Cook Papers.
56. George Cook, "Notes and Reflections on Nietzsche," Holograph Notes, Cook Papers.
57. Edward Cook Diary, Cook Family Papers.
58. Cook to Mollie Price (August 23, 1906), Cook Papers.
59. Cook, Holograph Note ("Sunday 1 A.M."), Cook Papers.
60. Cook to Mollie Price (August 23, 1906), Cook Papers.
61. Nilla Cram Cook, *My Road to India* (New York, 1939), p. 46.
62. Cook to Mollie Price (January 15, 1907), Cook Papers.
63. Cook to Mollie Price (August 16, 1906), Cook Papers.
64. Cook to Mollie Price (Summer, 1906), Cook Papers.
65. Cook to Mollie Price (December 9, 1907), Cook Papers.
66. Floyd Dell, *Homecoming: An Autobiography* (New York, 1933), p. 154.
67. Cook to Mollie Price (November 25, 1907), Cook Papers.
68. *Ibid.*
69. Cook to Mollie Price (November 29, 1907), Cook Papers.
70. Cook to Mollie Price (November 30, 1907; December 9, 1907), Cook Papers.
71. Dell, *Homecoming,* pp. 171-172.
72. Glaspell, *The Road to the Temple,* p. 192.
73. *Ibid.,* p. 191.
74. Cook, "Concerning Sex," unpublished essay, Cook Papers.
75. Cook, Holograph Note (1910), Cook Papers.
76. Cook, "Fragment," Holograph Note, Cook Papers.
77. Laurence Langner, *The Magic Curtain,* p. 70.
78. Quoted in Glaspell, *Road to the Temple,* p. 224.
79. Cook, "Letter to Editor," newspaper clipping in Floyd Dell Papers, Newberry Library, Chicago.

80. G. Thomas Tanselle, "George Cram Cook and the Poetry of Living, with a Checklist," *Books at Iowa* (April 1976), p. 7.
81. Dale Kramer, *Chicago Renaissance: The Literary Life in the Midwest 1900-1930* (New York, 1966).
82. Quoted in Glaspell, *Road to the Temple,* pp. 224-225.
83. Cook to Floyd Dell (April 13, 1912), Dell Papers.
84. Glaspell, *Road to the Temple,* pp. 227-246.
85. William Zorach, *Art is My Life: The Autobiography of William Zorach* (New York, 1967), p. 46.
86. Hutchins Hapgood, *A Victorian in the Modern World,* pp. 374-375.
87. Louis Sheaffer, *O'Neill: Son and Playwright* (Boston, 1968), pp. 320-323. William W. Vilhauer, "A History and Evaluation of Provincetown Players," Vol. 1 (unpublished Ph.D. dissertation, University of Iowa, 1965), pp. 18-123.
88. Helen Deutsch and Stella Hanau, *The Provincetown: A Story of the Theatre* (New York, 1931), pp. 7-17. Edna Kenton, "The Provincetown Players and the Playwrights' Theatre," *The Billboard,* Vol. 34 (August 5, 1922), p. 6.
89. Glaspell, *Road to Temple,* p. 253. Vilhauer, "History of Provincetown Players," p. 28, p. 33.
90. Dell, *Homecoming,* p. 267.
91. Quoted in Kenton, "The Provincetown Players," *The Billboard,* p. 15.
92. Sheaffer. *O'Neill: Son and Playwright,* p. 358.
93. Oscar Brockett, *The Theatre: An Introduction* (New York, 1974), pp. 311-364.
94. George Cook, "New York Letter" (*Friday Literary Review*) *Chicago Evening Post* (March 12, 1915), p. 8.
95. Quoted in Deutsch, *The Provincetown,* p. 39.
96. Quoted in Sheaffer, *O'Neill: Son and Playwright,* p. 377.
97. Glaspell, *Road to the Temple,* p. 262.
98. Cook to Susan Glaspell (December 13, 1916), Cook Papers.
99. Agnes Boulton, *Part of a Long Story* (New York, 1958), p. 219. Sheaffer, *O'Neill: Son and Playwright,* p. 442.
100. Bryant to John Reed (December 2, 1916), envelope postmark, Louise Bryant Papers, Houghton Library, Harvard University.
101. Dell, *Homecoming,* pp. 265-266.
102. Glaspell, *Road to the Temple,* p. 265.
103. Quoted in Sheaffer, *O'Neill: Son and Playwright,* p. 401.
104. Cook to Glaspell (December 23, 1916), Cook Papers.
105. Deutsch, *The Provincetown,* pp. 26-29.
106. Cook, *The Athenian Women* (Athens, Greece, 1926), p. 270.
107. Glaspell, *The Road to the Temple,* p. 266, pp. 276-285. Sheaffer, *O'Neill: Son and Playwright,* p. 468.
108. Quoted in Glaspell, *The Road to the Temple,* pp. 286-287.
109. Cook, "The Emperor Jones," undated holograph essay, Cook Papers.
110. Deutsch, *The Provincetown,* pp. 68-69. Louis Sheaffer, *O'Neill: Son and Artist* (Boston, 1973), pp. 31-33.
111. Sheaffer, *O'Neill: Son and Artist,* p. 35.
112. Glaspell, *The Road to the Temple,* pp. 292-297; p. 307.
113. George Cook, *The Spring* (New York, 1921).
114. Sheaffer, *O'Neill: Son and Artist,* p. 78.
115. *Ibid.,* pp. 78-79.
116. Quoted in Glaspell, *The Road to the Temple,* pp. 308-309.

117. Cook to Edna Kenton, undated, Cook Papers.
118. *Ibid.*
119. Quoted in Glaspell, *The Road to the Temple,* p. 361.
120. Cook to Ida Rauh, undated, Cook Papers.

CHAPTER FOUR

John Reed:
The Poet on Horseback

Born into the upper reaches of Portland society in 1887, and educated at private schools, first in Oregon and then in the East, John Reed received the preparation and opportunity for conventional success. At college he relentlessly sought acceptance and recognition in literary, social, and athletic activities. Little in his background or development suggested that Reed might one day become a partisan of revolutionary politics, and no one in his graduating class could have predicted a hero's funeral in Communist Russia. But the long journey, measured in miles and in politics, from Portland to Moscow began with his father's fortunes and his childhood experiences.

John's father, Charles Jerome Reed, grew up in Auburn, New York. After graduating from high school in 1870, Charles or C. J. became a salesman for the D. M. Osborn Company, a manufacturer of harvesting machinery. It was this position that brought him to Portland in 1882. A friendly, witty, outgoing man, C. J. won favor with the city's upper classes, and, in 1887, the hand of Margaret Green, a young woman from one of Portland's oldest families.[1]

Henry Green, Margaret's father, had died in 1885, and thereafter the family's resources began to dwindle. Nevertheless, during the early years

John Reed and Louise Bryant in Croton. By permission of Houghton Library, Harvard University.

of their marriage, Margaret and C. J. resided at the Green mansion, "Cedar Hill," an imposing gray chateau surrounded by "formal gardens, lawns, stables, greenhouses and glass grape-arbor."² The trappings of prosperity, however, proved to be a facade hiding the realities of future economic hardships. C. J.'s career suffered when the long depression of the 1890s wiped out the Osborn Company. Subsequently, he became a life insurance salesman, an occupation he pursued intermittently without success.

In 1905, C. J., a fervent supporter of Theodore Roosevelt, was appointed United States Marshall, a position which he held until 1910. His annual salary of four thousand dollars enabled him to provide his sons, Jack and Harry, with a superior education.³ Consequently, he sent them to Portland Academy, Morristown preparatory school in New Jersey, and Harvard.

Although Jack enjoyed the advantages of a middle-class childhood and adolescence, he realized after college that these benefits were made possible by his father's sacrifices. When C. J. died in 1912, Jack told a friend:

> My father worried himself to death—that's all. He never let any of us know, but he was harassed into the grave. Money! . . . At the end of twenty years of pain, physical and mental, . . . the terrific strain buckled him and he died fighting.⁴

Five years later Reed commented in an autobiographical essay:

> We never knew until later how our mother and father denied themselves . . . and how he poured out his life that we might live like rich men's sons. He and mother always gave us more than we asked, in freedom and understanding as well as material things.⁵

A sense of indebtedness to his father was crucial in the development of Jack's social conscience. Unable to repay his father, he would make amends by helping those who never had his advantages.

As United States Marshall, C. J. worked with special prosecutor Francis J. Heney in investigating a land fraud ring. Their efforts resulted in the prosecution of government officials and prominent men in the community. As a result, C. J. lost favor with Portland society. Lincoln Steffens, the muckraking journalist who covered the story, recalled that C. J.'s role "well-nigh ruined [him] financially and socially."⁶ Several years after the scandal, C. J. took Steffens to the exclusive Arlington Club where he had once been an active member. Pointing out his old associates, C. J. told Steffens:

> That's the crowd that got the timber and tried to get me. And there, at the head of the table, that vacant chair, that's my place. That's where I sat. That's where I stood them off, for fun, for years, and then for months in deadly earnest. . . . I haven't sat in that place since the day I rose and left it, saying I'd never come back to it and saying that I would like to see which one of them would have the nerve to think that he could take and hold and fill my place. I have heard, and I am glad to see, that it is vacant yet, my vacant chair.[7]

This episode contributed to Jack's estrangement from the community and provided material for an idealistic conception of his father. When C. J. died, Jack proudly remarked to a college friend:

> Sometime I'll tell you more of the brave, honorable, stainless life that he led so jauntily. I think he was the only honest man in Portland, — and they 'did' him [in?][8]

To his son, C. J. was a brave man who suffered because he would not compromise basic principles. Jack recounted that when "a man came around to brow-beat my father into contributing to the Republican campaign fund, he kicked the collector down the courthouse stairs — and was removed from the marshallship by President Taft."[9] In failing to understand that his father had been dismissed for supporting Roosevelt, Jack's imagination transformed an ordinary political conflict into a struggle between good and evil. In the process he invented a hero who exemplified his notion of manhood and bravery.

After his ouster in 1910, C. J. half-heartedly campaigned for a seat in the United States House of Representatives, and lost in the primary election to the Taft forces. Although the elder Reed had stood little chance of winning, Jack blamed himself for his father's defeat. He wrote later that C. J. "lost out by a slim margin, mainly because he came East to see me graduate from college instead of stumping the state." Finally, Jack attributed his father's death, at the age of fifty-seven, to the sacrifices for his sons — "on the day my brother graduated from college, he broke under the terrible effort, and died a few weeks later."[10] In assuming responsibility for his father's political defeat and premature death, Jack imposed a heavy moral burden on himself that he carried throughout his life.

Jack's compassion for others also developed out of a warm relationship with his father. In an affectionate letter, written a few months before his death, the elder Reed expressed admiration for his son's literary accomplishments:

> Dearest Lovey Boy,
>
> I am so out of the way of writing, being on the street soliciting life insurance all day and having, you know, no office conveniences, stenographer, etc. that I have almost forgotten how to write, . . . but I think and talk of you every day, and love you and am proud of you every hour. I am so anxious to see everything you write and your work is good stuff. . . .
>
> Write often and do try to keep out of debt and save a little. I have been cursed with debts all my life and one of my greatest griefs now is that I cannot afford to make you an allowance dearie boy. Don't forget that we are so proud of you and love you.[11]

More concerned about Jack's situation than his own, C. J. criticized himself for not providing additional assistance. Although C. J. appreciated the value of financial security, he did not pressure Jack to seek economic success. He urged his son to stay away from serious matters, particularly politics, and enjoy what he had missed in life. When Jack headed for New York after college, C. J. instructed Steffens "to take him on . . . and save him for poetry. Don't let him get a conviction, like me, and become serious. . . . Keep my boy laughing, laughing and singing."[12]

During his youth Jack would heed this advice, and pursue pranks and poetry instead of politics. Ultimately, however, his father's example proved more significant. By 1917 Jack viewed C. J. "as a great fighter, one of the first of the little band of political insurgents" who gave expression to the "new social conscience of the American middle class."[13] Jack would carry on his father's fight while advocating political programs that went beyond progressive reforms. If C. J. had labored for his advancement, he would repay that debt by freeing the poor.

Jack's early physical development was hampered by a kidney ailment, which made it difficult for him to hold his own against his playmates. When the family, beleaguered by economic setbacks, moved to an apartment-hotel in town, Jack faced the dangers of physical abuse. The route to school was particularly terrifying because it passed through "Goose Hollow," a Portland slum area inhabited by "brutal Irish boys." They threatened him and took his money because he was afraid to challenge them. He preferred, he recalled with self-contempt, "to be called a coward than fight." At school he fared no better.

> Outside of a few friends, I wasn't a success with the boys. I hadn't strength or fight enough to be good at athletics—except swimming . . . and I was a good deal of a physical coward.[14]

Consequently, other boys felt "a sort of good-natured contempt" for him. His failure to act bravely and measure up to classmate expectations left a permanent, psychological scar. In an autobiographical piece, written at the age of twenty-nine, he revealed that the memory of his cowardliness haunted him. He imagined that his father, "a great fighter," had been "disappointed" by his lack of courage, "though he never said much about it."[15] Unable to forget his childhood traumas, Jack resolved in adolescence and adulthood to live fearlessly, act nobly, and earn the respect of his peers. He would, therefore, forsake security for the perils of strikes, wars, and revolutions.

Sickness and weakness encouraged Jack to seek adventure in fantasy. He read tales of strutting kings and "the armored ranks of men-at-arms clashing forward in close ranks against a hail of cloth-yard shafts." But Jack did not rely entirely on books. Uncle Ray, "a romantic figure who played at coffee-planting in Central America, mixed in revolutions," and fought in the Philippines during the Spanish-American War, stimulated his imagination with first-hand accounts of daring escapades. Jack enjoyed recounting fairy stories about giants, witches, and dragons to neighborhood children and decided at an early age to become a writer. But Portland boys did not value literary talent. He had to wait for prep school, Harvard College, and Greenwich Village to find an attentive audience.

In 1904, Reed escaped the terrors of childhood when he arrived at Morristown School, a college preparatory institution. Looking back, he concluded:

> Boarding school, I think, meant more to me than anything in my boyhood. Among those strange boys I came as a stranger, and I soon found out that they were willing to accept me at my own value. I was in fine health. The ordered life of the community interested me; I was impressed by its traditional customs and dignities, school patriotism, and the sense of a long settled and established civilization, so different from the raw, pretentious West. . . . I had a fight or two, and stuck it out. . . . Busy, happy, with lots of friends, I expanded into self-confidence. So without trying I found myself; and since then I have never been very much afraid of men.[16]

Morristown provided outlets for his energies and fulfilled a need for recognition. No longer afflicted by a kidney disorder, he played football and ran track, lettering in both sports. He contributed short stories and poems to the monthly *Morristonian,* and edited the *Rooster,* a short-lived comic paper that published jokes and satirized the teachers.

Mainly, he achieved notoriety by organizing pranks and breaking rules. "There were perilous adventures, too," when he and his friends slipped away at night to country dances, returning to the dormitory in the early hours of the morning. Once he set a chamber pot atop a suit of armor in order to shock some female guests and embarrass the school officials.[17] When his joke resulted in punishment, Jack's popularity soared. Lacking the reserve of his Eastern schoolmates, Jack played the role of a wild boy from the West who knew all about the seamy side of life. One classmate recalled that Jack told "ribald and rather hair-raising tales about his wanderings on the Portland waterfront and in places of ill repute in that city; one never knew how much was true and how much made up to give us a thrill."[18]

In the fall of 1906, Jack entered Harvard, the leading college in America. Brash and exuberant, he expected to conquer Harvard as he had Morristown. But, as a Westerner without family connections, he had difficulty in making friends and distinguishing himself in a freshman class of nearly seven hundred men. Although he wanted "to be liked, to have friends, to be popular with the crowd," new acquaintances "were whirled off and up into prominence," and visited him "no more." Painfully he remembered:

> Fellows passed me in the Yard, shouting gayly to one another; I saw parties off to Boston Saturday night, whooping and yelling on the back platform of the street car, and they passed hilariously singing under my window in the early dawn.[19]

Isolated and lonely, he befriended Carl Binger, "a shy, rather melancholy" New York Jew, who was also an "outsider." But Jack became "irritated and morbid" about their association, which seemed to prevent him from partaking in "the rich splendor of college." Consequently, he decided against rooming with Binger in his sophomore year and "drew away from him."[20]

Since Jack was denied access to the "aristocratic" clubs, he sought recognition in sports and journalism. When he failed to make the freshman football team, he went out for the Harvard rowing crew, plugging away at the machines in the empty boathouse during his first Christmas vacation. Although dropped from the rowing squad, he achieved success in other fields. The swimming and water polo teams selected him as a member, the satirical *Lampoon* accepted some jokes, and the Harvard *Monthly* printed two of his poems.[21]

Other triumphs followed during the remaining three years. Jack was elected to the editorial boards of the *Lampoon* and *Monthly*, became

president of the Cosmopolitan and Western Clubs, manager of the
Musical Club, a member of the Dramatic and the Debating Clubs, and a
cheerleader. Plunging into an endless round of social activities, Jack
emerged, classmate Edward Hunt remarked, "a college celebrity." His
talents as a lyricist earned him admission to the Hasty Pudding, an
"aristocratic" club filled with those "fortunate and splendid" youths who
dominated "college society."[22] Jack fought no fights for democracy at
Harvard. He avoided the socially inferior yard dormitories for a private
one as he relentlessly sought recognition in a world which he had no intention of overturning.

In spite of these social successes, Jack subsequently viewed his experiences with ambivalence. Two years after their graduation, he told
classmate Robert Hallowell:

> The whole place [Harvard] seems mad about publicity. That I approve. But
> not the kind of publicity that judiciously cavorts over the West, making
> speeches that suppress the facts so as to lure Westerners under false
> pretenses. Harvard is not a democratic place.[23]

In an autobiographical essay, written in 1917, he denied that he had fran-
tically sought a place within the social elite. Instead he recalled how the
"cold, cruel stupidity" of "college aristocrats" had repelled him. He had
pitied "them for their lack of imagination, and the narrowness of their
glittering lives — clubs, athletics, society." This dissociation from the
"aristocrats" indicated the political and social distance he traveled after
graduation. By 1917, memories of college sharpened his antipathy for the
moneyed classes and socialist doctrines offered political justification for
his prejudices.

One activity, however, did not undergo reevaluation. Cheerleading,
Jack recalled, was his most satisfying experience at Harvard. "I had the
supreme blissful sensation of swaying two thousand voices in great
crashing choruses during the big football games."[24] Under his direction,
individuals joined in unison to spur others on to victory. Even at college,
Jack showed a need to live at a heightened pitch as he sought experiences that crackled with excitement. In a Lampoon editorial he spelled out the choice; it was either "happiness and experience, or money and
a rut."[25] Equating security with the humdrum monotony of ordinary existence, he intended to participate in momentous events that made life
thrilling.

Ignoring Harvard's most distinguished professors (Josiah Royce, Barrett Wendell, George P. Baker, and George Santayana), Jack was inspired
by Charles Copeland, an instructor in England composition.[26] In

Copeland, a former newspaperman, he found a counsellor and a teacher who encouraged his interest in journalism. On Saturday nights Jack was usually among those students who visited Copey's bachelor quarters in Hollis Hall. At these sessions, he wrote,

> everybody talks of the thing nearest his heart; everybody finds himself alert, quick, almost brilliant. Startling theories are expounded, and strange systems of philosophy. One tells of rowing, another of throwing the hammer, of 'parties' in town, of clubs and books and college politics.[27]

Camaraderie and conversation, not intellectual discussions or radical politics, consumed Jack's time in college. Despite later claims that he participated in "the modern spirit" at Harvard, Jack did not mix with the "radicals [who] sprang up, in music, painting, poetry, and theatre." Although he was friendly with Walter Lippmann and other advocates of socialism, Jack only attended one or two meetings of the new Socialist Club. But, he remembered, "no matter what you were or what you did — at Harvard you could find your own kind."[28] With his triumphs in sports, social activities, and literary enterprises, Reed left Harvard bursting with self-confidence.

After a walking tour of Europe and a sojourn on the Left Bank in Paris. Reed returned to New York. In March, 1911, he contacted Lincoln Steffens who placed him as an assistant editor on the *American Magazine*. Steffens recalled that "Jack was nothing but a bundle of fine nerves, bulging energy, overweening vanity and trembling curiosity, with an egotistical ambition to distinguish himself as a poet."[29] Having savored the freedom of France, Reed chose to develop his creativity in Greenwich Village, which was becoming a haven for budding artists and writers. With three friends from Harvard, he took third-floor rooms in a dilapidated rooming house on the south side of Washington Square. Other alumni lived nearby or frequented the area, so that Greenwich Village, like Harvard, offered freedom, escapades, conversation, writing, and fellowship.

Situated in the midst of a swarming metropolis, the Village was a point of departure for sorties into the forbidden sections of New York. Within a block of his house was "all the adventure of the world; within a mile was every foreign country." He wandered along East River docks, pushed his way through the crowded, "alien" streets of the Lower East Side, visited Chinatown and Little Italy, drank at McSorley's tavern and "Tenderloin dives," and talked to Bowery bums, streetwalkers, and disreputable dancers. He found out how to buy "dope," where to hire a killer, and how to enter "gambling rooms." Knowing the underside of city life was a source of pride because it demonstrated his ability to mix with a rough element and confirmed his status as a veteran journalist. Never fond of academic studies, Reed thought that experiences provided the best education, in the city he "saw that reality transcended all the fine poetic inventions of fastidiousness and medievalism."[30] Unlike "plutocratic New England classmates" who dawdled at the Harvard Club, Reed ventured forth to observe primitive life, poverty, danger, and illicit sex.

If Reed undertook excursions amongst the poor, his life centered in Greenwich Village where he wrote poetry and short stories, drank at the Brevoort Hotel, argued art and politics, and rollicked with friends. Not yet weaned from college interests, he joined the Harvard Club, ate lunch at the Dutch Treat Club (a gathering cf commercial artists, editors, and journalists), attended Harvard football games and the World Series, and saw popular Broadway shows.

Even though Reed was involved in conventional activities, he referred to himself as a Village bohemian. In *The Day in Bohemia, or Life Among the Artists,* a long poem published in 1913, he scorned commercial artists, middle class "philistines," and "unnumbered Jasons in their motor-cars." While there was "anaemia" in bohemia and a "tendency to let old Daily Bread gain ascendancy," Reed and his friends lived brazenly as they pursued art.

> Yet we are free who live in Washington Square,
> We dare to think as Uptown wouldn't dare,
> Blazing our nights with arguments uproarious;
> What care we for a dull old world censorious
> When each is sure he'll fashion something glorious?[31]

Since Greenwich Village encouraged free expression, Reed found the restrictions of commercial journalism unacceptable. Although the *American Magazine* and other popular journals printed a few short stories and articles, his more creative work was rejected because it violated middle class propriety. When he completed "The Harvard Renaissance," an article praising the student revolt against classical education, the *American Magazine* refused to use it. Similarly, he could not find a magazine willing to print "Where the Heart Is," a short story about a prostitute who chooses to return to her job at the Haymarket dance hall after a trip to Europe and South America. When the editor of *Adventure Magazine* advised him to restrain his "lawlessness" or be "conventionally lawless," Reed realized that commercialism meant censorship and conformity.[32]

Viewing himself as a serious writer, Reed resented the imposition of editorial standards that catered to respectable opinion. Therefore, when asked to write and direct a musical satire for the Dutch Treat Club's annual dinner, he presented *Everymagazine, An Immorality Play,* which ridiculed the editors and journalists in attendance. The songs rebuked the magazines for "abowing" to business men and "chasing" after advertising. In the finale, sarcastically entitled "The Freedom of the Press," the chorus sang:

> A silly tale I've heard
> That round the town is flying
> That every monthly organ
> Is owned by J. P. Morgan.
> Now ain't that absurd?
> Somebody must be lying.[33]

Although journalist Julian Street dismissed the "musical burlesque" as an example of "sophomoric" rebelliousness, there was a political undercurrent to Reed's attack.[34] In suggesting that J. P. Morgan, the powerful financier, controlled popular journals, Reed echoed socialist critics in the Village. Although still the exuberant rebel, he was developing an enthusiasm for bohemian values and radical ideas. He told Robert Hallowell:

> I hear that Andy is rooming with [Robert] Gook[in] Munroe, which I consider a calamity for Washington Square. Damn those business men, why can't they keep to their own part of town? They don't or won't learn anything by living with us live boys. . . . Tell Charley that I have become an I.W.W. and am now in favor of dynamiting; and that I have some good arguments which I shall be glad to discharge at him whenever he thinks he wants a debate.[35]

Interest in free-expression and an opportunity to publish unconventional writing brought him to *The Masses* in 1913. When Max Eastman accepted his story, "Where the Heart Is," he joined the staff as a contributing editor. Reed immediately asserted his views as to the nature of the magazine and drafted a statement for its mast head.[36] His nonideological manifesto reflected opposition to middle-class culture and concern for the fate of serious art. When Harriet Monroe, editor of the newly established journal, *Poetry,* asked him to submit a poem, he replied with a letter that applauded her efforts to save poetry:

> I am myself on the staff of a magazine [*American Magazine*], and have
> often heard the editors say that poetry is a declining art. . . . I have
> found that among men of whatever class, if they are deeply stirred by
> emotion, poetry appeals; as indeed all the arts appeal. The pathetic,
> mawkishly religious middle class are [sic] our enemies. A labor-leader,
> for example, who has been indicted for complicity in the dynamite plots,
> read aloud to me more naturally and beautifully than I have ever heard
> a verse read. And I think that wherever men are deeply stirred, all their
> living becomes attuned to the unheard systole and diastole of their pulses.
> Art must cease, I think, to be for the aesthetic enjoyment of a few high-
> ly sensitive minds. It must go back to its original sources.[37]

Reed's preference for simplicity, honesty, and the open expression of
emotions explains his empathy for the poor and his scorn for the rich. By
nature a boyish extrovert who liked people, Reed's personal inclinations
were inherently compatible with egalitarianism. His view of art,
something which "stirred" men's emotions, and his democratic impulses
made him, given an exposure to social injustice, a likely convert to
radical politics.

As a journalist Reed's contact with the disadvantaged was fleeting.
Although mainly interested in gathering material for stories, he was not
unmoved by what he saw. In "The Dinner Guests of Big Tim," a story for
the *American Magazine*, Reed reported on the Democratic party's annual
Christmas dinner for the denizens of the Bowery. Reed noticed that a
hearty meal miraculously altered the spirit of those who plodded into the
hall:

> Those who had been dull-eyed, those that had seemed bowed with all the
> hopelessness and weariness of the world . . . began to straighten up;
> a little fire flashed from their eyes, hope gleamed, tongues loosened,
> sparks flew—they were almost men.[38]

Reed could not forget this spiritual transformation; it provided concrete
evidence that the helpless could be resurrected. It was, he thought, a
miracle "to feel around you swell and flower the loving-kindness of
men." Cynics would rightly contend, he wrote, that the politicians and
the bums were motivated by self-interest, but they would overlook "that
little fire of divinity in every man, that fuses humanity into something
great whenever men do good to one another."[39] Initially a sensitive
observer, Reed became an idealistic participant when he encountered
downtrodden workers who had the courage to fight the rich and the
powerful.

Reed was first exposed to industrial strife during the Paterson silk workers' strike in the spring of 1913. When Bill Haywood recounted the wholesale arrest of strikers and the closing of all meeting halls to a group of Villagers, Reed decided to visit Paterson for a story. Shortly after his arrival, an Irish policeman, Officer McCormick, directed him to move off the street.

Reed replied defiantly: "I won't get off this street or any other street. If I'm breaking the law, you arrest me." When the policeman hesitated, Reed baited him: "I've got your number. Now will you tell me your name."

"Yes," McCormick replied, "and I got your number." Whereupon he hustled Reed into a patrol wagon and took him to police headquarters where James Carroll, who Reed described as having "the intelligent, cruel, merciless face of the ordinary police court magistrate," sentenced him to twenty days in the Passaic county jail.[40]

Incarcerated in a large, dirty room lined with three tiers of cells, Reed found himself among some eighty prisoners, half of whom were strikers. At first the workers avoided him, fearing that he was a police spy. But on the second day he met Haywood, who assured the prisoners that Reed was a sympathetic reporter. The immigrants then crowded around him, expressed their regret at his arrest, and hailed him as a hearty fellow. After the warm reception, he wrote Edward Hunt: "If you saw the strikers in here, you would realize it is a great strike." In signing his letter "from Reading gaol," a reference to Oscar Wilde's place of detention, he fancied a fellowship with famous poets who had suffered imprisonment. Beyond the sense of adventure, Reed relished the attention he received. Refusing to allow bail to be posted until the fourth day, he boasted to Hunt that he was "a personage in here," and instructed him to "save all the newspaper accounts for my delectation."[41]

Reed's arrest earned him the praise and envy of Greenwich Villagers who temporarily adopted this struggle as their own. After telling Hutchins Hapgood that the police had taken him because he "wouldn't be bulldozed," Reed became a topic of conversation at the Liberal Club.[42] In private Reed denied his political radicalism, telling Edward Hunt:

> It's nothing to make a roar about, anyway. I'm neither a hero nor a martyr—the whole business is a joke. I'm not even a socialist, you know. It's a clear case of injustice against a citizen who wasn't even mixed up in the business.[43]

Bristling like an indignant citizen, Reed contemplated a civil suit "for big damages for false arrest and brutality."

After his release Reed returned to Washington Square and wrote two accounts of his experiences in Paterson. In an article for the *Metropolitan* magazine he characterized the typical inhabitants of the county jail as "the petty criminals, the drunk-and-disorderlies, the little thieves, in short, the weak outlaws of society who have neither courage nor strength to commit state prison offenses." He condemned the county jail because it took in "weak men," sapped their strength, "diluted whatever little manliness they have left," and released them "to contaminate society." Since respectable society rejected the "sick men it manufactured," petty criminals sought out the company of "panhandlers," who, "being weak," understood "weakness."[44] Reed's preoccupation with strength, and his perception that petty criminals would never rebel against society, caused him to judge them harshly. This analysis unwittingly coincided with Marx's judgment of the *Lumpenproletariat,* a stratum of roués, vagabonds, gamblers, organgrinders, and ne'er-do-wells who were potential reactionaries. In effect, Reed groped his way towards a radicalism that assumed workers represented the hope for the future.

Reed's second account, which appeared in the June issue of *The Masses,* was a partisan narrative with himself in the thick of the action. There existed, he declared, a "War in Paterson" that pitted poor, immigrant workers against the police, the courts, the churches, and the newspapers. In short, the "machinery" of society had been mobilized against oppressed immigrants who only wanted decent wages and better working conditions. Disagreeing with other newspaper reports, Reed maintained that the "Mill Owners" or rather "their servants, the police" and hired "mercenaries" were responsible for the violence.

Although Reed admired Bill Haywood, Elizabeth Gurley Flynn, and the Wobbly leaders, the "slight, foreign-faced" workers were the heroes of the struggle. While the "English-speaking contingent" lingered in the background, the "wops," the "kikes," and the "hunkies" carried the brunt of the attack. These "gentle, alert, brave men, ennobled by something greater than themselves," served as the "vanguard of the battle-line of labor." Swept up by the excitement, Reed endorsed their cause. Having endured twelve years of defeats, "disappointment and incalculable suffering," they "must not," he declared, "lose again."[45]

After sharing a cell with striking workers, Reed was eager to become involved in their movement. While attending a Sunday rally of mill laborers and their families, he was asked by Haywood to address the crowd. Reed responded by leading the workers in a singing of the "Marseillaise" and the "Internationale." This experience, which recalled his days as a Harvard cheerleader, prepared him for the Paterson pageant. After writing the scenario, he drilled the workers in rehearsals, shouting directions at them through a megaphone. Unlike his Hasty Pudding production, Reed was in earnest about this performance. When several Harvard graduates arrived seeking amusement, Reed had them thrown out of the building.

If the pageant failed to raise money and dramatize the plight of the silk workers, it did produce a romance between John Reed (age 25) and Mabel Dodge (age 34). Two weeks after the show, the lovers were comfortably aboard the liner *Amerika,* bound for a vacation in Europe. When they reached Paris, Mabel opened her bedroom door to Reed and "learned what a honeymoon should be." After traveling by chauffeured motor-car along the Riviera, with a pause in Monte Carlo, they reached the Villa Curonia where Reed nightly descended "a silken ladder" to her four-posted bed.[46]

But their "mania of love" could not quench Reed's need for adventures. By day he was "carried away by people or things." Therefore, at night Mabel had "to reconquer him, triumphing over the day's loss."[47] When it became apparent that lovemaking could not extinguish his curiosity about the Italian countryside, she attempted to involve him in a circle of sophisticated friends that included Carl Van Vechten, Robert E. Jones, Paul and Muriel Draper, and Artur Rubinstein. Nonetheless, he remained a difficult pet to housebreak.

Although Reed felt "like a coward" for abandoning the fight in Paterson, he made no attempt to break free of Mabel. Returning from Europe at the end of August, Reed, now unemployed, moved in with his wealthy patroness. But he quickly became bored with domesticated life. He was, Mabel complained,

> ready at any moment to pop off into some new enthusiasm. He always seemed to have his lungs too full, and he would draw in his round chin in an effort to quiet his excited heart. *Always* there seemed some pressure of excitement going on in him. His eyes glowed for nothing, his brown curls rushed back his high, round forehead in a furious disorder, and . . . his eyebrows went further up. . . .[48]

As they breakfasted together (he on a little table by her bedside) Reed invariably became engrossed in the morning newspaper. "Listen to this," he would shout, his "honey-colored" eyes glowing with excitement. He would read her some item about Russia, Mexico or Poland. Then he was off, leaving the fallen newspaper on the floor, visiting friends at the Liberal Club, Polly's, *The Masses'* offices or enjoying a jaunt through the city streets. To add to her jealousy and frustration, he would sometimes return with boyish tales of a chance meeting with a "beautiful prostitute" or a shapely Village girl.[49]

Mabel tried to temper Reed's restlessness by entrapping him in her social activities. She revived the "Evenings," inviting "more and more people," with the hope that social "victories" would enhance her status and allure. But this plan miscarried because Reed was unimpressed by sophisticated idlers. He preferred to talk with Fred Boyd, an English anarchist who had been arrested at Paterson. When Mabel attempted to break up this friendship, Reed ran off to Copeland in Cambridge, leaving her a note:

> Good-by, my darling. I cannot live with you. You smother me. You crush me. You want to kill my spirit. I love you better than life but I do not want to die in my spirit. I am going away to save myself. Forgive me. I love you — I love you.[50]

Three days later, however, he came rushing back, knelt beside her bed, and cried: "I can't live without you. I missed your love, your selfish love."

Reed finally escaped in December when the *Metropolitan* magazine assigned him to report on Pancho Villa's activities in the Mexican Civil War. Here was an opportunity to become involved again, to write new chapters in his autobiography, and to test his manhood. He *"had to know"* how he would "act under fire," and how he would "get along with these primitive folks at war."[51]

Mabel, however, refused to give Reed up to the Mexicans without a struggle. She followed him to Chicago, and accompanied him on the train ride to El Paso. Writing to Edward Hunt en route, Reed poked fun at her attempt to bring Fifth Avenue to Mexico:

> I think [Mabel] expects to find General Villa a sort of male Gertrude Stein; or at least a Mexican Stieglitz.
>
> We hardly *ever* stir out of our drawing-room except at mealtimes, when we start with *caviar* and go right through to nuts.
>
> Mabel in her orange hat and satin-lined tiger-skin hunting jacket — with passports, and an expense-account, and a roll of blankets and fourteen different kinds of pills and bandages [was an amusing sight].[52]

But her elaborate preparations for the Mexican safari proved unnecessary. When it became apparent that Reed would not be diverted and that Mexico was too primitive, she hurried back to the comforts of home.

In February, 1913, General Victoriano Huerta seized power from Francisco Madero, a moderate liberal, and used his Federalist army to establish a dictatorship. Almost immediately a movement arose to restore constitutional government; its leaders were Venustiano Carranza in Coahuila, Pancho Villa in Chihuahua, and Emiliano Zapata in the South. Carranza, a conservative landowner, was primarily interested in re-establishing a constitutional government while Villa and Zapata desired agrarian reforms that would transfer land to peons and Indians who had been reduced to an agrarian proletariat.

Reed crossed the border and for four months lived with various elements of the Constitutional army, sending back written accounts of the bloody battles and his experiences. Three years later he romanticized his feats:

> That four months of riding hundreds of miles across the blazing plains, sleeping on the ground with the *hombres,* dancing and carousing in looted haciendas all night after an all-day ride, being with them intimately in play, in battle was perhaps the most satisfying period of my life. I made good with these wild fighting men, and with myself.[53]

Reed rejected the general assumption of Mexican inferiority, and in his writings he contrasted the generous peons with the greedy Americans he met: a mercenary who hoped to accumulate enough money "to go back to Georgia and start a child-labor factory," the manager of a silver mine who referred to the Mexicans he exploited as "a filthy lot of people," and Mac, who boasted about the purity of American women and sneered at the Mexican girls he compromised.[54]

As a correspondent Reed only had to write exciting tales. But he went further and identified with the cause of Villa and the peasants. To him the issues were easy to comprehend. The Federalists, which included rich *hacienda* owners, self-seeking politicians, and regular army officers, were determined to crush the peasant uprising. He maintained that a small number of landowners kept the peasants in "ignorance and religious superstition" in order to exploit them.[55] The division of adversaries into forces of good and evil, or the rich and powerful against the poor and the many, strengthened the radical cast of his thinking.

Reed denounced the demand for U.S. intervention because protection of European and American business interests, "all of them rich in the blood and sweat of peons," would mean the end of social reform. He warned American readers:

> We will leave things worse than they were before—an exploiting class firmly entrenched in the places of power, the foreign interests stronger, because we supported them, the great estates firmly re-established, and the peons taught that wage slavery and not individual freedom is the desirable thing in life.[56]

If he drew no obvious parallel with factory owners and workers in America, the implication was there. While socialists may have applauded Reed's views, it was classical history not Marxian doctrines that colored his analysis. To Reed, America was a modern version of imperial Rome. America's brutal policies in Cuba and the Philippines proved that "Anglo-Saxons" considered other races to be "inferior." Like Rome, America "civilized" the so-called barbarians by subjugating them; intervention in Mexico would "devitalize" the peons and "turn them into brown, docile American laborers."[57] Reed knew little about the "dynamics of capitalism," but he understood that imperialism meant enslavement of the poor.

Reed needed heroes. In the Mexican Civil War, Pancho Villa, a daring outlaw who took from the rich and gave to the poor, was his choice. Coarse, blunt, tough, and "natural," Villa displayed a decisiveness and cunning that educated men lacked. Unafraid to fight in the front ranks and unhampered by military tradition, Villa won the admiration of his ir-regular followers by confounding his enemies with a "Napoleonic" genius. Most importantly in Reed's view, Villa wished to establish an agrarian utopia for the common people. The idea of a yeoman democracy, unspoiled by "machinery, scientific thought, and political theory," showed that Reed's vision of the good society was preindustrial.

Reed's experiences in Mexico increased his empathy for the poor and politicized his attitudes about the rebellion. In December, 1913, shortly after his arrival in Juarez, he watched a band of Villa's ragged but color-ful cavalry on review and remarked:

> Two thousand nondescript, tattered men on dirty little tough horses, their serapes flying out behind, their mouths one wild yell, simply flung themselves out over the plain. . . . They had very little discipline, but gosh! what spirit. Not satisfied with that, they began to shoot into the air as fast as they could, on the run, with a reckless disregard for where the bullets went. They z-z-z-m-m-med over our heads, but a lot we cared. It was ten times as thrilling a sight as the cuirassiers charging at Longchamps.[58]

Reckless and free-spirited, they provided the dash and color which he sought in life. They were, he thought, a "great bunch," and excellent "pageant material"; everything, he reported, was "as romantic as can be." After his adventures with Villa, however, he spoke of the Mexicans as "an independence-loving race" who were fighting to win back lands and rights that belonged to them.[59] First-hand observation of exploitation and poverty, combined with the warmth and generosity of the peons, aroused Reed's sympathy for the "revolution" and transformed him into an advocate of social justice.

When Reed returned to New York, he called for American "recognition" of Villa as the legitimate head of a new democratic government, rejecting Carranza, who was against the distribution of land to the peasants. Reed concluded, however, that Villa would not receive American support because he was a "bandit" and a peon, not a "respectable" business man, and therefore "impossible in the eyes of a democratic nation."[60] Most readers of the New York Times undoubtedly missed the sarcasm of his message: America was concerned with business and respectability, not Mexicans and social justice.

Reed did not attack the American government because he believed that President Wilson could and would make a difference. Hoping that he might exert some influence and anxious to know more about future policy, Reed obtained an interview with the President in June, 1914. The talk persuaded or assured Reed that Wilson, "a sincere man of principles," would not meddle in Mexican affairs and would recognize "a bandit or a bull-fighter as President" so long as he represented the Mexican people.[61] If Reed had reservations about the President he said nothing, then or later, when Wilson authorized the Pershing expeditionary force against Villa, who had killed seventeen Americans in a raid on Columbus, New Mexico. By 1916, however, Reed had ceased to worry much about Mexico, for it was difficult to concentrate on a single problem when interests (and reporting assignments) were dictated by newspaper headlines.

Reed resumed his relationship with Mabel, but much of the old fervor was gone. He felt more self-assured, independent, and rambunctious; moreover, his sensational reports from Mexico made him, Mabel recalled bitterly, "more and more the Hero to everyone, especially to women." Although Mabel had enjoyed an affair with painter Andrew Dasburg during his absence, she refused to extend Reed similar liberties. Instead she attempted once more to entangle Reed in her private world, and jealously turned away real and imagined female rivals. But Reed refused to accept these restrictions. Mexico had strengthened his determination to live in "perfect freedom," for Pancho Villa and his soldiers practiced "free love" without embarrassment or vulgarity. Having endured the hardships of war, Reed expressed "nothing but contempt" for comfort, which he considered "only good enough for slaves."[62]

In April, Reed was off again, this time to Colorado to investigate the Ludlow massacre. Reed filed a long report for the Metropolitan in which he detailed how the managers of the Colorado Fuel and Iron Company, a Rockefeller interest, and other coal companies systematically exploited immigrant coal miners and their families.[63] Not only were the men under-paid for grueling and dangerous work, they were forced to live in company housing and buy from company stores. When the miners, under the auspices of the United Mine Workers, struck against the coal companies, they were driven from their homes and forced to live in tents. On April 22, 1914, company guards and state militia men machine gunned and then burned the largest tent colony at Ludlow, killing some twenty-six men, women, and children.

To Reed, who visited the smoldering ruins and talked to the survivors, it was another example of murder, industrial exploitation, and Rockefeller hypocrisy. While Reed spoke at meetings for the strikers' relief in Denver, he was not around for the denouement when the strike was defeated and indictments were served against one hundred and sixty-two miners. His attention had been diverted to Miss Virginia Bean, a young, refined woman whom he wished to liberate. He told her: "There isn't any law you have to obey, nor any moral standards you have to accept, nor in fact anything outside of your own soul that you have to take any account of."[64]

Although Reed remained "faithful" to Mabel, he wrote to her and described "gayly and frankly" his encounter with Virginia. Consequently, when he returned to New York, Mabel assailed him for his flirtation, and they separated. From Atlantic City where she took refuge, Mabel poured out her sorrow to Neith Boyce:

> Reed and I are at separation's point. . . . He says (and he does) he loves me and can't do without me—but he says that when he is away from me he sometimes wants other women. This he calls having 'amorous adventures' —and this, he says, he is *right* to have and to want—that it has nothing to do with our relation, that it doesn't touch it—or influence it or change it. That he feels he would be *wrong* not to respond to any impulse he has— that he believes in perfect freedom—that I may do the same and that he wouldn't feel it or mind it. . . . He *can't* change, he says, because he doesn't believe in it—that he makes it a *principle* to be free and to indulge in every whim. I tell him this isn't freedom—its being a slave to himself. He says he'd rather be a slave to himself than to me or to anyone who threatens withdrawal on account of his being as he is.[65]

While Reed's espousal of free love added to the disharmony and confusion, it was not responsible for their difficulties. The relationship played itself out in Paris where Reed, accompanied by Mabel, went to cover the early stages of World War I. Anxious to see the fighting, he hired a car and left Mabel in a Left Bank apartment where she languished in bed. When neither tears nor another simulated suicide could win Reed's solicitude, Mabel left for New York. The affair ended with an exchange of sentimental cablegrams as Reed fell in love (temporarily) with Freddie Lee, the wife of Village sculptor Arthur Lee.[66]

Riding on a train bound for New York shortly after the war began, Reed met a young English gentleman who was headed home to enlist. What prompted this young man's return home was not, Reed noted, hatred of Germans but a sense of duty to his class:

> He went to glory or the grave, fearless, handsome, unemotional, one hundred sixty pounds of bone and muscle and gentle blood, with the inside of his head exactly like an Early Victorian drawing-room, all knick-knacks, haircloth furniture, and drawn blinds.[67]

Reed's account, which disparaged British upper-class attitudes, illustrated a point: in Mexico men had fought valiantly for social justice, in this war unquestioning men marched off to the trenches like robots.

Arriving in England, Reed observed that there was "no enthusiasm" for the war. But the "centers of artificial stimulation" and the "military machine" welded the nation into a "mighty mechanism," and young men were bravely offering their lives for patriotism, "a humanly fine, stupid instinct," which entailed "self-immolation for something greater than self." It was even more depressing to see British socialists supporting a war "whose [sic] first result would be to put the working class back fifty years." Reed thought that the "aristocracy" was using the war to perpetuate its existence and convert "liberal England into a perfect despotism." Led by the cold and merciless Lord Kitchener, the aristocrats had revived "the stupid, sterile, gorgeous Imperial idea" of ancient Rome.[68]

To Reed the war was simply a struggle for commercial gain and none of the European powers, certainly not England, "the great intriguer, sitting like a spider in the web of nations," had justice on its side. He considered the hypocritical Allies, who shouted for a "peace which their greed had rendered impossible," as objectionable as the Kaiser. Germany had resorted to arms because it was being crushed economically by Britain, France, and Russia. Rejecting Britain's "campaign of lies and distortions," Reed maintained that there was "no right" in this war.[69]

In France, Reed encountered the same public indifference to the war. Soldiers did not understand how the conflict began or why the fighting continued. Reed was intrigued and depressed to see men leave for the front without a show of resistance. The reason, he decided, was the military system. Frenchmen were transported to "military centers," which crushed "all their impulses and ideas, and turned them into infinitesimal parts of an obedient machine to hurl against the youth of Germany, who had been treated the same way."[70] But this explanation merely raised the antecedent question of why men allowed themselves to be sent to the "military centers." Reed never pursued this problem; he only knew that he hated the acquiescence that existed everywhere.

Despite his aversion to the senseless killing, Reed could not suppress the itch to see the action. Turned away by French authorities, he traveled by train to Berlin and then to the German lines in France. There he observed the same blind obedience to "that superior intelligence, the Government." But, contrary to the bloodthirsty images painted by Allied propaganda, Reed found German soldiers to be "big, jovial, childlike people" who took pride in the "gallant pageantry" of "royalties, uniforms, [and] decorations." In spite of its efficiency, the German army suggested an earlier era when "show and ceremony" mattered in war.[71]

But pomp and splendor disappeared at the front. Visiting the trenches near Ypres, Reed discovered that men lived like moles in muck-filled dugouts. As unseen machine guns and howitzers discharged their deadly projectiles on German positions, Reed realized how impersonal war had become. Hence he felt no qualms about firing a rifle twice at the French lines. In modern wars individual responsibility seemed as obsolete as heroism.[72]

Returning to America at the end of January, 1915, Reed suffered from a sense of dislocation. While there was much discussion of the war in newspapers and magazines, most Americans, to his dismay, remained unconcerned about the European war. At the same time, he found nothing at home to match the excitement experienced in Europe. Needing danger and adventure to sustain his writing and mood, he asked for a new assignment in the war zone.

Since the French government had banned him from France as a result of the shooting incident, *Metropolitan* editor Carl Hovey suggested that he and illustrator Boardman Robinson report on the fighting in the Balkans. Reed jumped at the offer and sailed for Greece at the end of March. En route he told his mother that he would find the drama missing in France:

> Of course it will be different, and better in the East. The Caucasus is something like Mexico, they say, and I'm sure I'll like the people. It will be great to get on a horse and ride over the mountain passes where Genghis Khan invaded Europe.[73]

Exposure to wartime suffering had not shattered Reed's boyish delight in combat and adventure. In preindustrial eastern Europe he might again enjoy the company of artless peasants and transport himself imaginatively to a time when reckless, terrifying horsemen swept into the Balkans.

Arriving in Salonika, Reed was enchanted by his strange surroundings, and he reveled in images of the city's ancient past:

> Here Alexander launched his fleets. She had been one of the free cities of the Roman Empire; a Byzantine metropolis second only to Constantinople, and the last stronghold of that romantic Latin Kingdom, where the broken wreck of the Crusaders clung desperately to the Levant they had won and lost. Huns and Slavs and Bulgars besieged her; Saracens and Franks stormed that crumbling yellow wall, massacred and looted in those twisting streets; Greeks, Albanians, Romans, Normans, Lombards, Venetians, Phoenicians, and Turks succeeded each other as her rulers, and St. Paul bored her with visits and epistles.[74]

But these reveries faded when he crossed the border into Serbia, a country devastated by war, disease, and famine. Nonetheless, he liked the Serbs, a "strong, virile . . . race not far removed from the half-savagery of a mountain peasantry," because they displayed a spirit of fierce independence.[75]

Reed's preference for simple folk was coupled with a dislike for those who aped western Europeans. Consequently, he scorned the inhabitants of Bucharest who modeled themselves after the French. Romanian civilization, he wrote Copeland, was "so Frenchified that the people dress like caricatures of French fashion plates." Led by a "dinky" Hohenzollern king and a "fake" aristocracy, the Romanians had fabricated an effete culture. While pink and blue uniformed officers, "high-heeled cocottes," thieving shopkeepers, "bloated" millionaires, and "pederastic" Futuristic painters and poets did nothing but "screw, drink, and gabble," the peasants "sweated out their lives for a franc a day." Although the situation was "ripe for a revolution," the peasants, he decided, were too "cowed" to seize power.[76]

When news of a Russian retreat reached Reed and Robinson in Bucharest, they set out for the collapsing Eastern front. Unfortunately, immense distances, inadequate transportation, and military restrictions kept them from seeing any action. Finally Russian military personnel placed them under house arrest for entering the war zone. After two weeks of confinement in a tiny, hotel room, they were shipped to Petrograd, where they amused themselves, until their expulsion from

Russia, by playing pranks on the police spies who followed them everywhere.

Despite its bungling bureaucracy, exasperating secret police, a hapless army, dilapidated monarchy, and widespread anti-semitism, Russia appealed more to Reed than any other country in Europe. He thought that Russian ideals were "the most exhilarating, Russian thought the freest, [and] Russian art the most exuberant." Reed's infatuation with Russia stemmed from an overactive imagination and a disenchantment with modern America. Primitive Russia offered an alternative to the urban world of "narrow" streets and "congested" cities where people lived "self-centered and narrowly private" existences. In Russia, he wrote,

> houses are always open; people are always visiting each other at all hours of the day and night. Food and tea and conversation flow interminably, every one acts just as he feels like acting, and says just what he wants to. There are no particular times for getting up or going to bed or eating dinner, and there is no conventional way of murdering a man, or of making love. They are not restrained by the traditions and conventions that rule the social conduct of the rest of the world.[77]

In Russia, Reed envisioned the good society; it was a bohemian utopia where men and women would talk, play, love, and live in freedom and fellowship. But in 1915 there was little reason to think that utopia could be established anywhere.

By the time Reed returned to America in September, his interest in the fighting had flagged. Since the European war lacked moral purpose, the idealist could only look to the day when the killing stopped. Convinced that nothing useful or disastrous would result whatever the outcome, Reed hoped that America would not become involved. He would sit the war out, so should America. "The whole Great War is to me just a stoppage of the life and ferment of human evolution. I am waiting, waiting for it all to end, for life to resume so I can find work."[78] There was little to do but retire to a more private existence; accordingly, Reed turned to love, poetry, and Greenwich Village.

Visiting Portland in December, 1915, Reed met and fell in love with Louise Bryant, the slender, dark-haired wife of a local dentist. Since Louise wrote poetry, read *The Masses*, and proclaimed her opposition to middle class propriety, Reed thought her an ideal lover-companion. He told a friend:

> I think I've found her at last. She's wild, brave, and straight—and graceful and lovely to look at. In this spiritual vacuum [Portland], this unfertilized

soil, she has grown (how, I can't imagine) into an artist. . . . I think she's the first person I ever loved without reservation.[79]

But Louise, who aspired to become a writer and a bohemian, was less ingenuous than he imagined; she had known Reed by reputation and had arranged their meeting. Soon after his departure, Louise left her husband and followed Reed to New York.

Adulterous lovers, they rented an apartment at 43 Washington Square South and joined in Village activities. Reed escorted Louise to the Liberal Club, Polly's, the Brevoort, and other haunts, where he proudly introduced her to his friends. In May, they rode the Fall River ferry to Provincetown and rented a cottage that became a center of communal living for Fred Boyd, painter Marsden Hartley, actor David Carb, and Bobby Rogers. Hippolyte Havel arrived to feed the crowd, which included a newcomer, Eugene O'Neill, who found Louise's charms more inviting than Havel's cooking.[80]

In June, Reed left this boisterous gathering and covered the Republican and Progressive Party conventions in Chicago, and the Democratic Party's assembly in St. Louis. Bored and angered by the proceedings, which presented a show of democracy as the "Bosses" manipulated the outcome, he roamed the halls telling everyone that conventions were the "great American Farce."[81] Forced to restrain his criticisms in the *Metropolitan*, Reed vented his rage in *The Masses*. He lambasted Theodore Roosevelt, his father's standard-bearer, for betraying the trust of Progressives, "ordinary, unenlightened idealists" who yearned for social justice. There was, he wrote,

> virility, enthusiasm, youth in that assembly; there were great fighters there, men who all their lives had given battle alone against frightful odds to right the wrongs of the sixty per cent of the people of this country who own five per cent of its wealth. These were not Revolutionists; for the most part they were people of little vision and no plan—merely ordinary men who were raw from the horrible injustice and oppression they saw on every side. . . . We, Socialists and Revolutionists, laughed and sneered at the Progressives; we derided their hysterical singing of Revival Hymns; but when I saw the Progressive Convention, I realized that among those delegates lay the hope of this country's peaceful evolution, and the material for heroes of the people.[82]

Reed was not so estranged from conventional politics that he could not appreciate and idealize ordinary progressives. He was distressed by their ignorance, for in asking Theodore Roosevelt to run as their candidate, they selected a man who had "sold out" to the "munitions makers and the money trust."

The campaign for military preparedness worried Reed and the *Masses'* editors because they believed that defense spending was the first step to war. In the July "Preparedness Number," Reed argued that the country was "being scared into a 'heroic mood' by Wall Street," which wanted "a great army and navy to protect its foreign investments." Patriotic crusades, he maintained, were a hoax perpetrated by "imperialist bankers" and "predatory plutocrats" in order to launch the United States on a "gigantic adventure in World Imperialism."[83] To avert this disaster, Reed asked socialists to support Wilson's reelection.

After his depressing trip to the conventions, Reed was ready to shelve politics for awhile. Returning to Provincetown, he joined the theater group launched during his absence. He acted in one production and wrote *Freedom,* which was included in the players' first bill. At summer's end Reed enthusiastically supported a plan to continue the amateur theater in Greenwich Village.

But Reed's thespian career ended abruptly. After playing the role of "Death" in Louise's morality play, *The Game,* he entered a Baltimore hospital for diagnostic tests to determine the cause of his recurrent kidney pains. Although they had been secretly married before his departure, Louise remained in New York; she visited him just before the doctors removed his left kidney. During his absence, she resumed a secret affair with Eugene O'Neill begun that summer in Provincetown.[84]

Louise made no mention of O'Neill in her letters to Reed. Instead she worried him with her health problems, kept him informed of the latest gossip, and complained about several Village women, especially Ida Rauh, who wanted her part in O'Neill's play, *Thirst.* Louise recounted that Ida, "with true Jewish freshness, got up in the middle of [a play reading] and got something to eat, making as much noise as possible."[85] To allay any suspicions about her own behavior, she grumbled that their apartment had "suddenly become the center of the Village," for Dudley Tucker, Marcell Duchamp, Adell and Alan Norton, Charles Demuth, and others turned up for nightly drinking parties.[86]

The difficulty in concealing her affair with O'Neill made her jumpy. When Lucy Huffaker learned of their marriage, Louise became very upset and told Reed that the news would cause a "terrible scandal." The information could prove embarrassing because some Villagers suspected that she was seeing O'Neill. The impending revelation and the need to break with O'Neill prompted her to leave the theater group. Telling Reed that the Provincetown Players gave her "a pain in the stomach," she moved to their cottage in Croton and suggested that he join her there:

All the weeks before the operation I was so afraid you might not get through with it and I kept thinking to myself—the pity, the unpardonable

pity that you had always to waste yourself with Greenwich Villagers. . . .
That's why I think it will be so fine to do *work* out here uninterrupted,
and play in town. We can't put off real work year after year.[87]

The plan to leave the Village and concentrate on "real work" was never
put into practice. Given Reed's desire for action and his interest in
politics, it was improbable that he could ever live in isolation.
Withdrawal was particularly unlikely at that moment, for America was
drifting toward war.

In the spring of 1917, when Reed was "almost thirty" years old, he
reviewed his life as he approached "the end of youth." "In thinking it
over," he reflected, "I find little in my thirty years that I can hold to. I
haven't any God and don't want one; faith is only another word for finding oneself."[88] Although cognizant that his dissatisfaction stemmed from
the absence of a commitment, he saw nothing to which he could give his
allegiance. He wanted to believe that the working classes could reform
society, but doubted that they were "capable of revolution, peaceful or
otherwise." Nevertheless, Reed clung to the "idea that out of democracy
will be born the new world—richer, braver, freer, more beautiful."
Unable to distract himself for long in romances, literary projects, or
social activities, and knowing that his happiness was "built on the misery
of other people," he had to "write propaganda when [he] would rather
play."[89] Therefore, he resolved to fight the government's decision for
war.

Even before an American declaration of war against the Central
Powers, Reed prophesied "an ugly mob-madness, crucifying the truth
tellers, choking the artists, sidetracking reforms, revolution and the working of social forces." Although no one wanted war, the "speculators" and
the "plutocrats" would, he predicted, "whip up our blood until we are
savage—and then we'll fight and die for them."[90] Reed maintained that
this was a war of rival capitalists and nothing beneficial would accrue to
the workers. While his analysis exaggerated the amount of capitalist support for war and overlooked the extent of jingoism among ordinary
citizens, he accurately foresaw the onset of war fever and its repercus-
sions.

In April, Reed voluntarily testified before the House Committee on
Military Affairs and argued against a bill to establish national conscription. He maintained that Europe was "mad," that injustice existed on
both sides, and that the conflict was being waged for "commercial"
reasons. Overcome by emotion, he vowed never to serve in the army,
even if it meant his death by a firing squad.[91] But his dramatic plea,
betraying a wish to sacrifice himself for a cause, did not impress the con-
gressmen, and they voted for conscription.

In the June issue of *The Masses,* Reed recanted his support of Wilson: "I voted for Woodrow Wilson because Wall Street was against him. But Wall Street is for him now. . . . This is Woodrow Wilson's and Wall Street's war."[92] Wilson's action proved that the existing government could not control greedy capitalists. Unswayed by the President's plan to end all wars, Reed tacked a course that led him away from Wilsonian liberalism.

Reed's sense of alienation deepened as America was convulsed by a patriotic frenzy. His outspoken opposition to intervention made him unpopular at the Harvard Club and cost him a job with the *Metropolitan.* Old acquaintances avoided him and even his family was displeased with his behavior. His brother Harry, a volunteer in the army, advised him: "I wish you could see a little more clearly just what the situation is in this country and how useless it is to buck what can't be changed."[93] Similarly, his mother, invoking the memory of C. J., pressured him to abandon unpatriotic opinions:

> It gives me a shock to have your father's son say that he cares nothing for his country and his flag. I do not want you to fight . . . against us, by word and pen, and I can't help saying that if you do, now that war is declared, I shall feel deeply ashamed. I think that you will find that most of your friends and sympathizers are of foreign birth; very few are real Americans, comparatively.[94]

His mother's response reflected prevailing attitudes toward pacifists and political dissenters: those who opposed the war were "alien" elements bent on subverting the great crusade. Public opinion and administration officials demanded that these so-called traitors be punished or imprisoned.

As the government round-up of radicals and dissenters gathered momentum that summer, so did Reed's depression. "It's getting gloomier and gloomier around here," he told Louise. "Emma [Goldman] and Sasha [Alexander Berkman] are in the coop, with hundreds of others."[95] Although Reed decided to avoid an overt confrontation and stay out of jail, he was unhappy with his passivity, especially when one of Floyd Dell's girlfriends accused him of being a "coward for not getting arrested and raising hell."[96] Louise tried to console him: "You are too precious to waste your energy. . . . All of your best strength you'll need a little later for big, big things and it would be too terrible if you were out of the running by some rash deed when you are needed most—and you will be needed."[97] Isolated by his refusal to go to war or to prison, he felt "restless, aimless, and dissatisfied."[98]

Reed found temporary work with the German-financed *New York Evening Mail,* but admitted to Louise that there was "nothing much" for him in "newspaper work."[99] He continued to hammer away at the economic causes of the war and to denounce the "war profiteers." America, he insisted, was not engaged in a democratic crusade because democracy could not exist when "a small class of immensely wealthy" individuals owned the country. The enemy, he avowed, was capitalism, not autocracy, for the "power of money" ruled in all nations and none of the belligerent governments wanted real democracy. Although Reed refused to lose faith in the people, it was disheartening to see everyone acquiesce to "a regime of judiciary tyranny, bureaucratic suppression, and industrial barbarism."[100] But nothing, it seemed, could halt the government's preparations for war. Everything seemed futile.

Marital problems aggravated Reed's outlook, and the unhappy condition of his private life seemed to merge with the state of the nation. Louise condemned him for a passing encounter with another woman and suggested that they separate. Since, however, she had gone to bed with O'Neill, she was less than fair about his transgression. Nevertheless, she asked him to obtain a reporting assignment for her with the Wheeler News Syndicate and departed for Paris. En route she wrote: "Please believe me Jack — I'm going to try like the devil to pull myself together over there and come back able to act like a reasonable human being."[101]

Reed's ignorance about the O'Neill-Bryant affair was only surpassed by his tolerant response when he learned the details. Contrite about his shortcomings, he wrote to her: "Think about you and me a good deal, will you? It is not worth keeping going [sic] if you love someone else better."[102] He offered proof of his love by describing an incident in which he declined a sexual invitation:

One night I thawed out enough in Washington — I was walking with little Isabel Middleton — to be unable to control myself; and I burst out and talked of you and what you meant to me. . . .

That's all, my darling. I was decent and nice to a girl and pitied her — She wanted to make love. I didn't and couldn't. I've been true all right. But I think perhaps there's something terribly wrong about me — that I may be a little crazy, for I had a desire once, just the other day. I can't tell you how awful, how wretched that made me feel — how I have looked into myself and tried to know why those things happen. . . .

I am under repression a good deal of the time late years. I dare not let myself go. I feel that I am always on the verge of something monstrous. This is not as bad as it seems, dear — it is just that no one I love has ever been able to let me express myself fully, freely, and trust that expression.

I suppose you're right. I suppose it would wreck things to let nature take its course. I am perfectly convinced that that is so. And I am perfectly ready to admit that my nature is not to be trusted.

You will remember that among other things I told you in Portland, I said that I had reached the limit of my fighting strength, and that one more combat would bust me. Well, it has. I've had four or five of these things that have worn you down. Still, my *darling*, you've got to make up your mind to trust me to a certain extent, or our life together will be a farce.

In other words you've got to recognize the fact that I'm defective (if that is it) or at any rate different, and though I won't do anything you ask me not to, you must accept a difference in my feelings and thoughts.

It would be intolerable to both of us if you felt you had to direct and censor my thoughts, my actions — as you have in the past — as you did even in your letter telling me not to drink.[103]

Upholding a chivalrous conception of manhood, he berated himself like an erring Galahad for coveting other women. Reed had "cruelly disillusioned" Louise because she thought she was "getting a hero" when in fact he had become "a vicious little person" who was losing "any spark he may have had." He told her:

I have discovered, with a shock, how far I have fallen from the ardent young poet who wrote about Mexico. . . . I cannot help admitting that all this sex stuff is a symptom of that, perhaps. But please God I intend to get back to poetry and sweetness, some way.[104]

Reed doubted that anything of "artistic" value had been written since his Mexican accounts. To recharge himself morally and artistically he contemplated a trip to Russia. In revolutionary Russia he hoped to find the "idealism" and "spontaneity" he had seen in the Mexican revolt but missed in the European war. He asked Louise to accompany him because "of late years travelling alone has been the worst torture."[105] Whether it was the opportunity for new adventures or a desire to be with Reed, or both, Louise returned and together they planned an August departure.

At first, Reed had been only mildly interested in Russian political developments because he considered the overthrow of the Tsar to be a "middle-class revolution led by business men, publishers, and the progressive country nobles."[106] But subsequent reports describing a "Council of Workingmen's and Soldiers' Delegates" suggested that the February revolution was a "popular upheaval." Although the Provisional Government was still in power, Reed reported in the July issue of *The Masses*:

> The Council of Workingmen's and Soldiers' Delegates, which is the real
> revolutionary heart of the new Russia, grows stronger hourly as the power
> of the awakened proletariat bursts up through the veneer of capitalism
> smeared thinly over the face of things.[107]

Wartime hysteria and personal frustration enhanced the attractiveness of
Russia. He told his readers: "Events grand and terrible are brewing in
Europe, such as only the imagination of a revolutionary poet could have
conceived."[108] Brimming with optimism, he envisaged that the Russian
proletariat was about to erect "a new human society on earth." Eager to
become a part of this experiment, Reed left New York with blinkers
already in place.

He and Louise arrived in Petrograd in September. To Boardman Robinson, his companion on the earlier trip, he reported: "We are in the middle
of things, and believe me it's thrilling. There is so much dramatic to write
that I don't know where to begin. For color and terror and grandeur this
makes Mexico look pale."[109] With characteristic schoolboy enthusiasm,
Reed energetically threw himself into the exciting task of gathering information. His luck in being present as the Bolshevik coup unfolded made
Russia a stimulating assignment, for Reed wanted both to experience and
to write about revolution. His eyewitness reports became *Ten Days That
Shook the World,* a title which proclaimed his sense of the revolution's
significance.[110]

Using Marxist slogans as a guide, Reed immediately perceived a "class
struggle" with the "proletariat, the workmen, the soldiers, and the
peasants lined up against the bourgeoisie." He viewed the revolt as a
spontaneous uprising, a "stirring spectacle of proletarian mass organization, action, bravery, and generosity," and informed American radicals
that the "working class," for the first time in history, had seized control
of the state. The Bolsheviks were only "the ultimate political expression
of [the] popular will" and their program was "simply a formulation of the
desires of the masses." The decisive and pragmatic leadership of the
Bolsheviks ensured the establishment of a "proletarian republic."[111]

In Mexico Reed had been a partisan observer; in Russia he became an
active participant. Albert Rhys Williams, an American reporter who was
also present, commented in retrospect that Reed was "a rebel" whose
prior "identification with strikers and working people had been ardent
but fitful." But the "October Revolution made him a revolutionary." According to Williams, Reed taunted himself for having lacked revolutionary dedication in America. He told Williams: "It's easy to be fired by
things here. We'll wind up thinking we're great revolutionaries. What

counts is what we do when we go home."[112] Partaking in an event that promised to alter the course of world history, Reed was ready to make a commitment to bolshevism and revolution.

Reed did not, however, lose his love for fun and adventure. On hearing of an expedition to Siberia to find a cache of gold, he toyed with the idea of joining it. When officials in Kharkov went on strike, Reed proposed to Williams that they leave at once for the Ukraine and fill the vacant offices themselves. Reed wanted to become "Commissar of Art and Amusement" and, he told Williams,

> put joy into the people. Get up great pageants. Cover the city with flags and banners. And once or maybe twice a month have a gorgeous all-night festival with fireworks, orchestras, plays in all the squares, and everybody participating [sic].

Upon hearing that Leon Trotsky would appoint him Soviet consul in New York, Reed envisioned the indignation he could arouse. "When I am consul I suppose I shall have to marry people. I hate the marriage ceremony. I shall simply say to them, 'Proletarians of the world, unite.' "[113]

Learning of the federal indictment against *The Masses'* editors, Reed decided, though his appointment as consul had been rescinded, to return to America and stand trial with his friends. Neither the threat of arrest nor Trotsky's criticism of his bourgeois attitudes diminished his determination to act gallantly, and he left after the Third All-Russian Congress of Soviets. He was detained, however, in Oslo, Norway, on orders from the United States government, and did not arrive until April 28, 1918.

Despite the importance of his mission as unofficial envoy and propagandist for the new regime, Reed did not pass the time in exile plotting revolutionary strategy or studying Marx. Instead he composed a long, Whitmanesque poem, "America 1918," which extolled the sights and sounds, people and places of everyday America. It chronicled Reed's odyssey "from his free boyhood in the wide west" to "proud New York" with its medley of exotic peoples and cultures.[114] Much of the poem described how he learned about reality by experiencing the seamy side of lower-class life. Actually Reed had haunted Broadway and Greenwich Village more often than the Lower East Side, and rhapsodies on the rich variety of urban life could not conceal his preference for pastoral settings. But how could the socialist revolution bring back the peaceful, rustic world of preindustrial America? Reed chose not to wrestle with that problem.

Having joined the Bolshevik movement, Reed could no longer dissipate his time in conversation and art. In "America 1918" he served

notice that he had outgrown Greenwich Village, the playground of dilettantes:

> Old Greenwich Village, citadel of amateurs, Battle-ground of all adol-
> escent Utopias,
> Half sham-Bohemia, dear to uptown slummers,
> Half sanctuary of the outcast and dissatisfied
> Free fellowship of painters, sailors, poets,
> Light women, Uranians, tramps and strike-leaders,
> Actresses, models, people with aliases or nameless,
> Sculptors who run elevators for a living,
> Musicians who have to pound pianos in picture-houses,
> Working, dissipating, most of them young, most of them poor,
> Playing at art, playing at love, playing at rebellion,
> In the enchanted borders of the impossible republic.[115]

The contrast between his light-hearted celebration of the Village in *The
Day in Bohemia* (1913) and his critical views in 1918 indicate the growth
of a more serious attitude. Dedication to revolution had replaced poetry
and tomfoolery. Having witnessed the power of mass action and caught a
glimpse of the future, Reed no longer accepted the playful world of an
"adolescent Utopia."

After writing down his eyewitness account of the Bolshevik coup, Reed
set about to win support for the new regime. In speeches and articles he
explained that the "dictatorship of the proletariat" meant that soldiers,
peasants, and workers controlled the government through soviets, an arrangement that eliminated parliamentary government and insured the
establishment of "industrial democracy."[116] Reed denied the charge that
the Bolsheviks had installed a tyrannical government. Newspapers had
been suppressed, he explained, because they had violated "the Bolshevik
law making advertisements a Government monopoly."[117] Only those "involved in plots of armed counterrevolution" and grafters had been arrested. To Upton Sinclair, who expressed reservations about the
Bolshevik use of force and repression, Reed replied: "I was in a better
position to overlook the violence and injustice which cannot help going
on [sic] in times of Revolution, and see beyond them to the beauty and
bigness of the thing as a whole."[118] Later, he used the same argument
with Emma Goldman to defend the Bolshevik execution of five hundred
political prisoners. Reed told her: "You are a little confused by the
Revolution in action because you have dealt with it only in theory. You'll
get over that." Zestfully he shouted: "To the Wall with them. . . . I have
learned one mighty expressive Russian word, 'razstrellyat' [execute by
shooting]."[119] The wish to be as tough as the Bolsheviks, to be a revolu-

tionary and not a theoretician, to be a player on the field and not a cheerleader on the sidelines, made it easy to accept political executions.

Reed returned to America convinced that revolution was the only method to secure "industrial democracy." Direct action had proved effective in Russia and would work in America as well. Harboring a long-standing grudge against respectable "theoreticians," Reed told Sinclair that socialists ought to emulate the Bolsheviks. Although unable to define bolshevism, he viewed it as a political movement that expressed the will of "the people."[120]

In Russia, Reed perceived revolution and felt its exhilaration. He saw that the masses had "the power to make dreams come true." Converted by a dramatic event, Reed did not ponder the tremendous social, economic, and psychological problems that needed to be solved. The revolutionary deed and the proclamation of peace, land, and freedom were sufficient to win his allegiance. Reed returned to America filled with poetic inspiration and romantic dreams. He could advocate direct action, without specifying what that entailed, because the will to revolution was what mattered. While acknowledging that American workers were conservative, he predicted that governmental repression would produce a "revolutionary movement in this country in five years."[121]

Reed assumed that the *Liberator,* which Eastman had established after the November revolution, would break with liberalism and advocate bolshevism in America. But Eastman refused to take such a radical position because he believed that Wilson wanted to cooperate with the Bolsheviks in constructing a new international order. When Eastman refused to condemn the President, Reed resigned from the editorial staff. Although he continued to contribute to the *Liberator,* Reed's more militant writings appeared in *The Revolutionary Age,* a new publication formed by a small group of left-wing socialists.

As the leading promoter of Bolshevism in America, Reed became a target of police harassment and government persecution. Outlaw status only increased his intolerance of the Socialist party, which he finally joined in the summer of 1918. When he and other leftists could not gain control of the party, they walked out of the national convention in Chicago, and formed the Communist Labor party.[122] Although another faction, dominated by Russian-Americans, organized a rival Communist party, Reed hoped that his group would be recognized as the vanguard of Bolshevism in America.

Reed's career as a political activist pulled him away from Greenwich Village and its diversions. The abandonment of familiar footholds and old friends intensified his need for Louise, who also became a partisan of Bolshevism. But while she wrote a book, *Six Red Months in Russia,* describing the revolution, and toured the country praising the Soviet Republic, she lacked Reed's political zeal. The separations from one another, a result of political activities and traveling, encouraged infidelities. After failing to rekindle O'Neill's interest, Louise acquired a "French sweetheart" and then, with Reed's departure for Russia, moved in with Andrew Dasburg. Reed in turn enjoyed passing encounters with unattached women.[123] But the relationship endured, offering them a measure of security and romance.

Having progressed from a youthful rebel who enjoyed bumping against authority to a follower of international communism, Reed was prepared to become a revolutionary. Anxious to secure Bolshevik recognition for the Communist Labor party, he decided to make his appeal in person. In September, 1919, disguised as an ordinary seaman, he escaped illegally from America aboard a Swedish freighter. Arriving in Moscow after a difficult trip, he presented a report and his petition to the Executive Committee of the Communist International. While awaiting their decision, he learned that members of the Communist Labor party had been indicted for anarchy. Viewing the situation as a test of his mettle, he resolved to stand trial with his comrades. Even Louise could not change his mind. He told her: "My dear little Honey, I would do anything for you, but don't ask me to be a coward."[124]

The attempted return trip was unsuccessful; he was arrested by Finnish authorities and imprisoned in solitary confinement for thirteen weeks. Despite the physical debilitation and mental strain, Reed endured his suffering bravely; in his letters to Louise he constantly expressed concern for her well-being. When the Bolsheviks finally secured his release, he went back to Russia where he died in October, 1920, a victim of the typhus epidemic.

Reed's untimely death and hero's funeral confirmed the view in Village circles that he had been a valiant fighter who had "died at his revolutionary post." Although Eastman eulogized him as "a poet who could understand science" and "an idealist who could face facts," he overlooked Reed's propensity to view political events as the fulfillment of personal fantasies.[125] From childhood he had imagined an exciting world in which brave men struggled against the forces of evil. Unable to find heroic drama within modern society, he moved to the edge of respectability and traveled to countries where revolts, strikes, and civil wars threatened to undo the social order. The breakneck manner with which he ranged from Paterson to Ludlow and from Mexico to Russia demonstrated an addiction to fighting and violence. Class conflicts produced those moments of moral ferment and adventure that suited his restless temperament and mirrored his unstable existence.

To achieve acceptance from others, to be a member of a team, had always been a powerful need. Rebuffed by rich Harvard classmates, he sought approval from impoverished outcasts who knew alienation and injustice. It was important that he prove his physical bravery and have Paterson strikers, Villa's soldiers, and Bolshevik revolutionaries accept him as an equal.

Overwhelmed by the excitement and promise of Bolshevik revolution, Reed became a communist without fully understanding the party's ideological and organizational principles. To him the Bolsheviks were patriots, like Villa and Zapata, ready to distribute land, freedom, and justice to the Russian people. Captivated by his dreams and the Bolshevik leaders, he accepted all communist propaganda and became an apologist of the regime. He dismissed all criticism of the Bolsheviks and ignored the authoritarian nature of a government that was supposedly concerned with the needs of its people. Reed did not fret about the lack of democracy or the absence of civil liberties, and he did not live long enough to see that Bolshevism brought industrialization, not "industrial democracy" to Russia.

The transformation of a bohemian rebel into an active revolutionary was exceptional in the annals of Greenwich Village. While friends and influences in Greenwich Village had loosened Reed's ties with conventionality, they were not crucial in shaping his career. Experiences in Paterson, Mexico, and Russia had molded him into a romantic revolutionary. Reed burned his bridges, sacrificing money, praise, and security for poverty and the vicissitudes of a radical career. No on else in the Village could make that claim and no one else paid so high a price.

NOTES

1. Joseph Gaston, *Portland, Oregon: Its History and Builders* (Chicago, 1911), pp. 409-410. Harvey W. Scott, *History of Portland* (Syracuse, N.Y., 1890), pp. 535-537. Obituary, Portland *Oregonian* (July 3, 1912), p. 32. Granville Hicks, *John Reed: The Making of a Revolutionary* (New York, 1936), pp. 1-4.

2. John Reed, "Almost Thirty," *New Republic* (April 15, 1936), p. 268. This autobiographical essay was written in 1917, but did not appear in print until 1936.

3. *Official Register of the United States*, Vol. 1 (Washington, D.C., 1905), p. 1397.

4. John S. Reed to Edward Hunt (July 15, 1912), Reed Papers, Houghton Library, Harvard University.

5. Reed, "Almost Thirty," *New Republic,* p. 270.

6. Lincoln Steffens, "A Letter About John Reed," *New Republic* (May 20, 1936), p. 50.

7. Lincoln Steffens, "John Reed," *The Freeman* (November 3, 1920), p. 181.

8. Reed to Edward Hunt (July 15, 1912), Reed Papers.

9. Reed, "Almost Thirty," p. 270.

10. *Ibid.*
11. Charles J. Reed to John S. Reed (March 24, 1912), Reed Papers.
12. Quoted in Steffens, "A Letter About John Reed," *New Republic,* p. 50.
13. Reed, "Almost Thirty," *New Republic,* p. 270.
14. *Ibid.,* pp. 269-270.
15. *Ibid.*
16. *Ibid.*
17. Greenville Hicks, *John Reed,* pp. 17-18.
18. Quoted in Robert Rosenstone, *Romantic Revolutionary: A Biography of John Reed* (New York, 1975), p. 25. A recent, masterful biography of Reed which appeared after the first draft of this chapter, it should be read by those who desire a full account of Reed's life.
19. John Reed, "Almost Thirty," *New Republic* (April 29, 1936), p. 332.
20. *Ibid.*
21. Granville Hicks, *John Reed,* pp. 24-31.
22. Reed, "Almost Thirty," *New Republic,* p. 332.
23. J. Reed to Robert Hallowell (March 19, 1912), Reed Papers.
24. Reed, "Almost Thirty," p. 332.
25. Quoted in Robert Rosenstone, *Romantic Revolutionary,* p. 59.
26. Samuel Eliot Morison, Ed., *The Development of Harvard University* (Cambridge, 1930), pp. 76-77.
27. John Reed, "Charles Townsend Copeland," *American Magazine* (November 1911), p. 64.
28. Reed, "Almost Thirty," p. 333.
29. Lincoln Steffens, "A Letter about Jack Reed," p. 50.
30. Reed, "Almost Thirty," pp. 333-334.
31. John Reed, *The Day in Bohemia: or Life Among the Artists* (New York, 1913), p. 7; p. 14.
32. Quoted in Robert Rosenstone, *Romantic Revolutionary,* p. 89.
33. Quoted in Granville Hicks, *John Reed,* p. 88.
34. Julian Street, "A Soviet Saint," *Saturday Evening Post* (September 13, 1930), p. 65.
35. John Reed to Robert Hallowell (October 17, 1912), Reed Papers.
36. John Reed, "Unpublished Fragment," Reed Papers.
37. John Reed to Harriet Monroe (September 11, 1912), published in *Poetry* (January 1921), p. 209
38. John Reed, "The Dinner Guest of Big Tim," *American Magazine* (December 1912), p. 102.
39. *Ibid.,* p. 104.
40. John Reed, "War in Paterson," *The Masses* (June 1913), p. 17. *New York Times* (April 29, 1913), p. 2.
41. John Reed to Edward Hunt, undated note, Reed Papers.
42. Hutchins Hapgood, *New York Globe* (April 28, 1913), p. 1.
43. John Reed to Edward Hunt (n.d.), Reed Papers.
44. John Reed, "Sheriff Radcliffe's Hotel," *Metropolitan* (September 1913), p. 14, p. 60.
45. Reed, "War in Paterson," *The Masses,* p. 17.
46. Mabel Dodge Luhan, *Movers and Shakers,* p. 215, p. 218.
47. *Ibid.,* p. 219.
48. *Ibid.,* p. 232.
49. *Ibid.,* p. 211-234.
50. *Ibid.,* p. 242.
51. Reed, "Almost Thirty," p. 335.

52. Reed to Edward Hunt (December 10, 1913), Reed Papers.
53. Reed, "Almost Thirty," p. 336.
54. John Reed, *Insurgent Mexico* (New York, 1914), p. 131.
55. John Reed, "If We Enter Mexico," *Metropolitan* (June 1914), p. 4.
56. John Reed, "The Causes Behind Mexico Revolution," *New York Times* (April 27, 1914), p. 4.
57. *Ibid.*
58. John Reed, "With Villa in Mexico," *Metropolitan* (February 1914), p. 72.
59. Reed, "If We Enter Mexico," p. 4.
60. Reed, "The Causes Behind Mexico Revolution," *New York Times*, p. 4.
61. John Reed, "Presidential Interview," unpublished article, Reed Papers.
62. Luhan, *Movers and Shakers*, p. 261, p. 252.
63. John Reed, "The Colorado War," *Metropolitan* (July 1914), pp. 11-16, pp. 66-72.
64. Luhan, *Movers and Shakers*, pp. 259-260.
65. Mabel Dodge to Neith Boyce, undated, Hapgood Papers.
66. Luhan, *Movers and Shakers*, pp. 283-303.
    Hutchins Hapgood, *A Victorian in the Modern World* (New York, 1939), pp. 353-354.
67. John Reed, "The Englishman," *Metropolitan* (October 1914), p. 40.
68. John Reed, "Rule Britannia," unpublished article, 1914, Reed Papers.
69. *Ibid.* John Reed, "The Traders War," *The Masses* (September 1914), p. 17.
70. John Reed, "With the Allies," *Metropolitan* (December 1914), p. 14. John Reed, "The Worse Thing in Europe," *The Masses* (March 1915), p. 13.
71. John Reed, "German France," *Metropolitan* (March 1915), p. 13.
72. John Reed, "In the German Trenches," *Metropolitan* (April 1915), pp. 7-10, pp. 70-71.
73. Quoted in Greenville Hicks, *John Reed, p. 183.*
74. John Reed, *The War in Eastern Europe* (New York 1916), pp. 7-8.
75. *Ibid.*, p. 52.
76. Reed to Charles T. Copeland (August 8, 1915), quoted in J. Donald Adams, *Copey of Harvard* (Boston, 1960), pp. 212-214.
77. Reed, *War in Eastern Europe* (New York 1916), pp. 210-211.
78. Reed, "Almost Thirty," p. 336.
79. Reed to Sally Robinson, quoted in Granville Hicks, *John Reed,* p. 205.
80. Robert Rosenstone, *Romantic Revolutionary,* pp. 249-252. Louis Sheaffer, *O'Neill: Son and Playwright* (Boston, 1968), pp. 345-359.
81. John Reed, "The National Circus," *Metropolitan* (September 1916), pp. 12-13, pp. 62-64.
82. John Reed, "Roosevelt Sold Them Out," *The Masses* (August 1916), p. 19.
83. John Reed, "At the Throat of the Republic," *The Masses* (July 1916), p. 7.
84. Louis Sheaffer, *O'Neill: Son and Playwright,* pp. 348-350; Sheaffer, *O'Neill: Son and Artist,* pp. 242-44.
85. Louise Bryant to John Reed (November-December 1916), Bryant Papers, Houghton Library, Harvard University.
86. Louise Bryant to John Reed (November-December 1916), Bryant Papers.
87. Louise Bryant to John Reed (December 9, 1916), Bryant Papers.
88. Reed, "Almost Thirty," *New Republic*, p. 336.
89. *Ibid.*, p. 335.
90. John Reed, "Whose War?" *The Masses* (April 1917), p. 11
91. U.S. Congress, House of Representatives, *Hearings Before Committee on Military Affairs,* 65 Congress, 1st Session (April 14, 1917), Vol. 207 (Washington, D.C., 1917), p. 31.
92. John Reed, "Woodrow Wilson," *The Masses* (June 1917), p. 22.

93. Quoted in Greenville Hicks, *John Reed,* p. 235.

94. *Ibid.,* p. 236.

95. John Reed to Louise Bryant (June 17, 1917), Reed Papers.

96. John Reed to Louise Bryant (June 13, 1917), Reed Papers.

97. Louise Bryant to John Reed (July 4, 1917), Bryant Papers.

98. John Reed to Louise Bryant (June 28, 1917), Reed Papers.

99. John Reed to Louise Bryant (June 28, 1917), Reed Papers.

100. John Reed, "Too Much Democracy," *The Masses* (June 1917), p. 21. "The Great Illusion," *The Masses* (June 1917), p. 25. "One Solid Month of Liberty," *The Masses* (August 1917), p. 5.

101. Louise Bryant to John Reed (June 9, 1917), Bryant Papers.

102. John Reed to Louise Bryant (July 17, 1917), Reed Papers.

103. John Reed to Louise Bryant (July 5, 1917), Reed Papers.

104. John Reed to Louise Bryant (July 10, 1917), Reed Papers.

105. *Ibid.*

106. John Reed, "Russia," *The Masses* (May 1917), p. 5.

107. John Reed, "The Russian Peace," *The Masses* (July 1917), p. 35.

108. John Reed and Louise Bryant, "News From France," *The Masses* (October 1917), p. 5.

109. John Reed to Boardman Robinson (September 17, 1917), Reed Papers.

110. John Reed, *Ten Days that Shook the World* (New York, 1919).

111. John Reed, "Red Russia," *Liberator* (March 1918), p. 18, p. 14. *New York Call* (November 22, 1917), pp. 1-2.

112. Albert Rhys Williams, *Journey Into Revolution,* ed. Lucita Williams (Chicago, 1969), p. 43, p. 41.

113. Quoted in Granville Hicks, *John Reed,* p. 291.

114. John Reed, "America 1918," *New Masses* (October 15, 1935), p. 17.

115. *Ibid.,* p. 18.

116. John Reed, *New York Call* (May 25, 1918), p. 1.

117. John Reed, *Liberator* (June 1918), p. 26.

118. John Reed to Upton Sinclair (June 19, 1918), Sinclair Papers, Lilly Library, Indiana University.

119. Quoted in Emma Goldman, *Living My Life* (New York, 1934), p. 740.

120. John Reed to Upton Sinclair (November 6, 1918), Sinclair Papers.

121. John Reed, "A Message to Our Readers," *Liberator* (June 1918), p. 26; "Bolshevism in America," *Revolutionary Age* (December 18, 1918), p. 3.

122. Theodore Draper, *The Roots of American Communism* (New York, 1957), pp. 134-139, pp. 164-189.

123. Max Eastman to Florence Deshon (August 28, 1919), Eastman Papers, Lilly Library, Indiana University. Robert Rosenstone, *Romantic Revolutionary,* p. 360, p. 380.

124. Quoted in Louise Bryant, "Last Days with John Reed," *Liberator* (February 1921), p. 11. Writing a few months after Reed's death, Louise recalled Jack's "last days" in Moscow: At the funeral I suffered a very severe heart attack which by the merest scratch I survived. Specialists have agreed that I have strained my heart because of the long days and nights I watched beside Jack's bed and that it is enlarged and may not get ever well again. . . . The American and German doctors give a year or even two, the Russians only months." The pathos of her self-dramatized suffering served notice that she was in trouble. Thereafter, she sustained herself with alcohol. A pathetic figure, she lived out her remaining years in the Village and then in Paris, where she died in 1936 at the age of forty-nine.

125. Max Eastman, "John Reed," *Liberator* (December 1920), p. 5.

CHAPTER FIVE

MAX EASTMAN: Social Engineer and Moral Reformer

From 1913 until 1922, Max Eastman was editor in chief of *The Masses* and its successor, the *Liberator*. Since these Village journals satirized society, extolled sexual freedom, denounced capitalist exploitation, and supported the disadvantaged, Eastman achieved the reputation of a radical. An examination of his writings and activities, however, reveals that Eastman's political views and allegiances fluctuated wildly. He began his political career as an exponent of women's suffrage, advocated socialism after settling in Greenwich Village, championed Wilsonian liberalism during World War I, became a communist partisan in 1918, supported Leon Trotsky in the 1920s, repudiated Soviet Russia in the 1930s, and ended his political odyssey as a right-wing conservative and a zealous anticommunist.

Despite the lack of ideological consistency, there was an axis to Eastman's political gyrations — an indentification with certain leaders of intellectual aptitude and moral fervor who promised to reform society. The origins of this bias lay in the complex relationship between his

Max Eastman. Culver Pictures.

politics and the emotional needs and religious values acquired during
childhood and adolescence. Admiration of his mother, a figure of intimacy and moral leadership, was transferred to political leaders who
seemingly had the power and the principles to construct a new social

order. Thus, he identified with Woodrow Wilson and Nikolai Lenin because they were statesmen who could impose discipline and morality on the masses. Viewing himself as a member of the intelligentsia, Eastman longed to attach himself to a "philosopher-king" who would create Plato's Republic in the modern world. When his heroes failed to establish a utopia governed by intellectuals and engineers, Eastman became disillusioned with political reform and fearful of those who advocated it.

Born in 1883, Max grew up in small towns in western New York where his parents, Samuel and Annis Eastman, were both ordained Congregational ministers.[1] In his formative years, the personal and intellectual antagonisms that arose between his father and mother personified the conflict between cultural provincialism and nonconformity. Samuel, an "austere," pious man "obsessed by Christian virtue," adhered unquestioningly to Biblical teachings and conservative traditions. By contrast, Annis, a woman of "vivifying mind" and "impulsive candor," struggled "all her life with doubt" about Christianity, and finally resigned her ministerial position. Receptive to secular reformism, especially to the liberation of women, she instructed her three children "to live a life the core of which was doing, and not just being, good."[2] Given the power of their respective personalities, Samuel seemed narrow and ineffectual to Max. Rejection of his father and organized Christianity resulted from Max's deep attachment to his mother. It was her influence and example that led him to become a rebel and a reformer.

Samuel and Annis met at Oberlin College, and married when he graduated from Andover Divinity School in 1875. After holding several temporary positions, Samuel became pastor (1881) of the First Congregational Church in Canandaigua, New York, a small town in the Finger Lake region. Five years later, however, physical and "neurasthenic" disabilities forced him to resign, and thereafter he could only cope with part-time preaching and undemanding employment.[3]

The collapse of Samuel's health and standing in the home meant that he presented a figure of considerable weakness to Max, the youngest child. Accordingly, Max had difficulty in acquiring a traditional male identity. He tended, like his father, to assume a dependent role in the family. "I am pretty weak soup like my father," Max admitted in his memoirs. *"Anything to avoid a harsh scene* is the motto of my instincts, and that is one of the respects in which I most heartily despise myself."[4] But this sense of weakness would impel him to challenge conventional authorities and male stereotypes.

After Max's birth Annis refused to have sexual relations with her husband. This imposed celibacy, Max reflected later, contributed to Samuel's physical decline:

My father began mysteriously to lose his small vigor and fade out into the frail, hollow, weakly gesturing and half-whispering ghost of a preacher, and it seems fairly certain to me . . . that his mysterious malady was a sexual neurasthenia resulting from this secret fact.[5]

Whether this analysis was true or not, Max associated continence with weakness and compulsively sought, after he grew up, sexual relations with countless women.

Of medium height, with "light-brown hair and green-blue eyes," Annis was, Max insisted, "a gently curving beauty both of face and figure" who eclipsed her husband at home and in the community. Indeed, it fell upon Annis to support the family. She began as a teacher, but turned to preaching, which provided an outlet for her moral enthusiasm. She became, Max argued, "the most noted woman minister of her time," serving, first as associate and then as successor to Thomas Beecher of Elmira, New York.[6] Beecher's liberal attitudes and Park Church's nondenominational status provided an ideal situation for an energetic, unconventional woman.[7]

As breadwinner and authority figure, Annis Eastman dominated the family. She even punished misbehavior, whipping Max whenever he would wet the bed. The combination of strength and maternal love made her an overpowering figure; she was mother, moral counselor, religious adviser, and civic leader. Unfortunately, Annis lacked stability, and Max was "open as though at the pores to the influence" of her moods. Often she became "uncontrolled, unkind, unreasonable, [and] impatient." She was "melancholic to the point of moody madness; she could be cruel in passion, and her passions could keep foaming long enough to make that terrible."[8] Later Max concluded that her emotional explosions and her "morbid concern" with morality made him a "neurasthenic child."

"Normally sad" or "tired to the point of sickness," and often disturbed by a "vague, remorseful dread," Max was excessively devoted to his mother. In her diary Annis recorded:

Max is five. He is a very loving boy who can not bear to be away from his mother. He can not bear to have anyone else undress him. He is very shy and suffers a great deal from fear of everything. . . . Max is such a clinging kind of boy. Sometimes I weary of his climbing upon me and back of me on the chair, but what would I do if he were not with me?

Two years later he was, she reported, "still a baby, though seven — still timid and fearful of everything."[9] When Annis was away delivering sermons, Mary Linden, his mother's friend from college who lived with the family, and two spinster neighbors looked after him. Protected by nursemaids, including Crystal, his older sister, "the only playmate. . . with whom [he] felt completely at ease," Max became dependent on feminine company and the security of domestic life.[10] He realized later that this "gentle" upbringing did not prepare him for a "mean and illogical" world.[11]

When the family moved in 1894 to Elmira, a town of some thirty thousand inhabitants, Max felt out of place. Although he attended dancing school and social events with young people from the best families, he "did not belong—except in that rather shamefaced ex *officio* manner in which the minister's family rings in on everything."[12] But Annis, or the fictional mother in his novel, *Venture,* "did not agree with those parishioners who thought that her younger son was 'a little queer.' She thought he was all right, and he loved her with an unspoken feeling of pride."[13]

Max also found consolation in books. He liked George Henty's thrilling accounts of Hannibal's and Robert E. Lee's adventures; they helped to blot out his exclusion from boyhood activities. He recalled:

> While crossing the Alps with Hannibal, I had no pressing need to play hockey with a gang of boys on the Chemung River. And I never did play hockey, although I could skate as fast as they. I stood aside from the rough games of boys as though I were a girl. To put it more accurately, I was pushed aside by a social process with which I could not cope. I would gladly have played these games, and not minded getting hurt, but nobody seemed to believe in my adequacy for it, and I least of all.[14]

Henty's stories presented an exciting world in which he imagined himself riding bravely under the command of exceptional leaders. These fantasies left a lasting impression on Max's view of history and politics. His fascination with heroic figures made it easy to venerate Woodrow Wilson and Nikolai Lenin.

While Max suffered ridicule from other boys for his mother's activities, he also benefited from her position.[15] When sixteen boys from the better families left for Mercersburg Academy (Pennsylvania), Max joined them "on special terms as the minister's son." But lacking money, clothes, athletic ability, and a "celestial savoir-faire," he was out of favor with those "who set the social tone of the school."[16] The pain and humiliation of social exclusion caused him to malinger in bed. His only source of comfort was Annis, who disapproved of "a thoughtless going with the crowd." She urged him:

> Be an individual—nothing you can gain will make up for the loss of yourself. . . . *Live out of yourself persistently.* Become interested in all that is

going on in the world and train yourself to think about it. It's better to have your own thought, even if it's a mistaken one, than to be always repeating other people's better thoughts.[17]

She exhorted him to develop moral leadership, which required, she said, "something more than good clothes and money."[18]

Since his schoolmates surpassed him in athletic ability and "worldly grace," Max competed in the classroom. But his classmates dismissed his academic accomplishments and called him "wart." He would have gladly exchanged his "precious gifts of memory" for popularity as a humorist. At graduation he achieved a momentary sense of approval when his "class prophecies" were greeted by "roars of laughter."[19]

When Max entered Williams College in the fall of 1900, he decided to change his image by neglecting his studies. He joined the Delta Psi fraternity and self-consciously sought acceptance by advertising himself as a "hard drinker" and a heavy smoker, though he hated whiskey and never inhaled when smoking. He even accompanied fraternity "brothers" on evening excursions to taverns and theaters in North Adams, the nearest city in the northwestern corner of Massachusetts. But Max had no zest for "reckless" living and confessed his sins to Annis.[20] When she asked him to abstain from drinking and smoking, he complied with her wishes. "That," he recorded later, "was the end of my war for independence."[21]

In his first year at college Max befriended Sidney Wood, a rebellious classmate whose chief interests were physical fitness and American Indian culture. Wood bolstered Max's self-confidence by teaching him a "Greek conception of manhood" that combined poetry with outdoor living. When Wood campaigned for the Republican party ticket during the Presidential election, Max assisted him by speaking against the horrors of free silver and for the subjugation of Filipinoes.[22]

After Wood was expelled from college for ungentlemanly conduct, Max settled down to a more orderly existence. His closest friend became Ralph Erskine, a romantic dreamer who played the cello and knew about medieval furniture, *Till Eulenspiegel,* gothic architecture, and "other matters" that interested Annis.[23] To acquire sophistication and please his mother, Max devised a self-improvement program consisting of piano lessons, typing, studying, writing, and "making pencil copies of great men." In addition, he decided to better his character by overcoming "vanity, melancholy, lack of integration, and lust."[24] This ambitious plan to develop his talents and emulate virtues initiated a lifelong interest in moral regeneration.

Max achieved oratorical, literary, and academic success in college. He contributed poems and essays to the *Williams Literary Monthly* and joined its board of editors. In his junior year he became editor in chief of *The Gulielmensian,* the school annual, and participated in a literary "salon" of college students and liberal Christians.[25] Addressing this audience, he praised "great men" as "iconoclasts" and urged his classmates to be non-conformists. Education, he felt, could be more accurately defined as *"induction,"* or the practice of forcing everyone "into a strait jacket modelled after the average man." Although Max offered no proposals as to how the "college system" might nurture poetic sensibilities, he praised Woodrow Wilson, the new President of Princeton University, for introducing educational reforms.[26] Nevertheless, Max's criticism of college education did not deter him from seeking and winning a Phi Beta Kappa key.

In a speech at graduation, Max paid tribute to Giordano Bruno, a sixteenth-century philosopher who was burned at the stake for his rational attacks on Christian doctrines. Eastman maintained that Bruno, a "martyr of poetry and philosophy against churchly masterdom," presented an example of "courage in individual expression."[27] Identifying with a rebel against Christianity did not require a revolt against Annis because her concept of salvation was essentially moral, not spiritual. By repudiating Christianity he rebuked his father, a straw figure, and emulated his mother.

When Eastman completed college in 1905, he was suddenly incapacitated by severe lower-back pains. Later he realized that the prospect of leaving home had precipitated the malaise. Although Annis had always encouraged him to surmount his difficulties through an exercise of will, he was not ready to leave her care.[28] If she imparted the importance of individualism and toughness, she did not prepare him for independence. Dominated by an unstable mother, Eastman never developed a sense of inner security that enabled him to confront the world spontaneously. The gap between maternal expectations and psychological resources left him divided. To overcome deep-seated feelings of inadequacy, he fabricated an idealized version of himself that alternately produced feelings of self-adoration and self-contempt.[29]

Annis attempted to cure Max's ailments with various health schemes and quack medicines. When these treatments produced no relief, she concluded that his problems were "nervous" and sent him off to Dr. C. O. Sahler's "New Thought" sanitarium in Kingston, New York.[30] The "New Thought" movement was, Eastman explained, a "kind of practical-minded cousin to Christian science, a mixture of suggestive therapeutics, psychic phenomena, non-church religion, and a business of conquering the world through sheer sentiments of optimism." Dr. Sahler promptly ascertained that Eastman's problem was a "lack of vital force in the nerve centers." He prescribed a transfer of "psychic force," which was accomplished by laying his hand on Eastman's brow.[31]

Despite the persistence of his symptoms, Eastman liked certain aspects of the program, particularly the use of hypnotism, which he learned and practiced on a female assistant who functioned as Doctor Sahler's "medium" in diagnosing ailments. Eastman's experiments with this assistant were so successful that he was able to dictate to her diagnostic messages about himself. His fascination with this psychological technique foreshadowed an interest in Marxian socialism and Freudian psychology, which he thought could explain and control human behavior.

After three months at Kingston, Eastman returned to the family's summer cottage on Lake Seneca. There he tried to heal himself with "autosuggestion," outdoor living, and Walt Whitman's poetry. Realizing that "self-mastery" was the solution to his problems, he studied the lives of men who embodied his "ideals and resolutions."[32] From a reading of biographies he concluded that "the highest good is a union of the active and the contemplative life." Unfortunately, neither the self-improvement program nor his mother's raw food diets eliminated his backaches so that he might begin an active career.

In October, 1906, Annis dispatched Max, who was twenty-three, to Dr. John G. Gehring's Neurological Sanatorium at Bethel, Maine, where the doctor placed him on a strict regimen of work and rest accompanied by directives of self-discipline and positive thinking. Under Gehring's prodding and commands his pain eased. The results of this treatment converted Eastman to "suggestive therapeutics," which involved the "fixing" of "healthy mental habits" by means of "repetition from another person—without appeal to . . . reason."[33] This introduction to authoritarian techniques was not forgotten, for psychological engineering became an essential part of Eastman's social reform program.

Eastman was convinced that the "law of suggestion, one of the great discoveries of modern science," had worked a cure. But it was, by his own admission, the "suggestive power" of the doctor's presence and eloquence that stirred "moral and religious enthusiasm." Therefore, Gehring's methods were religious, not scientific. By assuming the role of father and spiritual leader, the doctor had temporarily freed Eastman from his mother's oppression. Although Eastman praised scientific "mind cures," he understood little about science and gained few insights into his own development. He venerated the authority of science as he once worshipped the power of religion. He attached himself to a new authority figure with whom he might "relax [his] critical faculty" without a loss of "moral dignity." He maintained:

I have not 'weakened my will,' or lost any moral dignity. . . . My relinquishment is an act of will. Persons of strong will when they cooperate with a physician are the best patients. Not only is such a voluntary subjection of one's self to a chosen master an act of will, but [sic] it is a high and difficult discipline. It is seen in all the history of religion and morals to be a victory.[34]

In viewing his submission to a "chosen master" as an act of self-mastery, Eastman prepared the way for future surrenders.

On the last day of 1906, Eastman left the Neurological Sanatorium and headed for Greenwich Village. Since Annis had constantly emphasized that "life consists largely of doing what you don't want to" do, he braced himself for a bold experiment in urban living. The decision to live in New York City, however, represented a small step toward independence, for he joined his sister, Crystal, and placed his fate in her hands.

After graduating from Vassar College in 1903, Crystal studied sociology at Columbia University. Like other college graduates of this decade, she was drawn to the settlement house movement and programs to help the urban poor. In 1904, she enrolled in law school at New York University (situated on the east side of Washington Square) and studied industrial labor laws. Managing a recreation center five nights a week, she came to know the radicals, reformers, social workers, and feminists who congregated in Greenwich Village.[35]

With Crystal's assistance Max became a "tuberculosis impresario," a job that required him to set up lectures for the prevention of tuberculosis and to operate a stereopticon during the presentations. After visiting dingy union halls and chapels on the Lower East Side, Eastman's "thirst for activity and experience" vanished. His backaches reappeared and he "had a desperate fight" to keep from lying in bed all day. Fortunately, Crystal found him a temporary position at Columbia University teaching a course on "The Principles of Science." When Crystal left for Pittsburgh to gather information on industrial accidents, Max decided to remain in the Department of Philosophy and Psychology. He obtained an assistantship under John Dewey and spent four years working towards a Ph. D. that he never completed.[36]

Eastman enjoyed a close relationship with Dewey, whom he admired for his "rigorous self-discipline" and "moral force." He was pleased "to find such a man in high place, and have him for a friend and boss." He approved of Dewey's experimental philosophy and agreed that ideas ought to be practical.[37] Yet, in telling his students that Walt Whitman represented "the culmination and ideal attitude to nature and natural science," Eastman demonstrated a reluctance or inability to separate poetry from philosophy or science.[38] In his first book, *The Enjoyment of Poetry* (1913), Eastman pleaded for the preservation of poetry, endangered by a society committed to "attaining ends."[39] He considered science and the formulation of generalizations inimical to the aesthetic pleasures of poetry and the novelty of individual experiences.[40]

When Crystal returned to New York, Max gave up his room in Morningside Heights and rented an apartment with her in Greenwich Village, where he could flee from the "baleful constraints" of respectability. It was Crystal and her liberated Village friends that pried him away from the "knowledge foundry" and thrust him into bohemianism and political rebellion. Shy, inexperienced, yet wanting romance and sex, Eastman's initial interest in Village life revolved around its women — exciting, "emancipated" tutors like Inez Milholland and Ida Rauh. Their work on behalf of women's rights encouraged his participation in the suffrage movement. Although he would have preferred to remain an observer, he realized that inactivity held the dangers of permanent invalidism and would not win him favor with liberated women. Spurred by Annis to embark on "a life of doing things," he became a suffrage lecturer like his mother. No "sissy," he told himself, would have the nerve to "champion the rights of women," or march down Fifth Avenue in a suffrage parade.[41]

At the head of the parade, sitting astride a white horse, was Inez Milholland, a tall, fragile graduate of Vassar who supported women's emancipation and working class reforms. Willful, candid, and intense, Inez suggested to him "a life of . . . venturesome audacity among ideas and social forces."[42] During the winter of 1909-1910, they participated together in a shirtwaist-makers strike. Romance was nourished by their adventures and the expectations of other rebels who thought that the tall, blond and handsome Eastman was a perfect counterpoint for Inez. "We were," Max recalled, "twin rising stars on the feminist horizon. Her female beauty and my masculine oratory providing just the combination that the movement wanted. There was almost . . . a public demand that we fall in love."[43]

Eastman was drawn to Inez because she had a superior "no-compromise mind" like that of his sister and mother. He transformed Inez into "an object of adoration," and told her in a sonnet that he no longer needed the imaginary heroes of childhood:

> I loved the impetuous souls of ancient story,
> Heroic characters, kings, queens, whose wills
> Like empires rose, achieved, and fell, in glory.
> I was a child, until the radiant dawn,
> Your beauty, woke me. O your spirit fills
> The stature of those heroes, they are gone![44]

But Inez criticized his "lazy-bashful drawl" and the "languid way" in which he slumped into a chair. He disliked her "high-geared, metropolitan, function-going rich girl's life."[45] Sexual inexperience and Max's devotion to his mother complicated the situation. He wrote Annis:

> How to combine being in love, and earning my living, and taking a Ph. D. and running a reform society, with the fulfillment of the desires of filial love is quite a problem—especially when your lady love [Inez] is spending part of the time in jail. . . . O my mother, how I love you—and how I long to put my head in your lap and have you touch my hair with your hands while I pray to God for her.[46]

In March, however, he told Annis that the romance with Inez had ended and that he was "back on [her] hands again." Nevertheless, it had been "a great adventure" and he had "grown in grace."[47]

Eastman longed for a relationship that combined "romantic exaltation with real companionship," but could find no one to satisfy his needs. Sexually he was attracted to Ruth Pickering, a tomboyish girl from Elmira who vacationed with her family at Lake Seneca. Despite a ten-year difference in their ages, he had an "insatiable desire" for her. That summer (1910), when Ruth was seventeen and about to leave for college, he attempted to embrace her. She rejected his advances, telling him: "I love to be close to you, but I wish you wouldn't be quite so physical." Embarrassed and chagrined by her remark, which made his romantic attention "seem like mere prurient exploration," he returned to New York a disappointed lover.[48]

In his state of depression he renewed a friendship with Ida Rauh, a plain-looking woman from uptown Manhattan whom he had previously viewed as "wilfully unalive." Suddenly she seemed to offer "a refuge from the problem of love." A graduate of New York University's Law School who did not practice law, she provided intellectual companionship without challenging his masculinity. In his memoirs he commented:

> My friendship with Ida persuaded me that I was a man. I did not have to exhibit myself in swimming and diving and sailing and baseball and pagan sermons in order to be happy.[49]

Ida introduced him to Marxist ideas and their discussions about socialism in her apartment overlooking Washington Square nurtured a more intimate relationship and cast a romantic glow over revolutionary politics. The question of marriage arose when Ida proposed a trip to Europe. They could not simply travel together because of his family's objections and his "prominence in the suffrage movement." Besides, Eastman claimed later, the free-spirited ideology of Greenwich Village encouraged him to regard marriage as a "negligible formality."[50] Therefore, he decided to marry Ida even though the relationship was not "built on passion." More important perhaps, the two women whom he needed for reassurance were no longer available—his mother died in October, 1910, and Crystal moved to Milwaukee and married an insurance salesman.

Married by a justice of the peace in May, 1911, the Eastmans left for a honeymoon in Europe. But the trip, like the marriage, became a disaster. On board the ship Max was seized by a desire to escape when he realized that his love for Ida was "factual, familiar, [and] everyday." He was then afflicted by "an attack of hives that placed [him] among the untouchables for more than a month."[51] Although the newlyweds continued their travels, they found nothing of interest in Italy and France. Max blamed Ida, for she lacked, he complained in his memoirs, the "eagerness," the "friendly delight in people," and the sense of humor that "would have made Sid Wood or my mother or Crystal so wonderful a companion on this journey."[52] In spite of his disappointment, Eastman decided to live "heroically," abandon his adolescent dreams, and accept the responsibilities of marriage. In any case, he lacked the "courage to break free from this anchorage, this guarantee of daily generous and tender companionship."

Returning to Greenwich Village, the Eastmans proclaimed their nonconformity (having yielded to the convention of contractual marriage) by placing their unmarried names on the mailbox—a gesture that ironically reflected the state of their marriage. When interviewed by a reporter from the New York World, Max asserted his commitment to sexual equality in marriage:

> I want [my wife] to be entirely independent of me in every way—to be as free as she was before we married. . . . [M]y wife works just as regularly at the Women's Trade Union League for the things she is interested in as she did before marriage. She has her regular hours of work, and devotes herself as zealously as she ever did.[53]

But Ida did not work regularly and had only a desultory interest in the labor movement. She contemplated a career in sculpturing, but then abandoned the idea, thereby undermining Max's vision of a "creative companionship."

Eastman's sexual novitiate with Ida dispelled his inhibitions, but did not generate romantic rapture. Although Ida professed her allegiance to free love ideals, she was "violently monogamous." Since Max dare not seek out Ruth or other women, he directed his imagination and energy to socialist politics. "For excitement" he read books about revolution, "cherishing the sole aspect of [his] urban and Ida-marrying self which could be called romantic."[54]

In the fall of 1912, Eastman attended a meeting at illustrator Charles Winter's apartment to discuss his becoming editor of *The Masses*. Besides Winter and his wife, there were painters John Sloan and Maurice Becker, cartoonist Art Young, humorists Horatio Winslow and Eugene Wood, poet Louis Untermeyer, and popular writers Mary Heaton Vorse and Inez Haynes Gillmore. Eastman was impressed by the group of "men and women who had made a name for themselves," and he liked the "free-thought talk" and the "radical" conversation. The editors exuded "a sense of universal revolt and regeneration" in art, literature, and politics. The scene, he recalled, "lent itself to my effort and my then very great need to romanticize New York life and . . . the revolution."[55] Eastman accepted the position with the assumption that his duties would leave him time for poetry and writing. But when his collection of poems, *Child of the Amazons,* received an unremarkable reception, he decided to focus on politics.[56]

The Masses was supposed to be a cooperative operation, but Eastman gradually assumed more influence than anyone else. Although monthly meetings were held to select entries, Eastman "did not feel bound to publish everything" chosen at the informal gatherings. Furthermore, he often prevailed on the "more flexible and congenial editors" to provide him with "a vital and timely contribution."[57] Floyd Dell, the managing editor, recalled that his boss was very adept at manipulating others:

> Max Eastman was one of the most selfish persons I ever knew, but he was so charmingly selfish that few people held it against him. He was fond of having his own way about everything, and he was so unscrupulous in exerting his persuasive charm that one had to be on fighting terms with him to call one's soul one's own.[58]

Despite his rudimentary understanding of socialism and radical politics, Eastman was the most important political commentator on the staff. While there was no rigid ideological policy, Eastman's lead editorials each month set the political tenor. He claimed to represent "extreme left socialism" and took credit for transforming *The Masses* into a radical journal.[59] But his opposition to violence, his silence about revolutionary plans, and his approval of President Woodrow Wilson placed him in the center of the American socialist movement.

When Eastman joined the Socialist party in February, 1912, socialism seemed to be growing in popularity. Since its founding in 1901, the party had achieved a remarkable increase in membership, rising from an initial figure of less than 10,000 to well over 100,000 in 1912. One thousand socialists held local political offices, and in the Presidential election of 1912, Eugene Debs, the party's candidate, received nearly 900,000 votes or six percent of the electorate. Since the vote for Debs more than doubled his 1908 total, there was reason to be optimistic about a working class victory.[60]

The Socialist party was a loosely bound coalition of unskilled workers, foreign nationals, small farmers, and Eastern intellectuals. This diversity of groups and interests produced a sharp disagreement over the question of tactics. One faction, headed by Wobbly leader Bill Haywood, favored "direct action," or the use of sabotage, violence, and a general strike to bring about a socialist revolution. These leftists opposed electoral politics and they criticized trade unions for a narrow interest in higher wages and better working conditions. By contrast, the moderate majority wanted to "bore from within" the existing political and economic structure to achieve a socialist society. Early in 1913, the moderates, led by Victor Berger of Milwaukee and Morris Hillquit of New York, organized a drive to oust Haywood by a national referendum. When Haywood was removed from the National Executive Committee, he and his followers resigned from the party.[61]

Although Eastman signed a petition protesting Haywood's "recall," he refused to side with either faction. He remained above the fight, advocating both "direct action and political action" while criticizing the timidity of the socialists and the militancy of the Wobblies. He argued against the use of violence, asserting that the "doctrine of class struggle" was "flatly opposed to class hate." The struggle between labor and capital involved "a conflict of interest" with "right on both sides." In maintaining that "some of the best people in the land [were] on the owning side," and in viewing "the tiniest concessions in wages or hours" as a "genuine advance in the social revolution," Eastman revealed his confusion and conservatism.[62] In his eagerness to be independent and current, Eastman steered The Masses on an erratic course shaped by external events and personal whims.

For Eastman, socialism promised the establishment of a Christian commonwealth without the necessity of divine intervention. Unlike Christianity, socialism advanced a program based on "the science of economics" or the assumption that "every man acts in the economic interest of himself and his family."[63] In stressing man's self-seeking drives (actually the premise of classical economists), Eastman ignored Marx's important insights into the social-economic structure of capitalism.

Eastman used elements of Marxism to attack Christian churches that taught the poor "humble subjection." His hostility to the "aristocratic," "hypocritical" churches showed the importance of personal grudges in his fight for social reform. Although churches were only the "hirelings" of powerful plutocrats, Eastman hated organized religion because it had subverted the teachings of Jesus Christ, "the informal well-doer, the poet of nature and candid life, and comrade of the rejected." Socialism promised a new, "scientific" force that would demolish the "animistic" religion of his childhood. In viewing Christ and Marx as "agitators" for truth and justice, Eastman demonstrated the persistence of Christian idealism. He wished to join with men and women who took the "declaration of faith in Jesus Christ seriously."[64]

Eastman's interest in domestic reform gave way in 1914 to a preoccupation with foreign affairs. The war in Europe, which a majority of socialists supported in every belligerent country, dealt a crippling blow to the socialist movement and exposed the tenuousness of its ideals. The decline of socialism deflated Eastman's interest in radicalism. One indication of political retreat was his growing support of Woodrow Wilson, who, he maintained, had the "character to resist the pressure of American capitalists" in foreign adventures.[65]

At the outset of the war Eastman dutifully repeated the socialist explanation that "commercial" interests had precipitated the conflict. But socialist slogans were then superseded by pseudo psychological analysis. According to Eastman, Germany was a "grandiose aggressor" because her "archaic rulers" suffered from a "pugnacious ego-mania." While opposed to American involvement, he called for Germany's defeat. To excuse his socialist heresy, Eastman distinguished between the German people and their militaristic rulers, an argument Wilson and his liberal supporters would use later to justify intervention. To free the German people from a ruthless military regime dominated by a feudal Kaiser and a Prussian aristocracy, Eastman favored the war's continuation until the military machine was smashed. Anticipating Wilson's speeches in 1917, Eastman predicted that Germany would become a republic in defeat and that "industrial democracy" would spread everywhere. Nonchalantly he reckoned that if the war wreaked great devastation and loss of life, it would accelerate social reform. When the numbers of available workers declined, business would be forced to "bow and beg" from those who were left.[66]

In December, 1914, Eastman asked for a moratorium on revolution so that plans could be implemented for the prevention of future wars. He urged capital, labor, and "awakening women" ("the three great powers of the day") to work together for a world federation. He maintained that labor-capital cooperation in erecting a bulwark against international war obeyed "the dictates of the Economic Interpretation of History."[67] Although he distorted socialist doctrines to suit new purposes, he was not distressed by his ideological inconsistency. He thought that these shifts demonstrated his pragmatic mentality, not the absence of a political center of gravity.

The failure of socialism to prevent aggression in Europe revealed to Eastman its weakness as a moral and scientific force in the world. Socialists thought that men could be taught to act rationally for their own interests. The war showed that men were captives of powerful, animal drives. Eastman found a "scientific" explanation for irrationality in the psychological theories of Sigmund Freud, which revealed the existence of uncontrollable instincts and "repressed impulses."

A superficial introduction to psychoanalysis stimulated Eastman's interest in Freudian psychology. The continuing deterioration of his marraige prompted him to seek psychoanalytic help from Dr. Smith Ely Jelliffe during the winter and spring of 1914. But these sessions, held four times a week, did not alter his behavior or outlook. In retrospect Eastman thought that "a more sceptical neurologist" than Jelliffe could have helped him. ("I believe that I might have learned something about my neurotic constitution. As it was, I merely learned about Freud's psychology.") Despite Jelliffe's heavy reliance on Freudian theory and terminology, the doctor did suggest some causes of Eastman's distress. Later Jelliffe recalled for Eastman:

> You weren't quite aware of the Oedipus situation, the hostility to the father working itself out in prejudiced radicalism. You were tied up also in a complex situation with your sister which made relations with your wife uncomfortable. There was a sister identification, and through that identification a fundamental narcissistic cathexis or investment.[68]

Dr. A. A. Brill, whom Eastman consulted later, was more to the point: "I think you have a strong mother-fixation. Your pattern is that you want to get away from your mother and yet be with her."

Eastman did escape from Ida one night and caressed a buxom, liberated Village girl. Then, however, he confessed his wrongdoing to Ida. "Armed with the authority of an irate parent," she forced him to recount "every detail" of his activities in bed. Mortified by this experience, Max vowed that he would be faithful in the future.[69] But alcohol and cigarettes proved easier to forswear than sex.

On the beach in front of Eastman's cottage. Provincetown, September, 1914. Left to right: Maurice Becker, Max Eastman, Daniel Eastman, and K. R. Chamberlain. Courtesy of K. R. Chamberlain.

That summer (1914) Max and Ida joined the trek of vacationing Villagers to Provincetown. But the change of scenery did not improve their domestic situation. Consequently, they decided that Ida would return to New York while Max remained behind to cure himself through self-analysis. In the process of filling three notebooks with "intimate findings," Eastman learned that he needed "romance, intense, flagrant, and mutually exhibitionistic."[70] This prescription, featuring the fantasies of a liberated existence, caused him to examine his motives in marrying Ida. It was, he recalled,

> her wish, and my devotion to her, together with some feeling of moral necessity, of my inferiority to her wish, and also a strained hope that this might *be* the unattainable—that with loving access to her beautiful body all my vagrant striving might cease—. . . that led me to commit myself to the word love.[71]

Then too, he "wanted to be *somebody's* lover" and thought that Ida was his last chance. He had refused to end the marriage after the trip to Europe because he had feared the reaction of his family and friends. Furthermore, he was too "sensitive through imaginative sympathy to the sufferings" of others to deliver "a clean blow" and tell Ida that he did not love her.[72]

Eastman was aware of certain personal "deficiencies"—his "instinctive infantile selfishness," indolence, and "neurotic pains." In his notebook he confessed:

> I think that with a very pronounced maturity of intellect and objective thinking, I retain an infantile attitude subjectively, and the foremost quality of this attitude is a supreme selfishness. In a life-crisis like this, or indeed any real crisis, I can not act, or think for any length of time, in terms of surrendering my happiness to any large degree *in* the happiness of another even though beloved. I can't face a life of unfulfilled craving. I can be wonderfully generous upon showy occasions, but in a large way, and in many small ways that do not show, it is the instinctive assumption of my thinking that I should have what I want.
>
> And the quality that has most mitigated this foremost trait of selfishness in me, giving me in the eyes of many friends a character of instinctive generosity, is exhibitionism. . . . My frequent dream of bodily exposure, as well as the exposure of various forms of nobility and heroism in my soul, confirm this knowledge.[73]

He blamed his "craving" for women on "an unconscious fixation of life-interest upon the early image" of his mother. In other words, he fashioned an ideal woman from early impressions of his mother and searched for someone who could measure up to her. But this explanation offered the convenience of a Freudian-inspired formula without the impact of a genuine discovery. He did not probe more deeply into the relationship with Annis to gain a clearer understanding of his development and relieve his distress.

Eastman realized that he was *"in love with the unattained,"* but refused to relinquish the illusion that the right woman could satisfy his needs.[74] Determined not to "sublimate" his sexual desires, he decided that he must be free of Ida. He wrote to her and explained that he wanted to stay married and yet be able to pursue Ruth Pickering and other women. Although Ida warned that he might "become a professional Don Juan," she consented to letting him have lovers "whenever and wherever" he wanted.[75]

Overjoyed at the prospect of enjoying "physical and semi-romantic gratifications" without losing Ida, Max invited her to leave immediately and meet him in Boston. But once they were together again, Ida discovered tearfully that she could not accept his terms. He justified his demands by explaining that he was a "creature of successive alarms of passion" and that love, "like life and poetry," came to him in a "surge of inspiration." Although he knew that love was "fleeting and unreliable," nothing else was "more precious" to him. He was a "gypsy lover" who wished to "dedicate his strength to poetry and truth and liberty."[76] Whether these explanations satisfied her or not, she agreed that Max should have a more independent existence. When they returned to New York, he rented a room not far from their apartment where he could live "flagrantly" without the encumbrances of a wife and son.

Viewing himself as an authority on Freud, Eastman explained psychoanalysis to the public in two articles for *Everybody's Magazine*. His facile presentation of "mental and nervous diseases" stressed situational dilemmas rather than deep-seated emotional disorders. Unlike Freud, who set modest goals for psychoanalysis, Eastman portrayed the new therapy as a simple but effective technique for ridding the patient of emotional distress. Likening psychoanalysis to surgery, Eastman argued that "mental cancer" could be "dissected out," leaving the individual "sound and free and energetic." The process was simple. Once the patient became aware of "desires and fancies" buried in the "unconscious" or "soul," the "morbid effects" disappeared. In contrast to Freud, who conceived of the unconscious as a headstream of animalistic drives difficult and unpleasant to restrain, Eastman placed reason at the center of the personality. Whereas Freud emphasized the unwitting determinism of human behavior, Eastman viewed "sickness" as a product of moral cowardice. "Instead of facing reality, admitting we are what we are, and thinking out a deliberate course of conduct in the light of the facts, we shudder at the cruel impulses of our hearts, hastily cover them up, and leave them to fester away, in the very core of our being."[77] In words that sounded like his mother's sermons, Eastman called on others to admit the presence of nasty impulses and sexual desires. In effect, he defined psychotherapy as a method of self-improvement that simply required intelligent probing, courage, and will-power.

Whereas Freud insisted on the importance of unconscious sexual desires in explaining the origins of neuroses, Eastman focused on individuals (like himself) plagued by unhappy interpersonal relations. Persons who could not establish a satisfying marriage were those who "failed to manage properly the business of growing up." While all individuals, he argued, were subject to non-sexual "infantile attachments," sensitive children, "too closely adored or too hideously nagged" by parents, were particularly susceptible to "chronic acute infantile homesickness." They were "foredoomed" to failure in the "hard and merciless" world because they faced "a man's reality with a baby's soul." The emotional attachment to a parent gave rise to an idealized image of a "perfect" lover. This "phantom" produced unsuccessful love affairs, chronic unhappiness, and psychosomatic disorders. Given the availability of psychoanalysis, however, Eastman was optimistic about the prognosis of "mama's boys." They could be cured if they would simply "go back and begin over again and *grow up*."[78] Had Eastman been more honest or insightful, he might have admitted that this was not an easy task. Eastman was closer to the truth when he remarked: "For many of us are chasing rather madly through this world, and just exactly what it is that we are chasing we will never guess, until some kind friend or physician of this newer school, some modern Socrates, teaches us to 'know ourselves.' "[79] But since Eastman rejected Jelliffe's insights, perhaps no psychiatrist could halt his obsessions.

Eastman argued that Freudian psychology furnished insights into "the art of educating young children." Eastman concluded (from his own experiences) that parents ought to allow children to grow into self-sufficient individuals. This did not mean parents should grant their children license to do as they wished, for children harbored "untoward impulses" that erupted into fighting and violence. A wise mother, he counselled, would not stifle this instinct because that would produce neurosis. Instead, she should interest her son (apparently daughters lacked this instinct) in games "of conflict" that safely discharged uncivilized impulses. As the boy matured he should be encouraged to *"lift that fighting instinct"* into "activities of real social or professional value which contain the element of fight."[80] The family could, therefore, become an agency of social reform once parents discarded overt coercion for stealthy manipulation. By democratizing Freud's concept of sublimation, Eastman reshaped it into a technique of social control.

Interest in social engineering was shared by other middle-class intellectuals in the Progressive Era. Walter Lippmann, Judge Ben Lindsey, and

John Dewey agreed that scientific management, not traditional repression, could best eliminate violence and socialize the citizenry.[81] Since the masses were immune to rational self-control (psychoanalysis was really for the intelligent members of society), Eastman believed that they needed authoritarian leadership. Consequently, he urged his Village friends to forsake bohemian activities for psychological studies; there was "other work to be done . . . than [sic] agitate and converse and write beautiful literature and poems of love and anarchy."[82] That work involved scientific control of mass behavior.

With money earned from the two articles on Freud, Eastman left for Europe in the summer of 1915 to "experience" war and find romance; he failed, however, on both accounts. Barred from visiting the trenches, Eastman remained in Paris with Arthur Bullard, a socialist supporter of the Allies. Instead of studying the current military and diplomatic situation, Eastman read and dreamed about a more heroic period — the French Revolution and the Age of Napoleon. Conversations with Bullard, however, did confirm his faith in the new methods of social control. Bullard told him how the German and French politicians had "pulled off the stunt of getting the people in motion in a desired direction." They had learned how "to harness this stupendous energy of crowd psychology and make it do the work of the will of man." While Bullard spoke of using these techniques to win the "social war," Eastman had more conservative goals in mind.[83]

After six uneventful weeks in France, Eastman left for England. But London proved almost as dull. The exception was a brief audience with playwright George Bernard Shaw. Eastman, who liked the company of famous people, was pleased by the friendly manner in which Shaw received him — "he knew me, he admired our magazine, he had even read some of my editorials." But Eastman was not otherwise successful. Except for a passing encounter with an "exquisitely shaped" prostitute ("to be intimate on a money basis was beyond my powers"), he could not find female companionship. He rented a hotel room and spent most of the time "lying on the bed, sick both at heart and stomach." Homesick and lonely, he returned from Europe "defeated," which was fitting, he reflected, "for one who had 'gone to war' in so unheroic a fashion."[84]

After the trip, Eastman commented in The Masses that the European war was "uninteresting," an observation which seemed in part to reflect personal disappointments. The war bored him because it only consisted of "a regular businesslike killing" of young men. Instead of a popular struggle against tyranny, there was a slaughter fueled by nationalism, "the most banal of stupid human idol-worships." Yet, he looked forward to Germany's defeat. Although Eastman claimed to be an "internationalist" who refused to label one side as "divine" and the other as "barbarity unveiled," he viewed Germany as uncivilized and the West as the repository of culture:

> France holds more of what is dear to us than any other country of Europe
> . . . . France has not only freedom but the arts of life more nearly won
> than any other country of Europe. Her culture is one of superior happiness,
> the habits of her people are more poetic, they realize more, live more, and
> with all that are more spontaneously intelligent than the Germans.

Even if England was a "land of snobs and servants," the people could express themselves freely and they were not shackled by "compulsory" national service. By contrast, Germany, the invading power, was "in a sophomoric stage of national egotism" and German soldiers, "trained to mere obedience," could not "control themselves quite so well as well-bred warfare demands."[85]

Eastman's commentary about modern warfare showed his quixotic attachment to the fancied conditions of a more chivalrous age. His inability to analyze political and economic structures, and his indifference to historical, diplomatic, and military factors, made it easy to advance romantic impressions of Britain and France. His stereotyped images, resembling the crude portraits painted by Allied propagandists, showed an inability to refrain from moralistic simplifications.

As an elitist who disliked mixing with others, Eastman had few incentives to idealize the masses. Since the outbreak of war, which released the "gregariousness and pugnacity" fixed in the "hereditary structure of all civilized races," he felt even less kindly towards them. By ignoring governmental complicity and coercion (except in Germany), he could blame the masses for the torrent of nationalism. The masses were vulnerable to "an instinctive emotional spasm" and truth was "a wholly inadequate corrective."[86] As he saw it, Marx and other socialists had overestimated the extent to which the proletariat could act rationally. "Scientific" studies of instinctual psychology had uncovered "the brute facts about human organisms in society, the unalterable data which must underlie all plans of progress."[87] Except in the case of pacifists, whose instincts were "abnormally weak" or "where the ideation is abnormally strong (as in the intellectual hero)," ideas had no impact. Because the "thoroughest teaching of class conscious inter-nationalism" could not produce a "human nature" able to withstand "the panic of patriotism," Eastman doubted the scientific validity of Marxism.[88] Instinctual psychology explained the failure of socialism and offered a surer guide to the future.

Eastman concluded that the prevention of future wars required manipulation of the masses. This could be accomplished by directing the "instinct of self-identification" to a larger group, preferably an international federation. He insisted that America lead the way by organizing all nation-states in the western hemisphere, and he exhorted socialists to support "bourgeois movements" for a world organization. Again he welcomed the support of powerful capitalists (who were evidently more rational than other citizens) in this venture; "as a matter of Christianity and good business" they would cooperate in the effort to abolish war. Eager to have a "great initiator" lead the crusade, Eastman announced in the December issue (1915) that President Wilson held "this hope of the future . . . in his hands."[89]

The Masses readers and editors apparently did not object to Eastman's political stance. In his memoirs he claimed that others readily accepted the "formula" of reconciling "bourgeois anti-militarism with a doctrine of proletarian class war." American radicals wanted, he explained, to be Marxian and Christian. They liked "pictures of a giant workingman rolling his sleeves" in preparation for a knockout fight with the capitalists, and they applauded pictures of Christ "being dragged into the barracks by a Christian recruiting sergeant."[90] But in supporting Wilson and a league of nations, Eastman had all but abandoned socialism.

Eastman's concern for international peace was strengthened by Crystal, who returned without her husband to New York in 1915. She became actively involved in the Women's Peace Party, a group clamoring for an end to the war and a permanent league of nations. Crystal, who was also secretary of the American Union Against Militarism, enlisted her brother's services in the fight against military preparedness. In May, 1916, she asked him to be a member of the Union's delegation to Washington. Although the pacifists were sent to protest defense appropriations, Wilson proved to be the most persuasive speaker. Eastman came away from the meeting much impressed with the President, a "graciously democratic aristocrat," and told his readers:

> You can easily see in an hour's conversation what power he wields over our country post-office politicians. It is the power of aristocratic and yet real knowledge. . . . He has an adroit logic as well as technical knowledge and the diction of the king's minister. He is the ablest man that has been in that office for years.[91]

Even though *The Masses* had consistently admonished that preparedness would lead to intervention, Eastman confidently asserted that the President would preserve American neutrality. He was certain that popular support for Theodore Roosevelt's jingoism, not a desire for war, had caused the President to endorse an increase in military spending. Eastman maintained that the President hated "preparedness policies," but tolerated them "by dwelling very strongly in his mind upon the idea of world federation and the international enforcement of peace." Accordingly, Eastman supported Wilson, not the Socialist party candidate, in the Presidential election of 1916.[92]

Since the President had not endorsed the federation plan, Eastman's infatuation with Wilson was not determined by political considerations. In his view, Wilson was a leader of "intellectual ability" and "pragmatic mentality" who could lead the masses from savagery to orderly progress. Moreover, Eastman entertained the illusion that he could influence Wilson's decisions. He had first met the President at a banquet during the 1912 campaign and had "instructed" him on the benefits of women's suffrage. Consequently, when Eastman visited the White House in 1916 to "lecture the President on the folly of enlarging the national army," Wilson, recalling their previous conversation, greeted him "with special warmth." For this reason, Wilson imparted to the delegation "his private and exciting plans to stay out of the war in Europe until both sides were exhausted and then step in with a proposal of peace and an association of nations to prevent future wars."[93]

After his talk with the President, Eastman lashed out against socialism and its blueprints for the future. "We shall," he declared, "have to renounce this alluring pleasure of drawing up plans for new worlds, which would run like a mechanical toy if we could only get somebody to start them."[94] Socialism, he concluded, was not a science, but a secular religion that helped believers to endure life. The working classes, who reacted to war with the frenzy of "a sexual or religious orgy," needed to be controlled by intelligent guardians. The German rulers had demonstrated "the value of popular welfare insured by a centralized government"; it permitted the ruling caste to generate "superior energy and capability in united action." Regardless of the war's outcome, "state-socialism attended by paternal discipline" would become the "common heritage of the world."[95]

Eastman's elitism became increasingly more visible as he repudiated the socialist ideals of equality and brotherhood. He considered competition to be congruent with man's egoistic nature, and he saw "beauty in the fluent orders that would continually form and dissolve themselves in a free society." With their "inherited propensities to domination and servility," the masses needed a "higher authority." The existing society erred in permitting "the crass and rigid aristocracies" of money to dominate. Eastman, like Plato, wanted a "genuine aristocracy" of intellectuals trained in the "art of instrumental thinking." He realized, however, that the establishment of what he called "scientific socialism" could only be accomplished through "the agitation and organization of the lower classes."[96] Eastman's readiness to use the masses for his own purposes suggested the likelihood that he would follow anyone daring enough to seize power and establish an updated version of Plato's Republic.

In the summer of 1916, Max and Ida returned to Cape Cod and participated in the formation of the Provincetown Players. Despite the excitement generated by this enterprise, their domestic unhappiess continued. When Ida visited friends in Maine, Max accepted the offer of a tango lesson from a dark-eyed sculptress. Although he tried to be discreet about his dalliance, Village friends informed Ida of his amorous activities. She became outraged, but did not leave him. They went back to New York and resumed their prior living arrangement.[97]

At the fourth annual *Masses* ball, held in Tammany Hall on December 15, 1916, Eastman met Florence Deshon and decided to end his relationship with Ida. Florence was a dark-haired, twenty-one-year-old photographer's model, chorus girl, and actress who wished to become a movie star. Eastman thought that she was the "most beautiful woman in America." Despite the fact that she was thirteen years younger, childish, uneducated, self-centered, petulant, and cared nothing for politics, Eastman "fell wholeheartedly in love." Florence's beauty and youth were as flattering as her high regard for his "superior knowledge." Therefore, he convinced himself that leaving Ida was an adventuresome "reconquest of freedom" and the beginning of adulthood.[98]

Max took Florence to his cottage at Croton where the rustic environment heightened a sense of romance. For the first time he enjoyed "the ideal rapture and the physical achievement of love." But if intimacy with Florence brought sexual ecstasies, it also entailed suffering, for her selfishness, ambitiousness, and moodiness took its toll. He welcomed the pain, however, because he no longer experienced "carnal or romantic" yearning toward the shapely breasts and delicately upward curving calves of summer-clad girls" who passed him on the street. He, the "frail one," was again forced to serve a "robust" woman.[99]

Public events, however, intruded into his private world. On January 22, 1917, President Wilson called for a "peace without victory" and a postwar "League for Peace." Eastman hailed this speech as the

most momentous event conceivable in the evolution of a capitalistic civilization. And it is also the one hope of preserving that struggle for a new civilization which we call Socialism, or Syndicalism, or the Social Revolution, or the Labor Struggle, from the continued corruption of militarism and the ravaging set-back of patriotic war.[100]

The specious connection between a league of nations and the social revolution testified to Eastman's persistent attempt to be a socialist and a Wilsonian liberal. While socialist critics might consider Eastman an apostate, he believed that flexibility and compromise were essential in "scientific thinking."

Eastman's optimism was abruptly deflated by a rapid turn in events. On January 31, the German Ambassador informed the American government that his country would resume unrestricted submarine warfare. Having previously committed his administration to a strong response if the German High Command revived this policy, Wilson severed diplomatic relations with Germany and asked Congress for authority to arm American merchant vessels. These ominous developments caused Eastman to forecast dire consequences if America intervened. War with Germany, he warned, would insure a decisive victory for England and would wreck the opportunity for a "peace without victory." Instead of a postwar federation of peaceful states, the "two dominant nations, bragging about Anglo-Saxon liberty," would impose "their commercial imperialism" around the world. Fulminating with socialist indignation, Eastman reminded his readers (and himself) that there was neither "liberty nor democracy anywhere in this capitalistic society." In the event of war and an "orgy of patriotism," he advised socialists to remain neutral in their sympathies and refuse to serve in the army.[101]

When the President asked for and received a declaration of war from Congress, Eastman expressed skepticism about the possibility of a democratic settlement. "We will," he forewarned, "Prussianize ourselves, and we will probably not democratize Prussia." But these perceptive observations were overruled by his loyalty to Wilson, and he consoled himself with the fuzzy notion that the war would "advertise the idea of democracy."[102] By ignoring his gloomy prognostications about the effects of American intervention, Eastman proved to be an inconsistent and uncertain critic. He simply refused to give up on Wilson and the dream of a league of nations. Consequently, he assured his readers that the "eradication of nationalistic war-policies" and the establishment of an international federation remained foremost "in President Wilson's mind."[103] Eastman believed that a single heroic figure could forge a better world.

Instead of criticizing the Wilson administration, Eastman attacked the super-patriots who considered the war a noble crusade. He maintained that patriotism satisfied that "craving for a sense of union with a solitary herd." He counted himself among those "few" individuals who withstood the stampede "by using their brains about truth." Pacifism, therefore, enhanced his sense of moral and intellectual superiority over ignorant "mobs" who needed "the religion of patriotism."[104] Eastman assumed that he represented one of the few voices of reason when in fact his allegiance to Wilson undermined critical detachment.

Eastman felt uneasy about the President's intentions. Since Wilson's plea for a "peace without victory" had apparently been superseded by the Entente's plan to defeat and dismember Germany, he wondered whether "this peace President," under "influences perhaps too subtle for political analysis," had not "changed into a man of the army and navy." Eastman pointed out that the President had not yet replied to the Russian Provisional Goverment's demand for an immediate settlement without spoils. Consequently, he asked Wilson in the July issue of *The Masses:* "Are we with revolutionary Russia, or are we with imperial Great Britain, in carrying war against Germany?" Patiently he awaited a reply.[105]

For weeks Eastman had ignored political developments in Russia. He made no mention of the revolutionary overthrow of the Tsar and offered no comment when the Provisional Government, under pressure from the Petrograd Soviet of Workers and Soldiers, renounced Russia's promised share of indemnities and annexations. When John Reed proclaimed in July that the "Russian proletariat" was establishing "a new human society upon the earth," silence became unbearable. It was difficult to ignore Reed because Eastman considered him to be a "broad-shouldered big brother who knew about rough life and was equal to it."[106]

In the August issue Eastman announced his support of the Russian revolution. Despite his previous criticisms of Marxism and his disdainful attitude toward the proletariat, he told his readers:

> What makes us rub our eyes at Russia is the way our own theories are proving true. . . . One by one the facts fall out exactly as they were predicted by Marx and Engels and the philosophers of syndicalism. To me the distance of Russia, combined with the almost comic patness of everything that happens, makes me feel that I am not watching history, but a kind of William Morris dream or a Gilbert and Sullivan staging of the Social Revolution in Comic Opera.[107]

Since Eastman had little solid information about Russia, he celebrated opera rather than history. The careless manner in which he tossed syndicalism and Marxism together testified to a lack of focus. There was no "patness" to the events and neither Marx nor Lenin had anticipated a revolution in Russia. Eastman, as in the past, forced theory and politics to conform to recent events.

Despite his previous defection from the socialist ranks, Eastman reasserted his claim as a Marxian expert. He noticed with dismay that "obtuse" socialist terms appeared on the front pages of "metropolitan dailies" and that newspaper "literati cut some ludicrous capers in their attempt to be glib with these names and facts." He dismissed the possiblity that "newspaper wise men," who had never heard of the economic interpretation of history or "the class theory of government," could understand developments in Russia. But to someone "already familiar with the idea of a workmen's syndicate simply taking over," the actions of the Russian people were perfectly comprehensible. He glibly explained that the workers had assumed command of the state because they controlled the forces of production. For Eastman, the revolution substantiated a "truth we learned long ago and have been telling ever since — that either through or aside from political forms, the economic forces always rule."[108] But Eastman did not explain what economic forces operated in Russia or how the working classes were able to seize power. Instead of gathering facts and data to arrive at an explanation, he applied rudimentary socialist theories to the Russian situation. He failed to understand the dynamics of this revolution or the factors that influenced its course. Socialist theories obscured the fact that the collapse of government and society resulted from Russia's inability to wage a protracted, modern war. The superficial analysis, however, allowed Eastman to acclaim the "scientific" validity of Marxism and to overestimate the possibility of revolution elsewhere.

Eastman announced his support of the Council of Workmen's and Soldiers' Deputies (the Petrograd Soviet) in its "diplomatic conflict" with the Western Allies. Britain's and Wilson's evasive responses to the Russian demand for a statement of war aims suggested that this was a "war of national prestige" and a crusade against "satanic" Germany. Since Wilson's league of nations would be founded "upon victory rather than peace," Eastman decided that only a new socialist international, formed by revolutionary forces in every country, would secure a lasting peace. "We believe," he declared,

> that if there were a Council of Workingmen's and Soldiers' Deputies, conscious of its power, in every belligerent country, they would join their voices and join their hands in this demand for a working class peace. The Council in Russia speaks for the working classes of every country, and for us the hope of democracy lies in those classes, and in none of the governmental institutions now in charge of the war.[109]

Formerly creatures of instinctual ferocity, the workers had become a
force for international justice.

By contrast, it seemed to Eastman that America had reverted to a
primitive stage of development. Everywhere government officials, cor-
poration executives, and private citizens harried socialists, anarchists,
pacifists, and workers. When scores of blacks were murdered in the East
St. Louis race riot, Eastman declared: "The United States has a more extended record of atrocities to her credit than any other nation of the
civilized world." The contradiction between America's "chivalrous
crusade to rid the world of German frightfulness" and its inhumane treatment of blacks and workers struck him as particularly hypocritical. The
"Prussian" dragooning of political dissenters resembled the enemy's
practices except that the administration's "imperial talent" was more efficient than the Germans.[110]

In July, Eastman and *The Masses* became one of the government's
many targets. The Postmaster of New York notified the editors that the
August issue was unmailable under the Espionage Act (June 15,1917),
which prohibited the mailing of material "advocating or urging treason,
insurrection, or forcible resistance to any law of the United
States."[111]Although Albert S. Burleson, the Postmaster General of the
United States, was behind this harassment, Eastman lodged no complaint
against the administration. Instead he blamed "the principalities and
powers of the economic world" who wished to establish "a feudal system
based on the control of industry." Unlike the "soft-headed idealists" who
thought that history could be controlled by "a man in the White House,"
Eastman knew that economic forces shaped history.[112] But this flimsy
analysis served mainly to exempt Wilson from complicity. Despite the
boastful claim to tough-mindedness, Eastman believed that Wilson
would make a difference.

Eastman conceded that President Wilson had "failed altogether as a
leader or even a defender of democratic life," but he refused to break
with him. He waited expectantly, eager to seize on some sign that indicated Wilson would lead the world to permanent peace. Finally, he
found his reassurance when the President replied, on August 29, 1917, to
Pope Benedict's proposal for an immediate peace based on a *status quo
ante bellum* and disarmament. According to Eastman, Wilson asserted
that America sought "no material advantage of any kind" in the war. The
United States only wanted to conclude "an enduring peace" based on
"fairness and the common rights of mankind."[113] Notwithstanding the noble phrases, Wilson in effect rejected the Pope's request for a cessation
of hostilities and a peace without victory. Most Americans approvingly
viewed this reply as a promise that the war would go on until Germany

was defeated. *The New Republic,* however, thought it was a commitment to anti-imperialism, showing Russian radicals that "their aspirations for a just peace are our aspirations."[114] Eastman drew the same conclusion. Wilson, he declared in *The Masses,* "acceded to the Russian peace terms" by binding America to a policy of no annexations and no punitive damages.

Eastman admitted that for a time he had been assailed by doubts about the President's intentions. Wilson's bellicose Flag Day Address (June 14, 1917) had caused him to wonder apprehensively if Wilson "had abandoned every elevated and just ideal and purpose that had been expressed by him in his Peace Without Victory message." But in renouncing all "vindictive intentions," Wilson allayed his fears. The President, Eastman stated, had separated America's "purposes absolutely from the imperialistic ambitions of the ruling classes in the Allied Countries," and thereby removed "a little of the insult, at least, from the injury of conscription."[115]

Although Eastman wondered why it had taken the President five months to respond to the "Russian Republic," he nevertheless credited "Woodrow Wilson with knowing what is going on." He speculated that the President waited until after the Allied powers received war materials "so that he would be in a position to tell them what their peace terms would be." If that was the reason, Eastman bowed "to him as the most astute and really powerful statesman of the world." Perhaps Wilson had reached this decision because the People's Council, pacifists "who insist upon using their brains," had "compelled him to." If that was the case, Eastman would "bow" to himself and other members of the People's Council.[116]

Not only did Eastman magnify pacifist (and his own) influence with the President, he abandoned his previous stand on a peace without victory. For Wilson's letter to the Pope implied that the United States intended to wage a vindicative campaign against Germany. The President declared:

> The object of this war is to deliver the free peoples of the world from the menace and the actual power of a vast military establishment controlled by an irresponsible government which, having secretly planned to dominate the world, proceeded to carry the plan out without regard either to the sacred obligations of treaty or the long-established practices and long-cherished principles of international action and honor; which chose its own time for the war; delivered its blow fiercely and suddenly; stopped at no barrier either of law or of mercy; swept a whole continent within the tide of blood—not the blood of soldiers only, but the blood of innocent women and children also and of the helpless poor; and now stands balked but not defeated, the enemy of four-fifths of the world.[117]

These observations portrayed Germany as an insatiable monster that needed to be exterminated. Eastman, however, dismissed Wilson's rabid characterization as "the necessary self-righteousness of the mood of combat."[118]

That Wilson demanded a democratic government in Germany before peace negotiations could begin did not disturb Eastman. On the contrary, he implied that the President followed his recommendations. Wilson declared, "as we demanded, that he will enter into peace negotiations as soon as he can treat with a government responsible to the people."[119] Eastman had previously argued that Germany should not be conquered and a democratic regime forced on her people—that was imperialism. The Allies only needed to oppose the military long enough until the army collapsed; democratic elements within Germany would then assume power—this would constitute internal revolution. The distinction between forcible imposition and natural revolution was not easy to define or implement. Wilson's refusal to negotiate with the existing government was certainly forcing the issue. But Eastman no longer viewed this demand as a violation of the "peace without victory" pledge; on the contrary, he took credit for the impending "democratic" peace. He then wrote a letter to the President thanking him for giving "concrete meaning to the statement that this is a war for democracy."[120]

In the same letter Eastman complained that American soldiers had attempted to "lynch" him in Fargo, North Dakota, when he delivered a speech calling for an immediate cessation of hostilities. Furthermore, he objected to the Post Office's harassment of The Masses, warning the President that the "support which your administration will receive from radical minded people the country over" depended on a correction of these abuses.[121] President Wilson responded with a short note of gratitude for Eastman's praise of his foreign policy, but said nothing about the charges of mistreatment. It was a prophetic answer, for The Masses had gone to press for the last time. In November, the Postmaster-General suspended The Masses' mailing privileges, thereby insuring its economic collapse.

In his memoirs Eastman maintained that the closing of The Masses, office was a "joyful" occasion because he had grown weary of editorial duties and radical causes. In August he had reluctantly agreed to undertake a speaking tour against the war under the auspices of the People's Council. He had to go, he confessed, because it was a "challenge to back up all the bold revolutionary things I had been saying in The Masses for the last five years."[122] In radical circles he was known as a poet and a firebrand. Joseph Freeman, a student at Columbia University, remembered hearing Eastman at a pacifist convention in Chicago:

> At last we saw Shelley plain. Out of the long array of speakers there emerged on the platform Max Eastman himself, tall and slim, with a pink handsome face and prematurely white hair. His voice was full of petition and persuasion. His well-ordered academic rhetoric carried to the farthest ends of the crowded hall. He seemed to embody in sensuous outline the New Spirit of the intelligentsia in rebellion against convention. He looked Beauty and spoke Justice.[123]

In spite of his success as a speaker, Eastman was temperamentally unsuited for activist roles, especially when it involved a confrontation with governmental authorities and unfriendly audiences. Once underway on the speaking tour, his old neurasthenic ailments reappeared. Despite attacks of anxiety and insomnia, he pressed on, determined to prove his toughness, even though he told Florence, he was really only a baby who yearned for her breast.[124] When unruly soldiers interrupted his speech in Fargo, he ended this unpleasant assignment and hurried home to Florence.

But isolation, intensifying his involvement with Florence, provided little stability in his life. She was too interested in her career to supply the attention that Max wanted. By contrast, he was "almost too devoted, too absorbed" in her. Although they quarreled frequently, they did not separate. We were, he reflected,

> both a little insane—at war with ourselves as well as with each other. My ambivalent behavior had divided Florence into two conflicting selves, the one proud and vengeful, the other tender and all-comprehending. We were fully conscious of this. We had a name—the Black Panther—for her vengeful self. And I . . . was similarly divided by my adoring love for her and my resistance to the self-surrender that love impels me to.[125]

Max was both attracted to and repelled by her self-centered independence; he enjoyed and resented his emotional dependence on her. He was pleased that other men were attracted to her and yet became "diabolically jealous" of potential rivals.

If the relationship with Florence did not produce tranquility, it did inspire poetry. In 1918, he published *Colors of Life,* which was mainly a collection of poems about her. In the preface he argued that while the struggle for liberty had often occupied his thoughts, he "never identified [himself] with it or found [his] undivided being there." Instead he discovered life in "individual experience" during "moments of energetic

idleness." Because life was "older than liberty" and "greater than revolution," he preferred to enjoy experience rather than dedicate himself to "a
general principle." "Earnest friends" expected him to "exemplify" a
single-minded, "monotonous consecration" to politics, but he preferred,
like Walt Whitman and the ancient Athenians, to "loaf" in nature.[126]

It was, however, impossible to escape from politics in 1918 because
The Masses editors were indicted under the Espionage Act for conspiring
to obstruct the draft. At the trial, which began on April 15, and lasted
nine days, the defendants (Eastman, Floyd Dell, and Art Young) soft-
pedaled their radicalism; to demonstrate their patriotism, they stood at
attention when a band marched by the courtroom playing "The Star-
Spangled Banner." Although Eastman admitted to the jury that he had
once counselled others not to stand for the national anthem, he argued
that his sentiments had "changed a good deal" after American boys arrived in Europe.[127]

Eastman told the court that democratic voting determined the selection of entries in *The Masses;* therefore, he accepted responsibility only
for the articles he had written. His editorials had urged the government
to accept the peace terms proposed by the Russians. Since the President
had agreed to a peace without victory in his note to the Pope, there was
nothing treasonable about his position. The trial involved "an attempt to
punish . . . that intelligent minority whose vigorous agitation was instrumental in securing the adoption of such policies." Eastman told the
jury that the war was being fought for "liberty and freedom," and he
thought it deplorable that Department of Justice officials wasted their
time "persecuting upright American citizens when they might be hunting" spies, profiteers, and "friends of Prussianism in this country and
prosecuting them."[128] Thanks to Eastman's patriotic performance, which
earned the disapproval of radicals, the trial ended in a hung jury.

At the second trial, held in October, Eastman again chose discretion
over heroics. In an eloquent three-hour summation he denied that the
defendants (including John Reed this time) had conspired to undermine
conscription. The editors, he explained, had been animated by a "mood
of extreme and proud and rather obstreperous individual expression,"
and their criticisms of "art and politics and society" had predated an
American declaration of war. Their satirical comments had simply continued "longer than was in good taste." Eastman had been "rather
shocked" at the "flip" manner in which Reed had placed the caption
"Knit a Strait-Jacket for Your Soldier Boy" over a report on mental
disease in the army. But then, being "older than Jack Reed," he "sobered
a good deal more quickly than some of the editors of the *Masses* to a
realization . . . that the United States had really got [sic] into a world war,

and could not get out except by carrying it forward" to a conclusion. While Eastman had asked for an endorsement of the Russian peace terms, he had not favored "withdrawing from the war." Socialists, he explained to the jury, were not unpatriotic; they believed in "liberty and democracy exactly in the same way" as Thomas Jefferson, Patrick Henry, Samuel Adams, and the "rest of the true revolutionary fathers." Finally, as the son of two Christian ministers, he assured them that "the teaching of Jesus" was closer to "the message of the Socialists than to the message of any other political body of men."[129] Needless to say, the jury could not find the defendants guilty.

Eastman considered abandoning politics, but returned to radical journalism after receiving exclusive rights to John Reed's eyewitness accounts of the Bolshevik revolution. With Crystal's assistance Eastman launched the Liberator as a successor to The Masses. To avoid democratic procedures and internal squabbles, Max and Crystal owned the new journal outright. Although many of the Masses, contributors joined the staff, the Liberator was less exuberant and more political than its predecessor.

In the first issue, which appeared in March, 1918, Eastman announced his support of the Bolshevik government in Russia. He proclaimed that the world was "entering upon the experiment of industrial and real democracy." With Reed leading the way, Eastman became a defender of Bolshevism. He accepted Lenin's decision to close the democratically-elected Constituent Assembly because it was, in Lenin's words, a "relic of bourgeois society." Eastman dismissed the majority vote against the Bolsheviks by arguing that "only after a general transfer of land and factories to the workers" could "an appeal to the people really be an appeal to the people." He pledged the Liberator to socialist goals in America and called for the nationalization of land, industry, public utilities, railroads, mines, and the telephone system.[130] Enchanted by revolutionary victories in Russia, Eastman uncritically transported the Bolshevik program to America.

Eastman offered little information on the Bolsheviks except that they were "intellectuals"—"thinking men set free from the old reliable motives of tradition and good business." Armed with Marx's "scientific" intelligence and the Communist Manifesto, the Bolsheviks had achieved such a "sublimely ordered and intellectual performance as to dispel all pessimism of propaganda forever, and raise intelligence and the dissemination of ideas to the highest place in their confidence." If the revolution, the "most momentous event in the history of peoples," represented the "orderly maturing and accurate enactment of ideas full-born in a great mind sixty years ago, and cherished and disseminated . . .

by all those who had strength to believe," then there was hope that intelligence could direct "every event." Although Eastman had once vilified Marx as a dogmatic obscurant, he now hailed him as the founder of scientific politics. Excited by the prospect of intellectuals in power, Eastman envisioned that the *Liberator* might play a significant role in a world "whose possibilities of freedom and life for all" had become "immeasurable." Never in all history, Eastman told his readers, "could one so joyfully and confidentally enter upon the enterprise of publishing and propagating ideas."[131] But the Bolsheviks had not yet consolidated their position, let alone begun the awesome task of reconstructing Russian society. Eastman was converted by faith, not by facts.

Eastman's enthusiasm for socialist Russia did not weaken his loyalty to Wilson. Since ideology counted so little in his politics, he assumed that the President and the Bolshevik leaders would work together to create a new international order. For him, the Bolshevik "Decree on Peace" (November 8, 1917), calling for an immediate, negotiated peace and freedom for all peoples, coincided with President Wilson's plan for a settlement based on national self-determination and "a general association of nations."[132] But Eastman's view was not, journalist Williams Hard reported in March, shared by *Pravda,* the Bolshevik party newspaper, which described the President as a representative of the "American Imperial dictatorship." Hard also pointed out that Wilson had repeatedly violated his so-called principles of "internationalism" and "national self-determination" by intervening in Latin American countries.[133] Eastman responded to Hard's accusations by arguing that "principles are, and . . . ought to be, things of times and places." Wilson's actions demonstrated "the amazing pliancy and free play" with which he held "abstract ideas in his mind."[134] Awe-struck by the "head of the most colossal industrial enterprise" in history, Eastman overlooked the imperialistic and conservative orientation of American foreign policy.

Eastman assured his readers that President Wilson endorsed the Bolshevik regime. Blaming the Allied governments for the administration's muted response to the Bolshevik plea for a general peace conference, he cited Wilson's "generous message of friendship and good luck" to the All-Russian Congress of Soviets (March, 1918) as "a different attitude from any other government toward industrial democracy." But the President's cable rebuffed a Russian request for "moral and material" assistance and the administration refused to recognize the legitimacy of the new government. Moreover, Eastman disregarded the subsequent response of the Soviet Congress, which slighted the President by addressing its remarks to "the exploited classes" of America and not to the administration. The Soviet Congress predicted revolutions in "all bourgeois countries" and the establishment of a "socialist order of society," which would secure peace and "the cultural and material well being of all the toilers."[135] Believing the President to be different from other Western leaders, Eastman promised his readers that Wilson would follow "the lead of insurgent labor" and not the lead of "bankrupt bourgeois diplomacy."[136]

In March, 1918, the German High Command forced the Bolsheviks to sign the Treaty of Brest-Litovsk, which deprived Russia of a large slice of eastern Europe. The harsh terms indicated that the German government had no intention of abiding by Wilson's "Fourteen Points" program. Since Social Democrats and ordinary Germans did not remonstrate against this unfair settlement, it seemed that the German people could only be freed by defeating autocracy. Consequently, many anti-interventionists changed their position on the war; they advocated an Allied victory in order to overturn the Treaty of Brest-Litovsk and save the Bolshevik government.[137] In the July issue of the *Liberator,* Eastman recommended a repeal of the Socialist party's "St. Louis Resolution," which committed American socialists to pacifism. He argued that the President's peace terms, "the growing menace of a Prussian victory," the German invasion of socialist Russia, and "the refraining of the Allies from such an invasion," made a policy reversal "imperative."[138]

William Bross Lloyd, the son of reformer Henry Demarest Lloyd and Socialist party candidate for Senator from Illinois, however, responded to Eastman's editorial by calling attention to the discrepancies between Wilson's platitudes and the intentions of the warring powers. Lloyd denounced Eastman's willingness to abandon socialist principles for "realism," and suggested that there was a "margin between Wilson's statements of war-aims and the actual terms of peace." It was "inscrutable" to Lloyd how Eastman could assume that the President would conclude a just peace when no western government had renounced the "secret treaties" promising spoils to the victors. Lloyd correctly foresaw "that short of revolution" none of the governments would "disrupt its *modus operandi.*"[139]

Eastman refused, however, to believe that Wilson would follow the dictates of reactionary Britain and France. Then, on August 3, 1918, the President announced that the administration would contribute American troops to an Allied invasion of Siberia. Eastman could not shrug off this evidence of an anti-Bolshevik policy. In sending American soldiers, Eastman declared in the *Liberator,* the administration had yielded "in practice if not necessarily in theory to the pressure of reactionary forces among the Allies." Discounting administration arguments that the Allies were merely seeking to defeat German troops, Eastman viewed intervention as "a counter-revolutionary attempt against the life of the Soviet Republic." In showing that he was not "brave or hard-headed enough . . . to *oppose the economic interest of those who possess the world,"* Wilson had failed altogether as a moral leader.[140] Consequently, Eastman turned against him with a vengeance. He regarded Wilson as an agent of international capitalism and the proposed League of Nations as "a system of international imperialism." Once thought to be the only organization capable of preventing future wars, the League loomed as the greatest single obstacle to "industrial democracy."[141]

The triumph of a "scientific" elite in Russia enabled Eastman to transfer his allegiance from Woodrow Wilson to Nikolai Lenin, "a statesman of the new order." Eastman proclaimed that Plato's philosopher-king had emerged as head of the Bolsheviks. A "technical authority" in economics, politics, and social psychology, Lenin had the expertise and toughness to create a new society. In contrast to "professors and idealists," Lenin knew *"how to think in a concrete situation."* A "forceful and fearless" general who crushed the Provisional Government with one call on the telephone, Lenin could command "practical men and *see to it that his orders are obeyed."* Moreover, Lenin was not afraid to impose social discipline on the masses, punishing those who stole or loafed. This concern for morality, Eastman observed, contrasted favorably with the concept of revolution enjoyed in "Bohemian parlors."[142] Anxious to be counted as a partisan of Bolshevism, Eastman dissociated himself from Village bohemianism. His zeal for revolutionary socialism, he told socialist Norman Thomas, distinguished him from "the puny, artificial, sex-conscious simmering in perpetual puberty of the grey-haired Bacchantes of Greenwich Village."[143]

To Eastman the Bolshevik revolution represented the accession of an intelligentsia "scientifically" trained to understand and control the forces of history. There would be, Eastman predicted, "something almost supernatural in the hold upon historic forces that Marxian science and the philosophy of change" would give to Lenin, the "scientific socialist." Lenin's strength lay in his pragmatic approach to politics and social problems. Unencumbered by doctrinaire Marxism, Lenin would borrow scientific techniques from any source, even capitalist countries; he planned to import the "Taylor System" of scientific management from America to improve economic production. In contrast to utopian levellers, Lenin realized that industrialization required a managerial hierarchy. Eastman declared in the *Liberator:*

It will be a hard lesson for revolutionists to learn that the productive labor or a free society must be strictly organized, and that strict organization requires subordination of individuals to authority *during work;* but it will have to be learned.[144]

Eastman's interest in efficiency, hard work, and morality for the masses indicated a willingness to subordinate freedom to industrial productivity. Unlike Reed, who mistakenly viewed the Bolsheviks as populist leaders, Eastman perceived that they were a ruthless group bent on industrializing Russia. It was precisely their ability to translate thoughts "into action with an iron will" that capitivated Eastman.[145] The *Liberator,* therefore, became a voice for authoritarian discipline, and by implication the enemy of bohemian freedom.

Eastman thought that Bolshevism could toughen "soft-headed" idealists who had "no taste for the hard mood of practical action." "Children of Light," individuals of "tender hearts and minds," were constantly outstripped by the "children of darkness"—the "James J. Hills, the E. H. Harrimans, the J. P. Morgans who determined the conformation of the earth." Bolshevism could redress the imbalance, for Lenin was "a J.P. Morgan Jesus . . . engineering our redemption from Moscow."[146] Eastman imagined that Lenin, a "revolutionary engineer" armed with the "science" of social control, would vanquish the captains of industry. In elevating Lenin to the stature of a secularized Jesus Christ, Eastman created a new authority figure as he lapsed into his mother's language of religion and moral redemption.

In Eastman's view, Wilson's "sentimental moralism" seemed pathetic by comparison with Lenin's realistic grasp of politics. Wilson had assumed that "he could turn a nationalist war into a war for peace and democracy by means of diplomatic evangelism," but the peace conference at Versailles proved that liberalism could not shape history.[147] By contrast, Lenin was a "socialist philosopher" who stripped away ideological disguises and "repressed motives" to uncover reality. He knew that the "facts and forces of mass-history are economic rather than moral or political." Just as the psychiatrist tried to find "egotistic and sex motives" beneath the "overelaborated ideas" of consciousness, so too did the socialist unearth "egotistic and economic motives under the grand language of politics and history."[148]

To dramatize Lenin's superiority, Eastman described a hypothetical session in which Lenin (acting for Eastman) psychoanalyzed Wilson, thereby reducing the President to a neurotic patient. Lenin, "the kind but deadly-candid" physician, remarked: "I notice, Mr. Wilson, a very frequent recurrence of the word *democracy* in everything you say." Lenin advised him to substitute "the dictatorship of the bourgeoisie" for "democracy" because it more accurately described the conditions in

America.[149] Lenin also recommended that the President discard the phrase "Open Diplomacy" because it caused Wilson to repress his "motives into the unconscious." Wilson would, Lenin prognosticated, experience a feeling of relief if he would tell the public: "I am absolutely incapable of public candor." Furthermore, the world would emit a "sign of relaxation and joy" if the Allied leaders at Versailles would admit that their discussions had nothing to do with "Justice or Democracy or the Rights of Small Nations."[150]

Administering a dose of socialist realism to Wilson served only to ridicule the President. Disgruntled and embarrassed at having squandered his idealism on an ineffective leader, Eastman scorned Wilson as a preacher, not a social engineer. Like his father, Wilson had proved to be a religious idealist hopelessly out of touch with reality. The virulence of his attack suggests the emotional character of his political loyalties. Instead of analyzing the political, economic, institutional, and psychological forces that influenced political decisions, Eastman continued to focus on dramatic statesmen. Unable to separate personal needs from public policies, Eastman searched for an heroic figure who could inspire him and reform the world. He embraced Lenin who had "fatherly or teacherly [sic] human understanding" and "a stern and lofty-certain mind." Lenin satisfied his desire for an authoritarian patriarch who "affectionately" appreciated "disorderly assemblies of masses" and yet realized "the absolute necessity of submission to authority during work."[151] Since Eastman had never seen or talked to Lenin, he conjured up an image from newspaper reports and revolutionary writings. Eastman assumed that he had advanced from liberal evangelism to scientific socialism. But he remained a moral crusader who wished to purify man's nature.

In his eagerness to think himself a tough-minded realist, Eastman defended the Communist regime against justifiable criticism. When cartoonist Robert Minor reported his dismay at the repressive policies of the Bolshevik government, Eastman dismissed him as a weak-kneed representative of anarchism—the philosophy of artists, which was "literary, not scientific."[152] Similarly, when Bertrand Russell condemned the methods and intentions of the Bolsheviks, Eastman called him a tender-hearted professor and a victim of Menshevik propaganda. Eastman applauded what Russell found distasteful, namely that the Bolsheviks had "created an aristocracy of brains and character" and they were "ruthlessly efficient."[153] Their apparent success in organizing an industrial society confirmed Eastman's grandest dreams about the new order. The Bolsheviks were creating a modern Republic, a stratified society commanded by an intellectual elite.

Eastman had no interest in becoming a revolutionary. He preferred to advise those who wanted to emulate the Russians in America. Unwilling to work with the poor and resistant to Communist party discipline, Eastman remained a sympathizer on the fringes of the movement. His refusal to become involved in the conspiratorial activities of an out-lawed Communist party gave him a more objective view of the political situation. In the summer of 1919, Eastman declared that the improbability of a revolt in America made revolutionary activities silly and futile. He argued that the "stage of development" was dependent on "the economic situation and not upon the degree of anybody's conviction or state of excitement."[154] Radicals would have to wait until the "system of capitalistic production" crumbled before they could hope to organize the mindless masses. Eastman's analysis of the proletariat had come full circle as he again edged away from revolutionary politics.

After covering the important Socialist party convention in Chicago, Max left for Hollywood to rejoin Florence who had just signed a movie contract with producer Samuel Goldwyn. The weeks of separation and the daily exchange of love letters enabled them momentarily to enjoy each other's company. But reality again intruded, and they were soon "snarling and caressing by turns."[155] Not even the charming company of Charlie Chaplin ("the most famous man in the world") and nightly games of charades in his house could offset their bickering, and Max returned to New York.[156]

Florence's movie fortunes experienced a short-lived upsurge when she became Chaplin's mistress. But this affair ended when she went to New York for medical treatment and had a miscarriage. Although she convalesced in Max's arms, "ugly quarrels" began again. After several months of "intermittent rage and rapture," Florence returned by train to Hollywood and renewed her quest for stardom. But her talents were not equal to Chaplin's support, and her career languished. In March, 1921, Max rejoined her and the tiresome pattern was repeated. He then went back to New York; she followed some months later intending to make a comeback on the stage. In February, 1922, the cycle was finally broken when Florence, depressed by her unsuccessful career, committed suicide in a Village apartment.[157]

The distressing loss of his "passionate wild gypsy" triggered the decision to undertake a "pilgrimage to Moscow." He resigned the editorship of the *Liberator,* and left in March to report on the European economic conference in Genoa, Italy, the first attempt by Western powers to admit Soviet Russia to a concert of European nations. At the meeting Eastman tried to ingratiate himself with the Russian delegates by translating a lengthy French document. When it became apparent that his knowledge of French was inadequate, he was dismissed by the Soviet press representative. Retreating in humiliation, Eastman spent the rest of his time in Genoa cavorting with Ernest Hemingway and courting Eliena Krylenko, a Soviet delegation secretary and the sister of the Commissar of Justice.[158]

When the conference ended Eastman went to Paris with the intention of captivating Edna St. Vincent Millay. ("And so much the better if she was famous—for I like to admire those whom I love.")[159] Despite his failure to have sex with Edna, Eastman delayed his departure for four months and frolicked with other expatriates. He attended the Quat'z Arts Ball, an annual event for art students, and, masquerading as an American Indian, marched through the streets of Paris in a jockstrap.

After Paris, he stopped for a week in Germany where he, journalist Albert Rhys Williams, and writer Josephine Herbst lived like "millionaires" thanks to a favorable exchange rate for American dollars. The dilatory manner in which Eastman proceeded to Russia revealed an absence of revolutionary ardor. It was, he claimed later, the "poet rather than the politico in me that set out on that journey." In the Soviet Union he studied Russian and enjoyed the freedom of nude bathing at Yalta, which symbolized to him the "candid realism" of the revolution. He also sampled the fruits of the proletarian revolution with the vacationing wife of a Kharkov engineer.[160]

Lenin's deteriorating physical condition denied Eastman "the prize of personal contact with the man in whose head and heart [he] trusted."[161] Nevertheless, Eastman was impressed with all of the Bolshevik leaders, and reported to the *Liberator* that Russia, in contrast to America, was ruled by "an aristocracy" of the "best engineering brains" who used Marxian ideas as "working hypotheses."[162] The Bolsheviks had not eliminated inequality or "emulation." They had swept away entrenched wealth and privilege, allowing artists and scientists to gain influential positions in society. Revolution, Eastman explained,

> does not produce a race of people educated in science and the poetic love of life; it enables the real idealists to go into schools and educate the race that way. Revolution does not produce liberty; it . . . enables those who love liberty to strive with sincerity and sound reason to produce the conditions which will make it possible. There is no short-cut to the goal of human culture.[163]

Arriving in Russia when civil authorities encouraged atheism, free love, legalized abortion, the liberation of women, education, and artistic expression, Eastman might have been persuaded that the Bolsheviks were constructing a utopian community, but only if he condoned a dictatorial government, a secret police, and the elimination of all political opposition.

Since Lenin was unavailable, Eastman cultivated a friendship with Leon Trotsky by proposing to write his biography. When Trotsky acceded to this request and granted numerous interviews, he replaced Lenin as Eastman's hero. Eastman told *Liberator* readers: "Trotsky's voice is so powerful that you rest when he talks. And his thought is so powerful that you rest when he is thinking. He is a born and inevitable leader of men."[164]

But the identification with Trotsky, "the most universally gifted man in the world," proved disappointing.[165] Trotsky did not make public Lenin's last "testament," which designated Trotsky as the new leader, and he refused to challenge Stalin at the Thirteenth Party Congress.[166] Although Trotsky surpassed other Bolsheviks "both in intellect and in self-dependent force," he lacked, Eastman concluded, the tactfulness to build a personal following. If Trotsky "had been a great politician and not just a great man," he could have continued Lenin's brilliant work.[167]

Before Eastman left Russia in June, 1924, he married Eliena Krylenko so that she could accompany him. Incurably cheerful and self-reliant, Eliena became a maternal figure who catered to his physical and emotional needs. "I never saw anyone," Eastman commented, "who could do so much, so swiftly, so *gladly*, and without nervous tension or the remotest thought of getting tired. My mother could *do* as much, but she compensated for it with sick-headaches and moods of melancholy."[168] Eliena was content to devote herself to Eastman. He was free to have any number of transitory affairs and afterwards return to her. At last he had an ideal arrangement, enjoying freedom and security without reponsibility or commitment.

Remaining in Europe, mostly on the French Riviera with other Americans, Eastman published excerpts from Lenin's "testament" and explained how the triumvirate of Stalin, Zinoviev, and Kamenev deprived Trotsky of his rightful place at the head of the state. He feared that the mediocre men who had gained power might transform communism into a religion and establish a "dictatorship of the officialdom" within the party.[169] To make Marxism more scientific, he advised socialists to jettison the metaphysical aspects of communism and retain only those elements that provided a practical guide to revolution. Eastman criticized Marx for proposing a course of history that ended with the inevitable triumph of communism. In so doing, Marx had imputed his own desires to history. Eastman believed that the Russian revolution had occurred because Lenin, who was a "scientific engineer" and not a "metaphysician" like Marx, and his cadre had guided the masses to victory. Lenin had used his "gigantic will," not a revolutionary ideology, for the "strength of his purpose." Eastman maintained that "scientific socialism" would incorporate Freudian psychology in place of Hegelian metaphysics, and it would "put a new emphasis upon the separate identity and unusual motivation of the revolutionary scientists." A "free and real human society" needed "intelligent control" of the population. Unfortunately, Lenin had failed to leave "in his place a body of men" who were engineers and not "priests."[170]

In the spring of 1927, Eastman returned to America where he was *persona non grata* with the Communist party for criticizing Stalin. He shared this outlaw status with Trotsky, who was excommunicated from the party in 1927, exiled to Alma-Alta in Soviet Central Asia, and then banished from Russia. Resuming communication with Trotsky, Eastman became his American translator and unofficial literary agent. When Trotsky relieved him of these duties, Eastman's interest in communism cooled. In July, 1932, he visited Trotsky, on Prinkipio Island in the Sea of Marmora, in an attempt to renew their business arrangement and establish a more personal relationship. But Trotsky, who was "deaf and dumb in an intimate relation," rebuffed his overtures. Eastman discovered that Trotsky had no appreciation of his intellectual abilities, showing a "total inward indifference to my opinions, my interests, my existence as an individual." Furthermore, Eastman complained in his diary, he "never asked me a question."[171]

Upon his return to America Eastman became an outspoken critic of Stalin and Russian communism. His condemnation of Stalin's dictatorship, an admirable voice of dissent among American intellectuals who defended communism and the Soviet Union, was valuable for its candor rather than its understanding.[172] His political perspicacity was quickly blunted by the narrow framework of ultraconservatism. Viewing Stalin and Hitler as demonic leaders who had learned totalitarianism from Lenin, he warned that the Communist party was plotting the establishment of a dictatorship in America.[173] After the war he became a fanatical anticommunist, applauded Senator Joseph McCarthy's witch hunt against liberals, defended the moral superiority of private property and competition, and became a "roving editor" of the conservative *Reader's Digest.*

Through the vicissitudes of his political career Eastman's elitism remained intact. Reducing politics and sociology to denunciations of human nature, Eastman longed for a social order that could insure efficient production and moral discipline. Men inherited "animal propensities" that were never successfully "repressed" and inevitably reappeared in their original form. The emergence of totalitarian societies in Nazi Germany and Stalinist Russia showed the baneful effects of innate "submissiveness" and the passion for "regimentation and discipleship [sic]."[174] To prevent the pernicious concentration of state-power and the evils of mass manipulation, Eastman recommended a return to laissez-faire capitalism as the best means of preserving freedom and survival of the fittest.

Travelling the political spectrum from left to right has not been that uncommon in modern times. In Eastman's case, personal insecurities and fantasies mainly accounted for his changing political views and loyalties. Ignoring social analyses and political ideology, Eastman gave his allegiance to powerful intellectual leaders who promised to reshape society. For all his adulation of science and logic, Eastman had little confidence in reason. Although counting himself among the intellectual elite, he was closer to the irrational masses than he realized. Eastman's conversion from "scientific socialism" to right-wing conservatism should have come as no surprise to those who knew him or read his columns in *The Masses*.

NOTES

1. Any attempt to study Max Eastman is hampered by the inaccessibility of personal letters and diaries; therefore, Eastman's two-volume autobiography, *Enjoyment of Living* (1948) and *Love and Revolution* (1964), constitutes, as Eastman evidently intended, the major source of personal information. While these memoirs seem exceptionally candid, containing intimate admissions and quotations from contemporary letters and diaries, the historian must wonder why Eastman chose not to make public those sources from which he supposedly drew his account. Some personal manuscript materials held by the Lilly Library, Indiana University, will be made available to researchers at a future date.
2. Max Eastman, *Enjoyment of Living* (New York, 1948), pp. 15-17, p. 23, p. 91.
3. *Ibid.,* pp. 31-43, pp. 51-67.
4. *Ibid.,* p. 16.
5. *Ibid.,* p. 51.
6. *Ibid.,* p. 23, p. 96.
7. *Ibid.,* p. 34.
8. *Ibid.,* p. 25.
9. Her diary accounts (March 14, 1888, March 25, 1888, February 1890, May 1891) are quoted in *Enjoyment of Living*, pp. 52-53.
10. *Ibid.,* p. 54, p. 85. The difficulty of learning a masculine identity was also enhanced by his mother's reforms, which dissolved the customary roles for children. The household was "run on feminist principles. The boys took their turns with the girls at making beds and washing dishes, and the girls took their turns at hoeing the garden and cleaning out the stable." *Enjoyment of Living*, p. 94.

11. *Ibid.,* p. 93.
12. *Ibid.,* p. 97, p. 102.
13. Max Eastman, *Venture* (New York, 1927), p. 3.
14. Eastman, *Enjoyment of Living,* p. 104.
15. Eastman, "Mark Twain's Elmira," in *Heroes I Have Known; Twelve Who Lived Great Lives* (New York, 1942), pp. 105-142.
16. Eastman, *Enjoyment of Living,* p. 116, p. 121.
17. *Ibid.,* p. 118.
18. *Ibid.*
19. *Ibid.,* pp. 119-120.
20. *Ibid.,* pp. 143-147.
21. *Ibid.,* p. 183.
22. *Ibid.,* pp. 134-142.
23. *Ibid.,* pp. 148-149.
24. *Ibid.,* pp. 206-207.
25. *Ibid.,* pp. 197-200, pp. 223-230.
26. Eastman, "O Mores," *Williams Literary Monthly* Vol. 18 (April 1903), pp. 341-346; "Systematic Suppression of Freshmen," *Williams Literary Monthly,* Vol. 20 (November 1904), pp. 49-55.
27. Eastman, *Enjoyment of Living,* pp. 231-232.
28. Annis Ford Eastman, *Have and Give: And Other Parables* (Elmira, N.Y., p. 37; Annis Eastman, "A Sermon For Children," *The Independent,* Vol. 98 (May 21, 1896), p. 704.
29. Eastman, *Enjoyment of Living,* p. 224.
30. *Ibid.,* pp. 233-241.
31. *Ibid.,* pp. 240-243.
32. *Ibid.,* p. 234.
33. Max Eastman, "The New Art of Healing," *Atlantic Monthly,* Vol. 101 (May 1908), pp. 646-647.
34. *Ibid.*
35. Eastman, *Enjoyment of Living,* pp. 265-266.
36. *Ibid.,* pp. 267-268.
37. *Ibid.,* pp. 282-286.
38. *Ibid.,* p. 268.
39. Max Eastman, *Enjoyment of Poetry* (New York, 1913), pp. 145-147.
40. *Ibid.,* pp. 170-171.
41. Eastman, *Enjoyment of Living,* pp. 313-316.
42. *Ibid.,* p. 309.
43. *Ibid.,* p. 319.
44. *Ibid.,* pp. 321-322.
45. *Ibid.,* pp. 323-324.
46. Letter quoted in *Ibid.,* p. 327.
47. *Ibid.,* p. 328.
48. *Ibid.,* pp. 329-338.
49. *Ibid.,* p. 343.
50. *Ibid.,* p. 356.
51. *Ibid.,* p. 355-360.
52. *Ibid.,* p. 362.
53. Undated newspaper clipping, Lilly Library, Indiana University.
54. Eastman, *Enjoyment of Living,* p. 378, p. 368.

55. *Ibid.,* p. 399.
56. Max Eastman, *Child of the Amazons: And Other Poems* (New York, 1913); *Enjoyment of Living,* pp. 434.
57. *Enjoyment of Living,* pp. 339-340.
58. Floyd Dell, "Review of Enjoyment of Living," *New York Herald Tribune Weekly Book Review,* Vol. 24 (April 11, 1948), p. 6.
59. Max Eastman, "Knowledge and Revolution," *The Masses, Vol. 4 (December 1912), p. 5.* (New York, 1970), pp. 377-390.
60. Albert Fried, *Socialism in America: From Shakers to the Third International* (New York, 1970), pp. 377-390.
61. *Ibid.,* pp. 446-456.
62. Eastman, "Dynamite Against Steel: A Tragedy and an Opportunity," *The Masses,* Vol. 4 (February 1913), p. 3; Eastman, "Knowledge and Revolution," *The Masses,* Vol. 4 (August 1913), p. 6.
63. Eastman, "Knowledge and Revolution," *The Masses,* Vol. 4 (April 1913), p. 5.
64. Eastman, "Knowledge and Revolution," *The Masses,* Vol. 4 (May 1913), p. 5; "Knowledge and Revolution," *The Masses,* Vol. 5 (December 1913), pp. 5-6.
65. Eastman, "Of Mexico," *The Masses,* Vol. 5 (December 1913), p. 7; "Knowledge and Revolution," *The Masses,* Vol. 5 (June 1914), p. 17.
66. Eastman, "War for War's Sake," *The Masses,* Vol. 5 (September 1914), p. 5; "Knowledge and Revolution," *The Masses* (October 1914), p. 5.
67. Eastman, "Knowledge and Revolution," *The Masses,* Vol. 6 (December 1914), pp. 14-15.
68. Eastman, *Enjoyment of Living,* p. 492.
69. *Ibid.,* pp. 484-489.
70. "Notebook" (July 27, 1914), quoted in *Ibid.,* p. 498.
71. "Notebook" (August 3, 1914), quoted in *Ibid.,* p. 505.
72. "Notebook" (July 30, 1914) in *Ibid.,* p. 502.
73. "Notebook" (July 30, 1914) in *Ibid.,* p. 500.
74. "Notebook" (August 2, 1914) in *Ibid.,* p. 505.
75. *Ibid.,* pp. 510-510.
76. *Ibid.,* pp. 512-518.
77. Max Eastman, "Exploring the Soul and Healing the Body," in *Everybody's Magazine,* Vol. 32 (June 1915), pp. 741-750; "Mr. Er-Er-oh! What's His Name?" *Everybody's Magazine,* Vol. 33 (July 1915), pp. 95-103.
78. *Ibid.*
79. Eastman, "Exploring the Soul," p. 749.
80. Eastman, "Mr. Er-Er," p. 102.
81. Christopher Lasch, *The New Radicalism in America; 1889-1963* (New York, 1965) See Chapter 5, "Politics as Social Control," pp. 141-180.
82. Eastman, "The First Few Books," *The Masses,* Vol. 6 (April 1915), p. 22. Eastman recommended that they read: Edward Thorndike, *The Original Nature of Man;* J.A.S. Watson, *Heredity;* Vernon Kellogg, *Darwinism Today;* Ernest Jones, *Psycho-Analysis;* Bernard Hart, *The Psychology of Insanity;* and Frank Boas, *The Mind of Primitive Man.*
83. Arthur Bullard, "The State of War," *The Masses,* Vol. 6 (August 1915), p. 8.
84. Eastman, *Enjoyment of Living,* pp. 535-536.
85. Eastman, "The Uninteresting War," *The Masses,* Vol. 6 (September 1915), pp. 6-7.
86. Eastman, "The Only Way To End the War," *The Masses,* Vol. 7 (December 1915), p. 9; "War Psychology and International Socialism," *The Masses,* Vol. 8 (August 1916), pp. 27-28.
87. Eastman, "The First Few Books," p. 22.

88. Eastman, "War Psychology and International Socialism," p. 28.

89. Eastman, "Way to End War," p. 10.

90. Eastman, *Enjoyment of Living,* p. 531.

91. Eastman, "The Masses at the White House," *The Masses,* Vol. 8 (July 1916), p. 16.

92. *Ibid.* Arthur Link, *Wilson: Campaigns for Progressivism and Peace, 1916-1917* (Princeton, N.J., 1965), p. 125.

93. Max Eastman, *Love and Revolution: My Journey Through An Epoch* (New York, 1964), p. 32.

94. Eastman, "Towards Liberty: The Method of Progress,"*The Masses,* Vol. 8 (September 1916), pp. 28-29. In the summer of 1916, *The Masses* absorbed a declining socialist journal, *The New Review,* and added it as a supplement called "The Masses Review." Eastman admitted later that his intentions were elitist—"the low-brows could read *The Masses* while the supplement was for "the high brows"; the "superelite, the true man of the future, would enjoy them both." Eastman, *Enjoyment of Living,* p. 544. Actually Eastman used the "Review" (which lasted a few months) to publish his "scientific" revision of Marx.

95. Eastman, "Understanding Germany," *Forum,* Vol. 55 (January 1916), pp. 43-47.

96. Eastman, "Towards Liberty," *The Masses,* Vol. 8 (October 1916), pp. 23-25.

97. Eastman, *Enjoyment of Living,* pp. 568-569.

98. *Ibid.,* pp. 570-587.

99. Eastman, *Love and Revolution,* p. 100.

100. Eastman, "Revolutionary Progress," *The Masses,* Vol. 9 (April 1917), p. 5.

101. Eastman, "In Case of War," *The Masses,* Vol. 9 (April 1917), pp. 7-8.

102. Eastman, "Advertising Democracy," *The Masses,* Vol. 9 (June 1917), p. 5.

103. Eastman, "A Separation," *The Masses,* Vol. 9 (May 1917), p. 15.

104. Eastman, "The Religion of Patriotism," *The Masses,* Vol. 9 (July 1917), pp. 9-10.

105. Eastman, "Conscription for What," *The Masses,* Vol. 9 (July 1917), p. 18.

106. Reed, "The Russian Peace," *The Masses,* Vol. 9 (July 1917), p. 35; Eastman, *Enjoyment of Living,* p. 564-565.

107. Eastman, "Revolutionary Progress," *The Masses,* Vol. 9 (August 1917), p. 5.

108. *Ibid.,* pp. 5-8.

109. Eastman, "A Working-Class Peace," *The Masses,* Vol. 9 (August 1917), p. 8.

110. Eastman, "Revolutionary Progress," *The Masses,* Vol. 9 (September 1917), p. 13.

111. H.C.Peterson and Gilbert C. Fite, *Opponents of War: 1917-1918* (Seattle, 1957), p.16.

112. Eastman, "The Post Office Censorship," *The Masses,* Vol. 9 (September 1917), p. 24.

113. Eastman, "President Wilson's Letter to the Pope," *The Masses,* Vol. 9 (October 1917), p. 5.

114. "Editorial Notes," *New Republic,* Vol. 12 (September 1, 1917), p. 115.

115. Eastman, "President Wilson's Letter to the Pope," p. 5.

116. *Ibid.*

117. Ray S. Baker, ed., *The Public Papers of Woodrow Wilson,* Vol. 5 (New York, 1925-1927), p. 94.

118. Eastman, "President Wilson's Letter to the Pope," p. 5.

119. *Ibid.*

120. Eastman, "To President Wilson," *The Masses,* Vol. 10 (November-December 1917) p. 21.

121. *Ibid.,* p. 24.

122. Eastman, *Love and Revolution,* p. 64, p. 49.

123. Joseph Freeman, *An American Testament: A Narrative of Rebels and Romantics* (New York, 1936), p. 103.

124. Eastman, *Love and Revolution,* pp. 50-51; Letter, Max Eastman to Florence Deshon (August 29, 1917), Eastman Papers, Lilly Library, Indiana University.
125. Eastman, *Love and Revolution,* p. 276, p. 222. See also a fictional portrayal of Florence and Max in Theodore Dreiser, *A Gallery of Women,* Vol. 2 (New York, 1929), pp. 529-564.
126. Eastman, *Colors of Life* (New York, 1918), pp. 13-14.
127. Floyd Dell, "The Story of the Trial," *Liberator,* Vol. 1 (June 1918), pp. 7-10; Eastman, *Love and Revolution,* pp. 85-91, John Nicholas Beffel, ed., *Art Young: His Life and Times* (New York, 1939), pp. 332-339.
128. *New York Times* (April 23, 1918), p. 9.
129. *Max Eastman's Address to the Jury in the Second Masses Trial* (New York, 1918), pp. 1-45.
130. Eastman, "Editorials," *Liberator,* Vol. 1 (March 1918), pp. 3-6.
131. *Ibid.*
132. *Ibid.*
133. William Hard, "Is America Honest?" *Metropolitan* (March 1918), pp. 15-16, pp. 66-69.
134. Eastman, "Wilson and the World's Future," *Liberator,* Vol. 1 (May 1918), p. 21.
135. George F. Kennan, *Russia Leaves the War* (Princeton, N.J., 1956), pp. 491, pp. 512-513.
136. Eastman, "Wilson and the World's Future," p. 21.
137. Christopher Lasch, *The American Liberals and the Russian Revolution* (New York, 1962), pp. 97-100.
138. Eastman, "Editorials," *Liberator,* Vol. 1 (July 1918), p. 5.
139. William Bross Lloyd, "Silence and the Resurrection," *Liberator,* vol. 1 (August 1918), pp. 30-32.
140. Eastman, "Editorials," *Liberator,* Vol. 1 (October 1918), p. 24.
141. Eastman, "Editorials," *Liberator,* Vol. 2 (December 1918), p. 5.
142. Eastman, "A Statesman of the New Order," *Liberator,* Vol. 1 (September 1918), pp. 10-11.
143. Quoted by Eastman, *Enjoyment of Living,* p. 548.
144. Eastman, "Lenin — A Statesman of the New Order," *Liberator,* Vol. 1 (October 1918), p. 30.
145. *Ibid.,* p. 11.
146. Eastman, "Editorials," *Liberator,* Vol. 2 (August 1920), pp. 5-6.
147. Eastman, "Editorials," *Liberator,* Vol. 2 (May 1919), p. 6.
148. Eastman, "Lenin and Wilson," *Liberator,* Vol. 2 (March 1919), p. 8.
149. *Ibid.*
150. *Ibid.,* pp. 10-11.
151. Eastman, "Lenin — A Statesman," *Liberator,* p. 31.
152. Eastman, "Editorials," *Liberator,* Vol. 2 (March 1919), p. 16.
153. Eastman, "Nietzsche, Plato, and Bertrand Russell," *Liberator,* Vol. 3 (September 1920), p. 5.
154. Eastman, "The New International," *Liberator,* Vol. 2 (July 1919), p. 31.
155. Eastman, *Love and Revolution,* p. 233.
156. Eastman, "Actor of One Role," in *Heroes I Have Known,* p. 165.
157. Eastman, *Love and Revolution,* pp. 183-189. pp. 204-208, pp. 231-234, pp. 273-282.
158. Eastman, *Knowledge and Revolution,* pp. 285-305.
159. Eastman, "My Friendship with Edna Millay," in *Great Companions: Critical Memoirs of Some Famous Friends* (New York, 1942), p. 84.
160. Eastman, *Love and Revolution,* pp. 311-327.
161. *Ibid.,* p. 333.
162. Eastman, "Moscow's Answer," *Liberator* (July 1923), p. 23.

163. Eastman, "A Permanent Revolution," *Liberator* (December 1923), p. 10.
164. Eastman, "Moscow's Answer," p. 23.
165. Eastman, *Leon Trotsky: Portrait of a Youth* (New York, 1925), p. v.
166. Eastman, *Love and Revolution,* pp. 419-431.
167. Eastman, *Since Lenin Died* (New York, 1925), p. 19.
168. Eastman, *Love and Revolution,* p. 340.
169. Eastman, *Since Lenin Died,* p. 106, p. 129.
170. Eastman, *Marx, Lenin and the Science of Revolution* (London, 1926), *passim.*
171. Eastman, "Problems of Friendship with Trotsky," in *Great Companions,* p. 156;
     Eastman, *Love and Revolution,* pp. 557-568.
172. Eastman, "Discrimination About Russia," *Modern Monthly,* Vol. 8 (September 1934),
     p. 482.
173. Eastman, "We Must Face the Facts About Russia," *Reader's Digest,* 93 (July 1943),
     p. 3.
174. Eastman, "Socialism and Human Nature," *The New Leader* (January 24, 1942), p. 5;
     Eastman, "Socialism and Human Nature," *The New Leader,* (January 31, 1942),
     p. 5.

CHAPTER SIX

FLOYD DELL:
The Bohemian
as Romantic Lover

O n a fall day in 1913, a pale, thin young man stepped from the Chicago-New York train at the newly-opened Grand Central Station on 42nd Street. Nervously lighting a cigarette, he left the huge terminal and walked a short way to Fifth Avenue where he boarded a double-decker bus bound for Washington Square. Floyd Dell knew the way to Greenwich Village because he had visited friends there a month earlier. After that visit he decided to quit his editor's job in Chicago and move to New York. He anticipated that in the Village, "where the pace of life slowed down a bit," he would find "friendship and art and love."[1]

Floyd Dell was born June 28, 1887, in Barry, a small town in central Illinois, not far from the Mississippi River. His family was poor because Anthony Dell, the father, had lost his butchering business during the depression of the 1870s. Forty-eight years old at the time of Floyd's birth, the elder Dell, who was small and combative, had difficulty finding work. Except for an occasional part-time job, Anthony spent his days at home where he washed dishes, read Ulysses Grant's *Memoirs,* and reminisced

Floyd Dell in flannel shirt. Photograph by Marjorie Jones, 1921. Newberry Library.

about his experiences in the Civil War. Since his father could not save the family from the suffering and humiliation of poverty, Floyd looked to his mother for protection, and she became his "all-powerful goddess."[2]

As the fourth and last child, Floyd reaped the advantages and disabilities of being the baby of the family. His "sweet and gentle" mother anxiously watched over a frail son who seemed to require special care. Discouraging traditional boyhood activities, Kate Dell, a former schoolteacher, entertained Floyd with stories about "real and imaginary people and places." She taught him "to understand words" and "no little bit of childish progress was too small for her to notice and reward with praise." She did not laugh at his "clumsy blunders" but led him "into the universe to be its prince." She was a gentle "Lawgiver" who imposed "inexorable *oughts* and *musts*" that he always tried to follow. The result was a shy, well-behaved boy who felt that he *"had* to be all" his mother "expected."³

Indigent and sensitive, Floyd found solace in books. He spent hours at the public library to avoid "a home where there was always some painful reminder" of poverty. In retreating from reality, he invariably mused about a "jolly and exciting companionship with a girl" who read poetry to him. This "dream-companion" of early adolescence inspired his search for poetry, love, and girls.⁴

In 1899, Floyd and his parents moved upriver to Quincy, Illinois, where they lived with the older children who worked in a factory there. However, Anthony Dell found no work. The family's lack of respectability precipitated Floyd's revolt against conventional values. In high school he became a disciple of Robert Ingersoll, the famous agnostic who attacked the doctrines of organized Christianity. At the age of sixteen Floyd was converted to socialism by a successful farmer who told him that radical politics would produce the "kind of world a poet would want to live in." Then he read a red-covered, socialist pamphlet that "said not a word about economics," but described a paradise of classical beauty. It told, he recalled,

> about Greek ideals of beauty in art and life; and it was illustrated with photographs of two Greek statues, the Venus of Melos and the Discus Thrower, which were interpreted in the text as examples of the gloriously alive and happy nature of Greek manhood and womanhood.⁵

This pamphlet and other utopian romances persuaded him that socialism would mean a pastoral idyl where love and freedom flourished. He came to think of revolutionaries as a cadre of young men and women living like Robin Hood and Maid Marian, robbing "the rich" and helping "the poor." He imagined that a "girl student revolutionary" might spend the night with a "comrade" and not expect him "to make love." To a young, inexperienced idealist like Dell, it was a "relief" to think that he could have a girl who would not test his sexuality. He fancied himself part of an heroic movement that would redress injustices and free his mother from the drudgery of housework. Since socialism emphasized the importance of the working class, he need not "belong to the respectable world nor try to struggle for a place in it."[6]

When the family moved to Davenport, Iowa in 1904, Floyd discovered "an intelligentsia who knew books and ideas." Marilla Freeman, a librarian, took a motherly interest in his development as a poet and "bossed" him with "angelic sweetness and patience." She introduced him to the town's literary circle and the Monist Society where he met Rabbi William Fineshriber and George Cram Cook. Floyd became a celebrity and was admitted into middle-class drawing-rooms where women, who "alone had time" for poetry, praised his work and discussed "life" with him. Greatly pleased with his identity, he began to wear a black silk scarf instead of the customary celluloid collar.[7]

Skipping his final year of high school, Dell became a cub reporter on the *Davenport Times*. In addition, he contributed to and edited the *Tri-City Workers Magazine*, a local socialist publication that concentrated on muckraking and municipal reform. Keeping with the "progressive" character of Davenport socialism, Dell advocated the establishment of a kindergarten system to counteract the immoral influences of street life. To discourage drifting from job to job, he urged that schools inculcate "community ideals" and offer "manual training."[8]

Despite Dell's lower-class background, industrial conditions and economic injustice did not engage his attention. It was the sexual exploitation of innocent working-class girls that aroused his indignation. In a piece on "Brick Munro's saloon" he exposed (though never venturing inside) what he assumed was the prostitute mill of Davenport.[9] He reported that working-class girls went there in search of fun and fell prey to "the men of the business and professional classes [who] get what they are after." While hypocritical "respectable businessmen" were responsible for this "malaria of vice and disease," Dell criticized working-class men for permitting this contagion to continue; a "true socialist," he scolded, would never "laugh at the spectacle of a fallen woman."[10] Typically he depicted women as innocent victims sacrificed on the altar of male lust.

Dell presumed that his interest in women was beyond reproach and his romances with Davenport women enhanced his favorable self-image. He was "not a seducer"; if a girl gave herself to him, "it must be with a clear conscience; she must believe that what she was doing was right." Since "slightly older young women" regarded it as "a duty as well as a pleasure to initiate an inexperienced young man," he felt free of any culpability.[11]

Dell became involved with a married woman, "a fellow-Bohemian," who was "so kind as to flirt" with him and praise his verses. Then he fell in love with a daring, "yellow-haired," upper-class girl who introduced him to the wondrous pleasures of sex. "It was," he recalled, "a magical experience to take a girl utterly into my mind and heart and senses and imagination." The "fire of sexual love" liberated their "individualities" into a "fearless existence," and there was "peace for a fevered head against her soft breasts." Since she did not want to marry him, he likened the romance to the "stolen" loves of Elizabethan poets. Nevertheless, he was "bruised with pain" by the break-up of what he "considered a marriage."[12] He was also fired from the *Davenport Times,* apparently for neglecting his work.

When Dell lost his job, Cook invited him to stay at the Cabin in Buffalo and become his helper. Since the work was not strenuous, there was ample time for endless conversations, especially about the "Girl Question," which they discussed "from the scientific, the Socialistic, the Anarchistic, the Nietzschean, the biological, and the experimental-opportunist point of view."[13] They made plans to write novels and began a story about themselves.

This project was postponed by Cook's marriage to Mollie Price, who first arrived at the Cabin after the wedding in Chicago. Dell immediately became enamored with this "adventurous" anarchist girl who knew New York bohemians and their haunts. Dell thought that he and Mollie had much in common. Since George was engrossed in writing a novel, they spent hours together talking, laughing, telling each other their life histories. But when Cook became aware of their intimacy, he ordered Mollie to stop seeing Floyd. Finding it impossible to continue his relationship with Mollie, Dell decided to leave Davenport and look for newspaper work in Chicago.[14]

On the eve of departure Dell boldly sent a letter to George Bernard Shaw in which he reprimanded the British playwright for his "supercilious attitude toward the literary achievement of America." While Dell discounted "the greater part of what New England took the trouble to say," he defended the "revolutionary work" of poets Walt Whitman and John Greenleaf Whittier. An "iconoclast" and a "disreputable person," Whittier had stood with the abolitionists "who rushed in where statesmen dared not tread" to upset "law and order in an absurd attempt to secure the overthrow of slavery." Whitman's achievement had been even more remarkable, for he taught "a new and purer attitude toward sex." Dell attributed Whitman's remarkable accomplishments to bohemian experiences. "To write the 'Children of Adam' poems [the section in *Leaves of Grass* which exalts sexual love], it took a man who had loafed, . . . steeped his youth in the glory of the metropolis, chummed with roughs and cab drivers, and begotten children of love."[15] Dell was prepared to follow Whitman's example.

Using a letter of introduction from Marilla Freeman, Dell found work with the *Chicago Evening Post*. Initially hired as a reporter, he was promoted in March, 1909, to assistant editor of the *Friday Literary Review,* a new supplement which printed book reviews, literary news, editorials, and gossip. The editor was Francis Hackett, a twenty-five-year-old Irish immigrant, who rejected popular romances and sentimentality for realism and European writers, and thereby set a high standard of literary achievement. Discarding his socialist views, Dell accepted Hackett's guidance without displeasing the conservative managing editor. His discretion paid off; when Hackett left for New York in July, 1911, Dell succeeded him. Later he admitted: "Suffice it to say that I evidently knew on which side my bread was buttered and could be depended upon to say the right word at the right time."[16]

Hackett remembered Dell as "an appealing and exasperating young man [who] would tilt his head superciliously and utter pitying comments on poor devils who did not happen to be materialistic monists."[17] Dell's remarkable rise from self-educated journalist to literary critic at the age of twenty-one in part explained his arrogance. He conceived of book reviewing as "an intellectual preoccupation" that permitted him to "talk about religion or politics or art"; his reviews, therefore, only indirectly discussed the books or authors under consideration.[18] His criteria for good literature were entirely subjective: he admired realism about sex and romances that lauded rebellious youth. His preference for tales about young rebels accounts for his selection of H.G. Wells as the foremost writer in the world. He thought that J. B. Beresford's trilogy about Jacob Stahl (an indecisive young writer who falls prey to pretty manipulative women), and Eden Phillpotts's melodramas about love and suffering were superior to Henry James's novels, which offered "an inventory of petty and foolish things, the minutiae of cerebral and nervous functioning, [and] a catalogue of dead thoughts and feelings."[19] Dell appreciated significant writers when their work touched upon love and adventuresome men and women. He thought that Leo Tolstoy possessed a remarkable understanding of "discontented women" and he applauded Stendhal for his female characters. Finally, he praised Henrik Ibsen's *A Doll House* because Nora Helmer courageously broke convention and slammed the door on an unhappy marriage.[20]

While Dell criticized American writers for failing to "deal sympathetically and soberly with sin," he refused to accept "nineteenth-century theories of determinism" or acknowledge the importance of social forces and biological impulses. The environment did not, he maintained, "create an individual, nor dictate his actions." Contrary to what America's "best writers" believed, a man could "do what he pleases" and his actions could be judged "by the old theological terms of 'good' and 'evil.' " Neither socialist doctrines nor his family's experiences caused him to question the traditional notion of individual freedom and responsibility. It was important to show "reality" in all "its pain and ugliness," particularly the "heartbreak and despair" of "personal relationships"; "unpleasant literature" taught one "how to live" and it tested "what manner of man one is."[21]

Dell considered Frank Norris the most important writer in America. Not surprisingly he preferred *Blix* (1899), a popular love story about Travis Bessemer (Blix), a comely, blond-haired girl who breaks with San Francisco "society" and runs off with Condy Rivers, a newspaperman with literary ambitions. Blix, a tall, "healthy-bodied" heroine helps Condy overcome his weaknesses and become a writer. Their free-wheeling camaraderie delighted and enchanted Dell. He commented in his review:

> The adventuring of the unconscious lovers thru San Francisco and its environs, the things they see and do together, the people they meet, the healthy animal environment they take in the sun and air, the things they talk about: these make an idyll of 'togetherness,' of all that which is so much longed for and so infrequently achieved by lovers. . . . One envies them their happiness, their frank, free comradeship, the blithe sharing of a wonderful world, the gay communion of their untroubled spirits.[22]

In evaluating fiction and poetry, Dell offered a narrow interpretation of literary achievement. While he attacked "victorian" writers for their self-censored and sentimental treatment of life, he expected sensuousness to be portrayed as the definitive aspect of romantic love. Absorbed by picaresque stories about romance and liberated women, he excluded or rejected novelists who probed the mind or exposed unhealthy social conditions. Nevertheless, his demand for more candor advanced the cause of literary freedom.

In the summer of 1909, Dell married Margery Currey, a thirty-three-year-old high school teacher whom he had met in Davenport. Plump, outgoing, brown-haired, and ten years older, Margery offered security and intellectual companionship instead of romantic exhilaration. She was not one of those young, rambunctious girls who inflicted pain; she was a self-supporting, liberated woman with literary and artistic interests.[23]

To offset their compliance with propriety, they were married by Rabbi William Fineshriber, Dell's fatherly advisor from Davenport, in a ceremony that adopted certain Jewish practices. This unconventional beginning served notice that their marriage would be an experiment in rebellion. To dramatize their boldness they posed in the nude for miniaturist Martha Baker and hung the drawing on the wall of their Rogers Park apartment. Opposed to patriarchy, they endeavored to forge a union of equals. Each partner worked, contributed to household expenses, and shared in performing domestic tasks. Each was free to maintain premarital friendships and to establish new ones. Dell took pride in their arrangement and believed his lack of authoritarianism proved his commitment to feminism.[24] Although pleased with himself for accepting the mature role of a working husband, this experiment in equality offered him freedom but brought few responsibilities. Margery provided a snug harbor from which he could sally forth to find romantic adventures.

With Margery serving as hostess, the couple's four-room apartment became a gathering place for writers, artists, and journalists. Margaret Anderson, founder and editor of *The Little Review,* remembered that Margery "created a sort of salon for Floyd who was so timid he would never have spoken to anyone if she hadn't relieved him of all social responsibility and presented him as an impersonal being whose only function in life was to talk."[25] The participants, most of whom subsequently moved to Greenwich Village, included writer Edna Kenton, her sister, Mabel Reber (society reporter for the *Chicago Tribune*), journalist Lucy Huffaker, painter Jerome Blum, and the staff of the *Literary Review*—Charles Hallinan, Lucian Cary (his wife, August), Llewellyn Jones, and George Cram Cook.[26] Everyone thoroughly enjoyed the informal dinner parties and the California wines that enlivened them. Margaret Anderson said that the "Dell soirees" were the only social functions she attended, and Eunice Tietjens recalled that her "awakening" as a poet began in a "blaze" when George C. Cook and Floyd Dell recited poetry "boldly into the open, with no apology, as though it were indeed one of the great facts of existence."[27]

Conversations revolved around avant-garde literature and poetry, Havelock Ellis's studies of human sexuality, the Montessori method of education, and feminism. Many of the participants had ambitions to write fiction, and they discussed contemporary writers and "theorized" about the "technique of novels, short stories and plays." Dell, Cook, Hallinan, and Cary met regularly over lunch and at night to abuse "ignorant, mean, and base employers" for exploiting their talents and to plan for the day when they could begin serious writing. They imagined that the end of "hired" slavery would mean the beginning of a "creative" existence.[28] When Charles Hallinan quit the *Evening Post,* he headed for Provincetown where he hired a "towncrier" to announce his intentions: "Notice. Mr. Charles Hallinan is resigning as editorial writer of a Chicago newspaper. He is going to write his novel and hopes to freelance it for the rest of his life."[29]

For Dell there were other consolations besides the fellowship of disaffected newspapermen. He made love "happily and solemnly" to another woman and was transported from the everyday world into a realm of romantic liberty. He recalled:

> There was a girl; and we kissed. And then, suddenly, I was in a realm more real to me than the world. . . . I was happy and free; not a literary editor; not a husband; only myself. All the values in my universe were suddenly transvalued. I felt like a wanderer, long absent in alien lands, who sets eyes upon his native place. . . . This, the realm of liberty, was one in which I could be at ease. There need be no effort here to be what one was not, only infinite sincerity of oneself to another in love and talk and laughter.[30]

Suddenly he realized how much he longed for "enchanting intimacy" and how "multitudinous" were the opportunities for romantic ecstasies beyond the "walls of custom and habit." In his mind indiscretions represented a revolt against social repression, and he convinced himself that yielding to sexual impulses required great courage. Infusing each relationship with transcendent meaning, Dell placed himself on an emotional pendulum that oscillated between exhilaration and depression as each affair began and ended.

After Dell terminated this affair, he became involved with someone else. Margery learned of his infidelity and suggested that they end the marriage. But Dell opposed a divorce and promised to remain faithful. His resolve, however, was not equal to his emotions, and he "fell in love" twice more. Margery then decided that the marriage had deteriorated beyond the point of reconciliation and filed for a divorce. As a show of bohemian civility, they conducted their separation without "reproaches or recriminations" and remained friends. They rented separate apartments on the South Side near Jackson Park where small, wooden shops, hastily constructed for the World's Fair of 1893, had been converted into studios by artists and writers. There they reestablished the salon in a freer but more spartan milieu.[31]

After disposing of their Marshall Field's furniture, Dell self-consciously accepted the discomforts of a poet's quarters. He told poet Arthur Ficke:

> It is 11:30 P.M. I have just returned from the north side, where I have been seeing the [Lucian] Carys, to my ice cold studio, where I have built a fire with scraps of linoleum, a piece of wainscoting, and the

contents of an elaborate filing system of four years' creation. I am
writing at a desk spattered with Kalsomine, and lighted by four candles.
The room contains one bookcase and nine Fels-Naptha soap boxes full
of books . . . —a typewriter stand, a fireless cooker, a patent coat
and trouser hanger, and a couch with a mattress and blanket. In this
blanket I roll myself securely, and sleep till 5:30 A.M., when I am
awakened by a flood of daylight, also by the fact that my shoulders
are cold. I wrap myself tighter, and sleep till 8 o'clock when I get up,
take a sketchy bath at a faucet, and go around the corner for breakfast.[32]

On his excursions from the apartment Dell wore a high white collar,
black stock and carried a walking stick and gloves. In adopting the
costume of a dandy, Dell demonstrated his commitment to bohemianism
and attracted the attention of neighborhood artists who sculptured and
painted him.

The move to Jackson Park represented a rejection of middle class life
for bohemianism. The group of painters, poets, sculptors (which included
B.J.O. Nordfeldt, photographer Marjorie Jones, writer Ernestine Evans,
and sculptors Kathleen Wheeler and Mary Randolph) were the most important colony of bohemians in Chicago. From 1890 to 1905, the first
generation of Chicago writers and artists (sculptor Lorado Taft, painter
Charles Francis Brown, and writers Hamlin Garland, William Vaughn
Moody, Henry Fuller, Robert Morss Lovett, and Robert Herrick) wrote or
expressed themselves within the tradition of genteel culture.[33] Most of
them came from an urban setting and they retained either institutional
or informal connections with the upper classes. By contrast, Dell and his
friends, who were from Midwestern towns and provincial backgrounds,
had no stake in urban culture and no interest in reforming the city. Since
few personal or intellectual ties existed between the two generations of
writers, tradition did not shape bohemianism. Isolated from genteel
culture and opposed to respectable society, the bohemians pursued a
life-style that aimed at liberating the individual from all standards. But in
emphasizing the importance of private over public life, the bohemians
created a colony in which individuals became absorbed in themselves
and one another.

The Dells' bohemian salon was apparently a success. Sherwood Anderson, newly arrived from Clyde, Ohio, and as yet unpublished, was overjoyed at finding this coterie. He remembered the summer of 1913 as the
"happiest period" of his life:

What nights we had, what excursions at the weekends. There was in us
. . . something of the fervor that must have taken hold of those earlier
Americans who had attempted to found communistic communities. We

were in our own mind a little band of soldiers who were going to free life from certain bounds.[34]

Unrestrained by conventional codes, they thought themselves a rebellious vanguard promoting individual freedom, sexual equality, and artistic creativity. Margery's parties, commented Lawrence Langner, began with "cocktails and food, and ended with discussions of books, plays, music, pictures, all of which were undergoing in thoroughgoing revolution."[35] There were picnics on deserted beaches where men and women sat around bonfires, chanted poetry, sang songs, and went swimming in the nude. It was, Sherwood Anderson reflected, "all quite innocent enough, but such a wonderful feeling in us of leading a new free bold life, defying what seemed to us the terribly stodgy life out of which we had all come."[36]

Determined to eliminate the barriers created by conventional concepts of masculine and feminine roles, they elevated candor to the highest virtue. Sherwood Anderson recalled the easy companionship with "liberated" women and the frank conversations in which sex was discussed freely without embarrassment. This did not, he maintained, lead to dissipation; "indeed sex was to bring [them] a new dignity." Dell used the same argument in explaining his affairs; to him "intimacies were beautiful, good in themselves, seemingly a part of the enchanting intimacy of self-revealing talk."[37]

Candor also had its liabilities. Once when Sherwood Anderson introduced the subject of homosexuality, those in attendance "pounced" on him with insinuations about his real sexual interests. Anderson recalled that Freud had just been discovered and everyone was "analyzing each other":

Floyd Dell was hot at it. We had gathered in the evening in one of the rooms. . . . Floyd walked up and down before us. He was at that time wearing a stock and looked I thought like pictures I had seen of [Edgar Allan] Poe. . . . And now he had begun "psyching" us. Not Floyd alone but others in the group did it. They psyched us. They psyched men passing in the street. It was a time when it was well for a man to be somewhat guarded in the remarks he made, what he did with his hands.[38]

Dell did use these occasions to expound his views and to demonstrate his erudition. He confessed to Arthur Ficke: "A party always makes me despise my fellow beings, and sets me up accordingly in my esteem." He did not always seek out troubled personalities; individuals talked freely to him and told "secrets for which they needed the relief of a confessional." But, he admitted later, intimate revelations "didn't solve anything"; most importantly, they "didn't heal the cruelties of love."[39] The probing of personalities had an unhealthy effect on the group, breeding a sense of superiority toward ignorant outsiders while placing insiders on the defensive, especially since, Dell confessed later, they "were much given to laughing at each other." In their haste to tear down the niceties of social etiquette, bohemian rebels subjected each other to the rude shock of blunt, if not inaccurate, analyses. Truth was one thing; destructive comments, accompanied or motivated by personal competition, resulted in intimidation. Terrified by his ignorance and uncertain about his literary talents, Sherwood Anderson sought out Margery Currey who offered him encouragement, not scrutiny.

The availability of unattached men and women also generated sexual rivalries. Dell "fell in love" with Elaine Hyman, a twenty-year-old, dark-haired beauty who dabbled in painting and acting. He met her at Maurice Browne's "Little Theatre" when she appeared in Euripides's The Trojan Women. He decided that Elaine, who took the stage name of Kirah Markham, was the girl he wanted. His plans were upset, however, by the arrival of forty-nine-year-old Theodore Dreiser, already a well-known author, who was in Chicago collecting information for the second volume of the Cowperwood trilogy. Much to Dell's chagrin and anger, Dreiser, "somewhat pudgy and no great talker," was able to dazzle Elaine.[40] When Dreiser returned to New York, Dell hoped that his romance had only been temporarily interrupted. He told Ficke, that despite being crazy with jealousy, he was "perfectly certain that we shall marry and live happily ever after." Four days later, however, he admitted that the love affair was over, bracing himself with the romantic notion that it was "better to surrender oneself utterly and to get smashed up, than to fool around on the edge." Chiding Ficke for remaining in Davenport, he told him: "Ordinary existence is all very well, the walking on the solid earth, but when you can stamp your foot and break the crust and tumble into fairyland—that is another matter."[41]

Early in the fall of 1913, Dell left Chicago to visit Greenwich Village. Perhaps the loss of Elaine, who followed Dreiser to New York, had a significant impact, for he intended to begin a novel. Edna Kenton had written to him: "The Village broke loose this month and what has not happened to theories is microscopic in quantity. 'Possessive love'—horrible thing!—'the tie that binds' even the strongest; treachery to a fellow woman; lies and lies and lies—all these have poured down like torrential floods upon the Village, and we are all quite wrecked." She and social worker-psychoanalyst Grace Potter planned to "reduce the month's experiences to writing, and then swap MSS and points of view."[42] Dell, already familiar with this technique, was led to believe that the Village was an excellent place to work. Most of his old friends were already there. It was almost as if one could not hope to become a writer, or consider oneself an apprentice, unless one lived in Greenwich Village or Provincetown, its summer counterpart. After visiting Susan Glaspell and George Cram Cook, he decided that "the life at Provincetown is the life for me."[43] He returned to Chicago, resigned his position with the *Friday Literary Review,* and set off once again for the East coast.

From the club-car of the Empire State Express, Dell wrote a long letter to Rabbi Fineshriber in which he attempted to summarize his experiences in Chicago before he commenced "all over again the adventure of life." But this bravado was mainly designed to raise his spirits. "Now, as then [when he left Davenport], I have been advised, and urged, and pushed into making the break." Each time he had just been painfully "bruised" by an ill-fated romance. Nevertheless, he was "ready to expose [himself] again to the dangers and the pain of love." He maintained that the Chicago experience had been worthwhile because he had "really lived" and had come to know himself and "people of [his] own world." Heretofore he had existed for ideas, which had made him hard, "callous," egotistic "in his relations with men," "hypocritical with women," "unsatisfactory as a lover," and "intolerable as a husband." The five years in Chicago had "freed" him from a "superstitious reverence" for "reason and logic," and he would not "use them in the future save as tools and weapons in the service of [his] enthusiasms and instincts." At the age of twenty-six he was finished with idealism; now he cared "a great deal for people and damned little for ideas."[44] In short, Chicago had prepared him well for Greenwich Village.

Dell eagerly submerged himself in Village life. He joined the Liberal Club, wrote plays, romanced, whiled away hours in cáfe conversations, and attended Village balls where he "would have given anything to be able to dance." His financial problems were solved by a position (at a salary of fifteen dollars per week) as assistant editor of *The Masses.* Bowing to its political stance and the thrill of political dissent, he reasserted his socialist sympathies and jettisoned his high collar and black stock for a proletarian flannel shirt. He continued, however, to wear silk underwear.[45]

The presence of rebellious artists and liberated women made it difficult for Dell to concentrate on writing. While he told others of his project, he achieved little progress. Initially he told Ficke and himself that working as a literary editor, albeit a "less worthy occupation than writing novels," was nonetheless "honorable and exciting."[46] Later, when editorial duties and bohemian activities began to lose their luster, the unfinished novel became a source of self-recrimination.

Soon after his arrival Dell became involved with photographer Marjorie Jones, whom he had known in Chicago. They rented an apartment together and practiced free love with the zeal of a crusade, for they were going to "behave better than any husband and wife." In promising to be candid and unpossessive about their "inevitable faithlessness to each other," they felt "superior" to married couples.[47] Following the usual custom, they placed both surnames on the mailbox. But this gesture lacked public significance. Except for indifferent postmen, no one outside Village circles witnessed their rebellion. Safely tucked away in the Village, they enjoyed being rebels without suffering the social consequences.

Publicly Dell agreed with Max Eastman's political and editorial positions. Confidentially, however, he told Ficke that he wanted to establish a journal of "ideas" that would be "sufficiently free from the bonds of party or creed or clicque [sic] allegiance as to be under no obligation to lie about anything." He perceived that The Masses' rebels were "revolutionalists without a revolution."[48] Holding to a romantic conception of individual freedom and yearning for simple communities of the past, he was unsympathetic to economic determinism and the socialist concept of a centralized government. When asked to recommend books to the Masses' readers, he suggested Alfred Zimmern's The Greek Commonwealth and Euripides's plays, arguing that "the most significant books of recent years are those which relate more or less directly to the Greek world." His selection seemingly denied the importance of socialist writings or contemporary politics. In praising classical Greece and its supposed belief in "free will", Dell underscored his disdain for the notion of "superior forces." The Greeks viewed life as "a glorious and comic and sublime adventure," and Dell wanted "romance."[49]

Aside from criticizing Theodore Dreiser for not writing the "American novel of rebellion," Dell did not require social realism in literature. On the contrary, he was tired of "sociological generalizations," and advised writers to give attention to the "romantic, un-modern, eternally fascinating facts of human nature." He praised Joseph Conrad, "a great romanticist," for his "emotion-rousing tales of love and adventure and mystery."[50] Rejecting "such magnificent failures" as Tolstoi's Anna Karenina, Dreiser's Sister Carrie, and "anything" by Honore De Balzac and Emile Zola, he extolled picaresque tales—Henry Fielding's Tom Jones, J.B. Beresford's trilogy about Jacob Stahl, Romain Rolland's Jean

Christophe, and Gilbert Cannan's *Mendel,* a story of a Jewish painter who has "adventures in a London bohemia which in many ways resemble[d] Greenwich Village."[51] Favoring literature that conformed to personal fantasies, Dell could appreciate Beresford's continuing story about "a person without ties, a wanderer. . . , a discoverer of one's own life, a person responsible to no fixed and preexisting group or institution for one's mistakes, and one to whom success, if there be any success for such an one, comes with a breathless flush of accident and surprise." Romantic capers and personal quests were Dell's "recipe for modernity."[52]

If politics and working class struggles did not inspire him, Dell was enthusiastic about feminism, which he regarded as the liberation of women from domestic roles and constraints. Even before his arrival in the Village he wrote a series of sketches on important "feminists." For Dell, feminism was inseparable from bohemian causes, hence he classified dancer Isadora Duncan as a feminist because "she made us despise the frigid artifice of the ballet, and taught us that in the natural movements of the body are contained the highest possibilities of choregraphic beauty." As a reformer, Isadora belonged in the tradition of the Greeks and Walt Whitman who "made us see, without any obscure blurring by Puritan spectacles, the goodness of the whole body."[53] Feminism, therefore, promised more sexual freedom for women and more sensual pleasures for men.

Above all feminism would free women from the home and allow them to become worldly companions to men. Marriage extinguished the excitement lovers shared during courtship, and the home was not "one of the delightful corners of the world." Dell, therefore, proposed that women venture out into society. Emancipated men, those who accepted women as comrades "in the adventure of life," would offer "lessons in Socialism, poetry, and poker, all with infinite tact and patience." They would gladly introduce women to the "mysteries" of drinking and smoking, thereby undermining the "tabooes" set by conventional males who wished to remain "sultans in little monogamic harems." Feminism, Dell maintained, would give men "back their souls," so that they could "risk them fearlessly in the adventure of life."[54]

Dell felt that women needed to raise themselves out of traditional roles. If his program placed the responsibility for reforms on women, he credited men with initiating the change. "The Woman's movement" was, according to Dell, "another example of that readiness of women to adapt themselves to a masculine demand." A new feminine type appeared because men were "tired of subservient women." The modern woman, he predicted, would become "that self-sufficient, able, broadly imaginative and healthy-minded creature upon whom we have set our masculine desire."[55] In effect, his feminism meant that women should serve his fantasies and ideals.

Although Dell argued that feminism would aid the fight against capitalist employers who wished to tie laborers down with wives and children, his proposals were irrelevant to the problems of the working classes. His description of the battle for women's rights was merely an exercise in fantasy. "We males, who have so long played in our politics at innocent games of war, we shall have an opportunity to fight in earnest at the side of Valkyrs [sic]."[56] That Dell depicted feminists as Valkyries suggested the attractiveness of bold and strong-minded women. Infatuated with the "modern" woman of independent temperament and sexual precocity, he praised the Village "playfellow" because she absorbed "the shock and jostle of life's incidents more bravely, more candidly and more lightly."[57] Believing that acceptance of liberated women demonstrated a superior sensitivity, Dell congratulated himself for rejecting women who retreated from life into domesticity. "To disregard the claims of dependent women, to risk their comfort in the interests of self or of society" took, according to Dell, a "good deal of heroism—and some scoundrelism too."[58] Therefore, bohemian men who shunned traditional marriage were leaders in the fight for freedom.

Since Dell disliked facing the "jostle" of life alone and lacked close relationships with men, he emphasized the importance of women as lover-companions. He scoffed at the idea that feminism might result in a conflict between the sexes:

> There is no possibility of a war between beings who hunger and thirst after each other, who go insane and die when deprived of each other's society, who cannot have even ordinary good health, let alone peace of mind, without the most intimate association with each other.[59]

But not all men and women experienced the same obsessions as Dell. Having idealized his own needs, he could not foresee that some women might resent his feminism and view male feminists as oppressors.

Dell's "illicit domesticity" with Marjorie Jones ended in 1916. They separated, Dell told Arthur Ficke, because they "had become too good friends [sic] to be lovers any more."[60] He had originally undertaken this arrangement, he argued later, "to keep from becoming involved in other love affairs." But the availability of "beautiful and intelligent" girls undermined his experiment with domestic stability.[61] He hoped "that in each new and charming girl-companion" he would find "the ultimate goal" of his wanderings. If there were disappointments, his life was "enriched" by "intimate talk and romantic lovemaking."[62] Neither painful experiences nor Freudian insights caused him to doubt the magic of love; to become a "successful lover" required more courage, ability, pain, and "spiritual enterprise than most people have."[63] Several short-lived affairs, earning Dell the reputation of a "fickle and inconstant lover," only made him question his ability to form an enduring relationship. Retaining his illusions, Dell could not perceive the compulsive components of his search for love.

While Dell celebrated the enchantment of romantic experiences, misgivings about his relationships with liberated women were revealed in two Village plays. In Enigma, which concerns the dissolution of an affair, Dell expressed bewilderment at love's volatility.[64] He implied that free love often led to destructive personal relations. Ironically, the play, a reflection of Dell's solipsism, explains why Village affairs produced so much unhappiness. In the narrow confines of the Village, rebels had difficulty transcending personal relations.

In The Angel Intrudes, a "comedy" produced by the Provincetown Players in December, 1917, Dell demonstrated how much unfulfilled love continued to trouble him. He suggested that the weakness of men and the shallowness of women resulted in unstable romances. In The Angel Intrudes it is Annabelle who decides to end the affair with Jimmy Pendleton. Jimmy admits that he is completely dependent upon her: "I'm a doddering lunatic, incapable of thinking of anything but you. I can't work. I can't eat. I can't sleep. I'm no use to the world. I'm not a man, I'm a mess." This confession only increases Annabelle's indifference to him. She then captivates Jimmy's guardian angel, an accomplishment which underscores her power over men. Utterly bewitched, the angel offers to burn his wings as proof that he will never leave her. But Jimmy warns: "Keep your wings, my friend, against the day when the glamor of sex has vanished and you see in her, as you will see, an inferior being . . . who does not know how to work, nor how to talk, nor even how to play."[65]

Dell obviously suffered from his dependence on women and his need for love. Two short stories, published after he quit the Village, made it plain that his affairs brought him grief. In "The Kitten and the Masterpiece," Paul Sherwood, an autobiographical character, saves his money so that he can move to the Village and become a writer.[66] His plans are upset, however, when he becomes infatuated with June Glory, a bohemian girl. After spending his savings on her, Paul proposes marriage, even though it means abandoning his novel. June, announces that she has no intention of marrying because she wants to write poetry. In the second story, "A Piece of Slag," a young bohemian wife discovers that her husband's commitment to ideas is a pose that conceals his consuming in-

terest in her. She cries out in anguish: "Why he's only a child."[67] As Dell
perceived the situation, whenever a man fell in love he lost control of the
relationship, and was reduced to a tormented weakling. Women,
especially those he wanted, placed their artistic ambitions before love.
Since women were attracted to successful writers, he needed to finish his
novel to achieve "distinction."[68] But he found it impossible to work
steadily without the support of a companion.

Despite an awareness of the dangers involved, Dell could not resist a
new femme fatale, red-haired Edna St. Vincent Millay. Ironically, he met
her when she tried out for and won the part of Annabelle, a role she
could play both on and off the stage. Edna, or Vincent as she called
herself, was a pert, willful, and self-centered woman with a penchant for
tragic romance in life and poetry. Believing that the "joys" and "pain" of
love "nourished" her imagination, she became involved in numerous, intense relationships only to end them abruptly to the disappointment of
her suitors.[69]

Edna arrived in New York after graduating from Vassar College. She
had received national attention for her poem, "Renascence," which was
published in The Lyric Year. Dell, who had admired her poetry, was soon
under her "spell," for "her hair, falling softly about [his] face, was a shield
against the threats of an evil time." She insisted that they go to bed
together, fully unclothed, but would not have sexual intercourse. For
some weeks Dell agreed to this "platonic" arrangement, but wondered
about the "Freudian explanation" for her behavior. The next time they
were in bed together he confronted her: "Now I understand you. I know
your secret. You pretend that you have had many sexual love affairs—but the truth, my dear, is that you are still a virgin. You have merely had homosexual affairs with girls at college." According to Dell, she
was "astonished" at his "deductive powers" and replied: "No man has
ever found me out before." Feeling that it was his "duty" to rescue her,
he made love to her. The second time they set up a huge gilt-framed mir-
ror so that they could watch themselves; conventional lovers viewed sexual intercourse as a "ludicrous and ugly" sight, but they thought "the
spectacle was beautiful and charming." While Edna considered their
lovemaking "wonderful," she did not take their relationship as seriously
as Dell, for she refused to believe in the permanence of love. He begged
her to marry him, but she declined and began having other affairs.[70]

Believing Edna to be a genius, Dell submitted to "her heroic egotism"
and staked out a humble destiny for himself. He explained that there was
"in her something of which one stood in awe—she seemed, as a poet, no
mere mortal, but a goddess; and though one could not help but love her,
one loved her hopelessly, as a goddess must be loved."[71] Small and

fragile, she had the charm of a tomboy and the dedication of a professional artist. Like the unattainable upper-class girls in Davenport, Edna, or "Vixen" as he sometimes called her, was always beyond reach. The more she ignored, rejected, and humiliated him, either by retreating into herself or into the arms of other men, the more he wanted her.

Their relationship adversely affected Dell. Already seeing a psychoanalyst, he pressured Edna to undergo analysis so that their relationship might be saved. She refused and complained about his constant study of her personality. Some weeks later, however, fearing that she was pregnant, she agreed to marriage. Contrary to custom, she gave him an engagement ring—nothing better symbolized the reversal of traditional roles. After discovering she was not pregnant, Edna broke off the engagement, sending Dell into a depression that necessitated a return to the couch.[72]

Dell had alternated between safe relationships that did not engage his emotions and intimate romances that annihilated him. Neither option gave him a sense of well-being. The succession of unsuccessful romances caused Dell to wonder if, at thirty, he was a rake, a Village type he "heartily despised."[73] He did not want to be a promiscuous lover and yet his transitory encounters seemed to place him in that category. A lasting relationship, an ideal at once conventional and romantic, was the goal of his incessant searches. To strengthen his stability and direct his energies to writing, he underwent psychoanalysis.

Dell had come to Greenwich Village in part to overcome personal difficulties that had bothered him in Chicago. Surrounded by rebels who encouraged his earlier patterns of behavior, Dell failed to achieve a more satisfying and independent existence. He thought that psychoanalysis could cure "an inability to achieve results in one's work" and "infelicity in personal relationships." He assured himself that it would also eliminate "a sense of not being able to get at grips [sic] with the realities of life."[74]

Dell considered psychoanalysis a form of confession; the individual divulged "his most carefully guarded secrets" and "felt better for it."[75] Once the patient realized and accepted the existence of forbidden sexual desires, he could rid himself of guilt and repression. Since sexual repression was not a problem for Dell, he refused to accept a sexual etiology of neurosis. After reading Carl Jung's *Psychology of the Unconscious,* he concluded that neurosis resulted from a "refusal or failure to meet the difficulties and dangers of life in the actual world." Furthermore, there was nothing sexual about infantile behaviour; regression involved a wish "to return to the rest and comfort of the mother's breast, or the more perfect peace of the mother's womb." This explanation corresponded with his own difficulties, for he thought that the "too-sensitive soul recoils into a dream which is an imaginative restoration of the conditions of infantile irresponsibility and peace."[76] Viewing mental health as a matter of personal responsibility, Dell denied the unconscious, deterministic components of human behavior and affirmed the individualistic ideology of Greenwich Village. Having simplified the process of emotional catharsis, he exaggerated the effectiveness of psychoanalysis in alleviating mental distress.

Dell underwent analysis ("often interrupted and never completed") for six months because he was "filled with remorse and self-disgust" at his inability to write a novel. Since he had already resurrected memories of childhood and was familiar with the technique of associating to words, no time was lost resisting therapy. It was "easy" to relate the "wicked things" he had done. What was "hard was the history of [his] foolishness—silly little things of no importance whatever that nevertheless made [him] squirm to think of."[77] He "discovered" that he was "afraid of life" and "of women." His timidity stemmed from his mother's overprotectiveness, which had made the world outside of her arms seem "indifferent and harsh." Consequently, he "unconsciously" looked at "the world with the eyes of a hurt child." He wanted to fall in love, settle down, have "a houseful of children," and be "happy ever after," but feared that he would fail to achieve this dream.[78]

Psychoanalysis, Dell claimed, provided a "new emotional center" to his life. He "felt free for the first time" because he was no longer the "blind victim of unsuspected motives."[79] But the ease with which Dell seemingly uncovered and solved his difficulties suggests a superficial experience. His enthusiasm rested on the acquisition of an intellectual stimulant rather than the discovery of personal insights. He failed to explain how the fear of women was consistent with his remarkable attraction to them, and psychoanalysis did not stabilize his personal life so that he could work on a novel.

Dell's spirits were buoyed by the attention he received. Having learned first-hand about the new science, he advanced his standing in the bohemian community. Other Villagers told him their "painful secrets" and asked for his advice, which he gave:

> I understood other people in a way I had not before. I knew why they acted as they did, and what they would do next, and—most magical-seeming of all—read their hidden secrets when I needed to do so, much to their astonishment.[80]

The role of pseudopsychiatrist made Dell a Village guru and a rebel of middle-class society.

Village rebels relied on American psychoanalysts to provide them with much of their information about Freud and Jung. A. A. Brill, Smith Ely Jelliffe, and Samuel Tannenbaum—the Village's chief psychiatrists—advanced interpretations that coincided with bohemian attitudes and perceptions. Although Brill was a disciple of Freud, he rejected the deterministic. implications of Freudian theory and celebrated sexuality as a great life-force. Jelliffe, an eclectic practitioner, considered the libido a source of creative energies to be tapped for useful purposes. Tannenbaum linked psychoanalysis and mental health with sexual liberation and antipuritanism. To these physicians, the "id" was not a mass of uncivilized impulses and the individual was not a slave to insatiable desires. Harboring an optimistic view of man's unconscious, they stressed the human potential for self-direction and happiness.[81]

Given the social and intellectual atmosphere of the Village, Freudian theory had an obvious appeal. It originated in Europe, the fountainhead of culture, and Freud was shockingly frank, examining subjects that the middle classes dared not discuss. Under the rubric of science, Villagers could talk about their sexual fantasies; silence was viewed as a sign of repression and an invitation to emotional disorders. Many Village rebels assumed that Freud vindicated the extension of social and sexual freedom. Freud purportedly plumbed the depths of personalities to uncover the most deeply buried truths about human motivation. With their interest in exposing reality and their experience in dissecting one another, Village rebels felt themselves qualified for the work of psychological exploration and reclamation.

Freud was also attractive to Villagers because of the special status he assigned to those who transformed primitive impulses into artistic creations. The artist's gifts, originating deep within the unconscious, emerged only after a terrific inner struggle. For some Villagers the presence of psychological problems seemed to verify the existence of unmined talent. Failure to develop and produce meant that repression had dammed up creativity. In a letter to H.L. Mencken, poet Louis Untermeyer expressed the common belief that inspiration germinated in the unconscious: "[James] Oppenheim is sending you his book—as good a piece of writing in poetry as psychoanalysis has given birth to."[82]

The Village popularized psychoanalytic theories and supplied American psychiatrists with patients to treat. Seeing a psychiatrist was considered avant-garde. While the rest of society ignorantly confessed their sins to clerics, the modern Villager explored the psychic forces at work in the world. Dell remembered:

There must have been . . . a half dozen or more people in the Liberal Club who knew a great deal about psychoanalysis, and a score or more who

were familiar enough with the terms to use them in badinage. . . . Everyone
. . . who knew about psychoanalysis was a sort of missionary on the subject,
and nobody could be around Greenwich Village without hearing a lot
about it.[83]

Psychoanalysis was fascinating, Dell admitted, because "it [dealt] with
ourselves, a subject in which we are all deeply interested."[84] While
psychoanalysis was embraced as a method of self-exploration, it enhanced and expanded the practice of mutual evaluation. Margaret
Anderson and Jane Heap spent their evenings searching for "the Achilles
heel of everybody's psychic set-up."[85] With its "recondite technical
vocabulary," psychoanalysis permitted "talk about morbid states of
health without seeming to indulge a vulgar predilection."[86]
Psychoanalysis provided new topics of discussion and a new form of
entertainment. Liberal Club members played parlor games of
"associating" their thoughts to lists of words and tried to unravel dreams
by following "the Freudian formula." Plain, everyday gossip was
elevated to scientific analysis, and commonplace dreams were assigned
intellectual and sexual significance.

The availability of a common language and the growth of social narcissism did not promote cohesion in the community. Using Freudian
techniques to detect personal flaws often subverted personal relations.
Susan Glaspell said that "you could not buy . . . a bun without hearing of
someone's complex."[87] Hutchins Hapgood recalled that psychoanalysis
was "overdone to such an extent that nobody could say anything about a
dream, no matter how colorless it was, without his friends' winking at one
another and wondering how he could have been so indiscreet."[88] Dell
discovered that his expertise in psychoanalysis did not lead to new
friendships. After confiding in him, fellow Villagers invariably regretted
their indiscretions and turned against him.[89]

Villagers hoped that psychoanalysis might alleviate psychological
distress and release latent talents. They erred, however, in assuming that
catharsis would provide the solution. No one suggested that the problem
may have been a lack of self-discipline rather than too much repression.
Anxious to chart a course away from respectable society, Village rebels
greatly minimized or rejected routine and an orderly existence. Structure, they assumed, was conventional baggage that had to be jettisoned.
What they considered so much flotsam, however, might have provided
them with ballast and aided the quest for a creative life.

To many bohemians the Greenwich Village setting became a
background for Freudian drama. Freudian ideas fused with Village concepts to give Village rebels their own view of reality. The presumption of

intellectual superiority over conventional society encouraged the belief that Villagers understood the springs of human motivation. Enthralled by the form rather than the substance of Freudian psychology, Dell and his friends concocted self-serving answers instead of genuine insights. Arrogance and naïveté generated a superficial interpretation of psychoanalysis. The efficacy of the Villagers' ideas was always assumed and seldom demonstrated. In concentrating on individual problems and in simplifying human dilemmas, Villagers failed to raise more serious questions about society, Greenwich Village, or themselves.

Already stimulated by psychoanalysis, Dell found the tempo of life accelerated by direct involvement in political dissent. Opposition to American intervention in the European war brought *The Masses* into conflict with the federal government. When the Justice Department charged *The Masses* with conspiracy to obstruct national conscription, Dell was among those indicted.

As literary editor, Dell rarely commented on politics or governmental policies, and when he did, it was usually in support of a position outlined by Eastman. While Dell disliked the "autocratic" methods of the Wilson administration, he hoped that the President would negotiate an end to the war and a fair settlement. Dell advocated, like Eastman, the establishment of a league of nations because he did not want "to rely exclusively on the possessive instincts of the working class to bring about a happier world." Nevertheless, an unsigned introduction to an article praising British "conscientious objectors" and his four-year association with *The Masses* was enough for the Justice Department attorneys.[90]

The courtroom drama was more effective than psychoanalysis in relieving him, at least during the trial, of his psychological burdens. Furthermore, as he faced the prospect of a long prison sentence, Edna became interested in his fate and accompanied him each day to the crowded courtroom.[91] Despite the seriousness of the charges, Dell greatly enjoyed the notoriety of a dangerous radical. He appeared in court wearing a silk scarf in place of a tie, offering a touch of bohemianism but not enough to give affront. He liked having his writings treated as "matters of social and political importance," and he found the cross-examination to be an exciting but "primitive game of wits."[92] He insisted that his reviews were never intended to obstruct recruitment or inspire objection to the draft. He told the jury that he had been a conscientious objector and had opposed American military intervention in the war. But President Wilson's reply to Pope Benedict had convinced him that the United States would pursue a peace without victory. Since that time, he had withdrawn his opposition to the war and had registered for the draft.[93]

After the trial ended with a hung jury, Dell was drafted, and he reported "cheerfully" to training camp.[94] It pleased him to know that he was young enough to serve in the army. He told his *Liberator* readers:

> I throw off the heavy weight of thought that has chained and bowed my spirit. Exultant in my new-found youthfulness, I look with scorn upon the senile decrepitude of friends who happen to be a few years or months or weeks older than myself, and hence beyond the age-limit. I am content to leave the task of thinking [about] the problems of the new age to tottering greybeards like Walter Lippman[n].[95]

That his father had served with distinction in the Civil War was a matter of pride to him. Here was a chance to emulate him and demonstrate an expertise in drilling he had learned as a boy. Later he commented: "I was rather good at it; and I think if the war had lasted long enough, and I had survived long enough, I should inevitably have risen to a corporal."[96] But he was not given the opportunity; when the army learned that a retrial had been set, he was discharged.

At the second trial, which began September 30, 1918, and lasted just five days, Edna returned to his side and recited her new poems to him while the jury tried unsuccessfully to reach a verdict. When the crisis had passed, Dell admitted that his interest in radicalism had cooled. During the trial he asked himself:

> What am I doing here; Why am I not at home writing a story? The fact was that I was an artist—not a politician. How in the world did I come to be mixed up in this political *cause celebre*? . . . For I am not ashamed to say that to me art is more important than the destinies of nations, and the artist is a more exalted figure than the prophet.[97]

After facing the perils of jail, he decided to concentrate once more on fiction and love. But his romancing would not be with Edna, for she had run off with John Reed.[98]

The pain caused by Edna's inconstancy convinced Dell that he did not want to marry a "girl artist." Since these women put less emotion into affairs, they dominated romantic relationships.[99] Dell accepted "the desire to sacrifice himself utterly to his love," but contemporary opinion looked with disfavor on the wish to be "trampled upon, humiliated, deceived and hurt." Whereas the medieval knight had been "openly proud" of the "tragic" quality of "romantic love," the modern lover was "ashamed" of this "neurotic desire." Although Dell disliked the change in attitude about "painful love," he realized that it was "romantic folly" for him to pursue destructive women like Edna.[100] Free love and liberated women had not solved the problems of his love life.

Dell's disillusionment with romance and feminism was paralleled by a growing dissatisfaction with Village life. in a *Masses'* review he praised poet Louis Untermeyer as a "pagan" even though he lived outside the Village. Untermeyer was more "Dionysian" than all the crowds he had ever seen "mournfully foregathered" in the basement of the Brevoort Hotel or at "The Hell Hole." A "pagan" knew about the "cruelty and ugliness" of life and yet enjoyed it. The Villagers knew about life, but that knowledge left them "saddened" or "intolerably earnest." If Walt Whitman were alive, Dell maintained, he would not live in Greenwich Village, for "he would find his fellow human beings as worried about their souls as ever, even though they called it psychoanalysis instead of religion." Dell had to leave the Village periodically and visit Untermeyer's apartment in uptown Manhattan just to refresh himself. He could feel the "Village Weltschmerz" lifting from "his soul" as the elevated train pulled out of the station at Fourteenth Street. By Fiftieth Street he felt "ten years younger" and he let loose with "an unpracticed laugh."[101] Here was the supreme irony; uptown Manhattan had become a refuge against the tyrannies of bohemia.

Dell's admission that Villagers sometimes depressed him was followed by a disclosure that Village social life was often uneventful. In an editorial defending prohibition, Dell confessed that he had drunk in the Village "just from a priggish desire not to seem priggish," an acknowledgement of his inability to withstand group pressures. He recalled the "hundreds of hours" spent in café-haunts with people he did not like, "waiting, in deadly boredom, hour after hour, for something to happen." But nothing ever happened except that "somebody ordered another round of drinks."[102] Despite a realization that the Village was at best a refuge for "amiable and interesting loafers" and at worst a gathering place for "bums and wastrels," Dell could not break away from the "tiresome egotisms" of other bohemians and work on his manuscript.[103]

Finally, early in 1919, ten weeks after their meeting, Dell married B. Marie Gage, a "golden-haired" and "blue-eyed" girl who "seemed to have stepped out" of a Frank Norris novel. B. Marie was a husky, twenty-three-year-old pacifist who had read his *Masses'* reviews as a student at the University of Wisconsin.[104] Although an ardent feminist, she was prepared to bear children and live through her husband's achievements.

Having "someone with maternal authority over him," Dell was able to escape bohemia, "a world dominated by the lazy and sloppy masculine ideals of freedom and pleasure: a world in which debts never came inexorably due, and in which one is whatever one pretends to be."[105] Aided by "psychoanalytical experiences," which uncovered the "sources of literary creation," Dell completed his autobiographical novel, *Moon-Calf*. The publication of his book, which sold more than thirty thousand copies, the purchase of a cottage in Croton, and the birth of a son provided a happy contrast to his existence in Greenwich Village. He concluded that he had finally attained maturity, a goal that had eluded him through "ten years of struggle."[106] Living comfortably in Croton with old friends and ex-radicals from the Village, he had reason to feel content. But accepting the responsibilities of parenthood did not mean that he had ceased to be a romantic. He married the girl of his dreams and avoided the worst of modern society.

NOTES

1. Floyd Dell, "Greenwich Village," *The Masses* (May 1918), p. 41.
2. Floyd Dell, *Homecoming: An Autobiography* (New York, 1933), pp. 3-6, p. 23.
3. *Ibid.*, p. 6.
4. *Ibid.*, p. 17, p. 46.
5. *Ibid.*, p. 64.
6. *Ibid.*, pp. 63-64, p. 57 p. 73.
7. *Ibid.*, pp. 80-94, p. 102.
8. Dell, "Socialists and Kindergarten," *Tri-City Workers Magazine*, Vol. 1, No. 4 (February 1906), pp. 7-11.
9. Dell, "Why People Go to Brick Munro's," *Tri-City Workers Magazine*, Vol. 1 No. 11 (September 1906), pp. 1-4.
10. Dell, "The Salvation of the Working Class," *Tri-City Workers Magazine*, Vol. 2, No. 9 (July 1906), p. 10.
11. Dell, *Homecoming*, p. 160; Dell, "The Kinsey Report," unpublished essay, Floyd Dell Papers, Newberry Library, Chicago.
12. Dell, *Homecoming*, p. 148, pp. 158-165. Letter, Dell to Rabbi William Fineshriber (Fall 1913), Dell Papers.
13. Dell, *Moon-Calf* (New York, 1921), p. 297.
14. Dell, *Homecoming*, pp. 172-180.
15. Letter, Dell to George B. Shaw (1908), Dell Papers.
16. Dell, *Homecoming*, pp. 189-191, p. 207.
17. Francis Hackett, *American Rainbow: Early Reminiscences* (New York, 1971), p. 250.
18. Dell, "Imaginary Reviews," (*Friday Literary Review*) *Chicago Evening Post*, (September 6, 1912), p. 4.
19. Dell, "Editorial," (*Friday Literary Review*) *Chicago Evening Post* (June 7, 1912), p. 4; "Theodore Dreiser's Chicago, *Review* (February 23, 1912), p. 1; "Failure" *Review* (June 21, 1912), p. 1. "Eden Phillpotts," *Review* (April 11, 1913), p. 1; "Marriott," *Review* (August 9, 1912), p. 1.
20. Dell, "Stendhal," *Review* (July 5, 1913), p. 9.
21. Dell, "Jeffrey Farnol," *Review* (March 21, 1913), p. 1; "Reality," *Review* (August 23, 1912), p. 1.
22. Dell, "Norris," (*Friday Literary Review*) *Chicago Evening Post* (July 11, 1913), p. 1.

23. Dell, *Homecoming,* pp. 178-180, pp. 184-187.
24. *Ibid.,* pp. 192-194; pp. 198-201.
25. Margaret Anderson, *My Thirty Years War* (New York, 1930), p. 37.
26. Dell, *Homecoming,* pp. 200-201.
27. Eunice Tietjens, *The World At My Shoulder* (New York, 1938), p. 17.
28. Dell, *Homecoming,* pp. 207-208, pp. 221-222.
29. George Cram Cook, "New York Letter," *(Friday Literary Review) Chicago Evening Post,* (September 26, 1913), p. 8.
30. Dell, *Homecoming,* p. 212.
31. *Ibid.,* pp. 232-233, pp. 240-241. Letter, Dell to Arthur Ficke (May 13, 1913), Dell Papers.
32. Letter, Dell to Ficke (May 26, 1913), Dell Papers.
33. Bernard Duffey, *The Chicago Renaissance in American Letters* (Michigan State College Press, 1954), pp. 3-142.
34. Sherwood Anderson, *Sherwood Anderson's Memoirs: A Critical Edition,* Ray Lewis White, Ed. (University of North Carolina Press, 1969), p. 341.
35. Laurence Langner, *The Magic Curtain* (New York 1951), p. 81.
36. Anderson, *Memoirs,* p. 345.
37. *Ibid.,* p. 341. Dell, *Homecoming,* p. 213.
38. Anderson, *Memoirs,* p. 339.
39. Letter, Dell to Ficke (July 21, 1913), Dell Papers. Dell, *Homecoming,* p. 239.
40. Dell quoted by W.A. Swanberg, *Dreiser* (New York, 1965), p. 169.
41. Letters, Dell to Ficke (June 15, 1913; June 19, 1919; June 2, 1913), Dell Papers.
42. Letter, Edna Kenton to F. Dell (March 28, 1913), Dell Papers.
43. Letter, Dell to A. Ficke (September 5, 1913), Dell Papers.
44. Letter, Dell to William Fineshriber (Fall, 1913), Dell Papers.
45. Floyd Dell, "On Being Sherwood Anderson's Literary Father," *Newberry Library Bulletin* Vol. 5, No. 8 (July 1961), p. 318.
46. Letter, Dell to Arthur Ficke (April 14, 1914), Dell Papers.
47. F. Dell, "The Ex-Villager's Confession," *Love in Greenwich Village* (New York, 1926), p. 243.
48. Letter, Dell to Ficke (March 28, 1914), Dell Papers.
49. Dell, "First Few Books," *The Masses* (February 1915), p. 17.
50. Dell, "Mr. Dreiser and the Dodo," *The Masses* (February 1914), p. 17; "A Vacation from Sociology," *The Masses* (June 1915), p. 18.
51. Dell, "The Adventure of Life," *The Masses* (May 1917), p. 28.
52. Dell, "Mr. Beresford and the Hero," *The Masses* (January 1917), p. 31.
53. Dell's sketches, which first appeared in the *Chicago Evening Post,* were collected as his first book, *Women as World Builders: Studies in Modern Feminism* (Chicago, 1913), p. 43, pp. 48-49.
54. Dell, "Feminism for Men," *The Masses* (July 1914), pp. 19-20.
55. Dell, *Women as World Builders,* pp. 19-20.
56. *Ibid.,* p. 40.
57. Dell, *Intellectual Vagabondage: An Apology for the Intelligentsia* (New York, 1926), p. 161.
58. Dell, "Feminism for Men," p. 19.
59. Dell, "Socialism and Feminism," *New Review* (June 1914), p. 352.
60. Letter, Dell to Arthur Ficke (November 2, 1916), Dell Papers.
61. Dell, "On Being Sherwood Anderson's Literary Father," p. 317.
62. Dell, "A Utopian Confession," unpublished piece, Dell Papers. Dell may have also enjoyed the notoriety of being linked with certain women. In her fictional account of Greenwich Village, Dorothy Day commented that "Hugh Brace" [Floyd

Dell] was "something of an exhibitionist in his love making. Or as one jealous rival put it in a moment of irritation, Brace's love encounters should really take place on the stage of the Hippodrome before a packed house." Day, *The Eleventh Virgin* (New York, 1924), p. 169.

63. Dell, "Fairy Gold," unpublished fragment, Dell Papers.
64. Dell, "Enigma: A Domestic Conversation," in *King Arthur's Socks: And Other Village Plays* (New York, 1922), pp. 131-140.
65. Dell, "The Angel Intrudes: A Comedy," *King Arthur's* Socks, p. 50, p. 59.
66. Dell, "The Kitten and the Masterpiece," *Love in Greenwich Village*, pp. 47-73.
67. Dell, "A Piece of Slag," *Love in Greenwich Village* pp. 203-235.
68. Floyd Dell, "All About Love," *Pearson's Magazine* (December 1918), pp. 76-77.
69. Dell, copy of unpublished memoir in author's possession (1967), p. 12.
70. *Ibid.,* p. 15, pp. 20-23.
71. Dell, *Homecoming,* pp. 301-303.
72. Dell, unpublished memoir, pp. 32-33.
73. Dell, *Homecoming,* p. 290.
74. Dell, "Speaking of Psychoanalysis: The New Boon for Dinner Table Conversation-alists," *Vanity Fair,* Vol. 5 (December 1915), p. 53.
75. *Ibid.,* Dell, "How It Feels to Be Psycho-Analyzed, "unpublished essay, p. 6. Dell Papers.
76. Dell, "Science of the Soul," *The Masses* (July 1916), p. 31.
77. Dell, "How It Feels to be Psycho-Analyzed," pp. 17-18.
78. *Ibid.,* pp. 21-22.
79. *Ibid.,* pp. 22-24.
80. Dell, *Homecoming,* pp. 293-294.
81. Nathan G. Hale, Jr., *Freud and the Americans: The Beginnings of Psychoanalysis in the United States, 1876-1917* (New York, 1971), pp. 332-396. A.A. Brill, *Psychoanalysis: Its Theories and Practical Application* (Philadelphia, 1914). Samuel Tannenbaum, "Sexual Abstinence and Nervousness," *American Journal of Urology,* Vol. 6 (June 1913), pp. 290-315.
82. Letter, Louis Untermeyer to H.L. Mencken (November 5, 1915), Mencken Papers, New York Public Library. Hale, *Freud and the Americans,* pp. 332-396.
83. Letter, Dell to Frederick Hoffmann, *Freudianism and the Literary Mind* (Baton Rouge, La., 1945), p. 56.
84. Dell, "Speaking of Psychoanalysis," p. 53.
85. Dell, "Speaking of Psychoanalysis," p. 53. Dell practiced analysis to the point of folly. This was easy to do, he recalled, because "most of my friends were presently being psychoanalyzed, and we could talk together without being thought mad." *Homecoming,* p. 294.
86. Margaret Anderson, *My Thirty Years War,* p. 186.
87. Quoted by Albert Parry, *Garrets and Pretenders: A History of Bohemians in America* (New York, 1960), p. 278.
88. Hutchins Hapgood, *A Victorian in the Modern World,* p. 382.
89. Dell, *Homecoming,* pp. 294-295.
90. Dell, "The Chances of Peace," *The Masses,* (August 1917), p. 25, p. 28. "My Political Ideals," *The Masses* (November-December 1917), p. 33.
91. Dell, unpublished memoir, pp. 27-28.
92. Dell, "The Story of the Trial," *Liberator* (June 1918), p. 11. The ease with which Dell assumed and discarded political and social roles was characteristic of his career. Lacking a strong self-identity, he tended to pick one on the basis of the group in which he found himself. This tendency was noted by two of his fellow

Villagers. Hutchins Hapgood commented in 1926: "The truth is that whether Floyd is emerging from capitalistic standards into socialism and bohemianism, or retreating into monogamy and rigid rules of virtue and success, the mainspring seems always to be the instinct to conform." Quoted in *A Victorian in the Modern World*, p. 316. Similarly, Max Eastman said retrospectively: "I thought it a fault in [Floyd] that he could give himself so generously to any entrancing idea he happened to find in a book. I should have said then, and probably did, that he lacked stability of opinion." *Love and Revolution*, p. 223.

93. *New York Tribune* (April 17, 1918), p. 18; *New York Tribune* (April 24, 1918), p. 9. *New York Times* (April 24, 1918), p. 9.

94. Dell, unpublished memoir, pp. 28-29. Dell planned to dramatize his opposition to the war by refusing induction into the army. He told Arthur Ficke that he expected to end up in jail and joked about "finishing his novel there." Dell to Ficke (July 18, 1917), Dell Papers. Brave words were not, however, followed by self-sacrificing action. Dorothy Day related how Dell and his roommates discussed, until three o'clock in the morning, their plans to fight conscription. "And then next morning, bright and early, they registered" with the draft board. Dorothy Day, *The Eleventh Virgin*, p. 174.

95. Dell, "Books," *Liberator* (May 1918), p. 40.

96. Dell, *Homecoming*, p. 321.

97. Dell, "Review," *Liberator* (December 1918), p. 45.

98. Dell, unpublished memoir, pp. 30-31.

99. Dell, "All About Love," *Pearson's Magazine* (December 1918), pp. 76-77.

100. Dell, "Love Among the Shavians," *Liberator* (November 1918), pp. 44-45.

101. Dell, "Review," *The Masses* (June 1917), p. 40.

102. Dell, "Beating Prohibition to It," *Liberator* (April 1919), p. 18.

103. Dell, "Should a Young Writer Live in Greenwich Village?" unpublished essay, Dell Papers. "Review," *Books*, Vol. 16 (September 24, 1939), p. 1.

104. Dell, *Homecoming*, pp. 330-331. Letter, B. Marie Dell to Robert Humphrey (August 25, 1971).

105. Dell, "Men, Women, and Books," *Liberator* (May 1920), p. 39.

106. Dell, *Homecoming*, pp. 340-363.

CHAPTER SEVEN

Greenwich Village:
The Playground of Utopia

The careers of Hutchins Hapgood, George Cram Cook, John Reed, Max Eastman, and Floyd Dell demonstrate the successes and failures common to those who experimented with a bohemian life-style. In reaction to painful childhood and adolescent experiences, Villagers evolved a romantic outlook that became the hallmark of their rebelliousness. Finding conventional society monotonous and oppressive, they sought a community where they might escape conformity in the company of other idealists. The appealing vision of a playground unfettered by respectability lured them to Greenwich Village. They anticipated that bohemia would provide a setting where potential might be realized and life made more exciting.

Since materialism, injustice, hypocrisy, and repression seemed pervasive in America, Greenwich Villagers agreed that their community should promote art, radical politics, freedom, and sexual equality. But few rebels considered how these lofty goals could be achieved. Villagers thought that removing customary restrictions was sufficient to generate creativity and community. Because liberty was the Village ethos, no one wanted a framework to guide the activities of the participants. Unity and organization brought to mind the society they had fled. It was assumed that a colony of like-minded individuals could live in peaceful and pro-ductive anarchy.

Villagers hoped to build a santuary for rebels and to revolutionize society; they wanted to live freely and to influence public policies. Village rebels thought that they could isolate themselves from society and yet have an impact on it. They assumed that there was a positive relationship between self-development and social reform, and they in-fused personal gestures with political meaning. Their first priority was an unstructured existence in Greenwich Village. They wanted to establish an open community ba$ed on social and sexual equality that could serve as a model for the rest of society. But expectations exceeded opportunities and capabilities.

Villagers acclaimed private acts of rebellion as significant attacks on conventional values. They congratulated themselves on their ability to enjoy life on scanty resources. In contrast to the materialistic middle class, they could appreciate simple pleasures—riding the Staten Island Ferry, taking a double-decker bus uptown, and making love in Central Park.[1] Harry Kemp believed that he and his friends "were doing something fine and radical" by swimming in the nude: they were liberating themselves from the "stupid codes" of ordinary people who were "ashamed and afraid" of the human body.[2] Floyd Dell thought it in-genious that a small group of painters and poets played "Up Jenkins," a "noisy, rowdy, childish" game, until dawn in Polly's restaurant. Behavior that departed from the usual pattern, staying up late or keeping irregular hours, seemed daring and was celebrated as a triumph over respectabil-ity. Dell boasted that Villagers played with "such gay and riotous aban-don" that they incurred the disapproval of "sober middle-class people." The spectacle of Villagers amusing themselves without money "enraged the virtuous bourgeois." But the impulse to have fun and violate tradi-tional mores made the rebels, Dell admitted, "incurably frivolous."[3]

Other Villagers were less enthralled by bohemian experiences. Harold E. Stearns, a Harvard-educated journalist, recalled that he lived "the characteristic pot-boiling existence of the time," but with "few of the proper ingredients to put into the pot." Stearns picked up publicity jobs and "played poker well enough" to supplement his income. Credit was available especially at the Hotel Lafayette where one could sit and talk with Villagers, "both the unsuccessful and the indigent hopefuls, without it costing very much." But, Stearns remembered, survival was a draining experience: "The constant worry as how to 'get by' would be enough to make anyone jumpy and irascible, let alone one with a rather high-strung temperament." Dell also admitted that a bohemian existence could be difficult. He described the fate of "Paul," a reporter who had "rashly thrown up a good newspaper job" to write short stories. Paul's "precarious and uncertain living," aggravated by "having too many love-affairs at one time," had resulted in "economic and emotional wretchedness."[4] For some, at least, poverty was as much misery as revelry.

Stearns abandoned a career in journalism to live in the Village because he wanted to withdraw from society. Others arrived with ambitious plans only to learn that a bohemian life did not confer discipline and talent. Dell described a fictionalized character, Dirck, as one of "those tragic-comic figures of whom the Village had its due share — a writer who did not write."[5] The enjoyment of rebellious gestures, sexual affairs, and bohemian activities distracted Villagers from artistic and intellectual pursuits. Social influences were too numerous and personal conflicts too demanding for most Villagers to achieve their goals. But under the best conditions, there would have been limits to what ordinary talents could hope to accomplish. At least the Village offered an alternative for those who disliked the restrictions of respectability.

The public or ideal image of the Village emphasized its classlessness and harmony. In 1916, Floyd Dell proclaimed that the Village was a community enjoying intimacy, curiosity, and friendly gossip. Unlike the oppressive villages of conventional society, bohemia was free, open, and "kindly."[6] Whereas small-town gossip and rigid moral standards curtailed freedom and individuality, Greenwich Village offered the advantages of communal life with none of its liabilities.

Other evidence indicates, however, that Villagers had trouble establishing a tolerant and supportive environment. After living in the Village several years, journalist Griffin Barry confessed to Mary Heaton Vorse: "I've been wanting to get away from that circle of grinning wrecks in the Village for so long. It's a humiliating fact, this not being able to avoid preying and being preyed on by a community."[7] In his fictionalized autobiography, More Miles, Harry Kemp described one poet who had grown to "hate" the "shifts and pitiable subterfuges of the Bohemian life." When Randolph Bourne moved to the Village in 1915, he enthusiastically endorsed bohemia as one of "the cornerstones of his intellectual world."[8] But two years later he reported to a friend that "Greenwich Village [w]as a poisonous place which destroys the souls, even of the super Villagers like ourselves."[9] Floyd Dell eventually concurred with Bourne's assessment. Having endured the tiresome company of idlers, Dell was "almost willing" to return to the town from which he had originally "made his escape so gladly."[10]

If, as former Masses cartoonist Kenneth R. Chamberlain says, the Village was originally a "homogeneous" community with "some talented off-beats" like poet Maxwell Bodenheim, Harry Kemp, and Hippolyte Havel, it did not remain unified.[11] Artists and writers split into cliques that sometimes were at odds with one another. These groups in turn were factionalized by personal preferences and conflicts. Despite common participation in *The Masses,* the Liberal Club, and the Provincetown Players, Villagers could not maintain a sense of solidarity.

Although the Village aspired to become an egalitarian colony, a rudimentary social hierarchy emerged. Floyd Dell recalled that upon his arrival in 1913 the Village elite decided that he was a promising candidate for their group. Anxious to be admitted, he allowed himself to be schooled by Village "aunts," who were "familiar with Village history," knew "all about everyone," and were "intent upon maintaining community standards." His "aunt," a leading member of "the Village intelligentsia," disapproved of the "bohemian riff-raff" and warned him to avoid their company or face the threat of ostracism.[12]

Dell was not a college graduate and had not published a novel, but he had literary ambitions, knew important Villagers, and seemed destined for success. If he worked hard and made a name for himself, Dell recalled mockingly, he might "assist the upward march of humanity," acquire a house in the country, and become one of the *"real* Villagers" who "paid their bills and bathed regularly." Those Villagers, he wrote,

> were schoolteachers, college professors, social workers, doctors, lawyers, engineers and other professional people. As for the artists and writers—such as John Sloan and Art Young, Mary Heaton Vorse, Inez Haynes Gillmore, Susan Glaspell, Theodore Dreiser—they already had positions of importance in the realm of art and letters. . . . They had most of the familiar middle-class virtues and in addition some of their own; they were an obviously superior lot of people.[13]

Dell claimed that all Villagers of "intellectual distinction" and some "who had artistic talent belonged to the socially superior group." Those who worked for or contributed to *The Masses* included themselves among the select. Eastman told Norman Thomas that he had to fight "off the encroachment of Greenwich Village's provincialism on *The Masses* from the beginning." Eastman maintained that the staff's dedication to socialism gave *The Masses* "a distinctly anti-Bohemian tenor."[14]

Dell argued that the upper crust wanted Villagers to observe certain standards of propriety, especially in regard to sexual behavior. According to their code, "one's sexual impulses were indulged, not impulsively or at random," but with taste and discretion. Dell admitted that members of the elite referred to some bohemians "as pigs or bums" regardless of their talents. Slovenly appearance and excessive promiscuity could, therefore, result in social exclusion. In spite of its radical aspirations, the Village was in some respects a subculture of middle class professionals who rejected both ostentatious materialism and, as Dell put it, "disorderly, pig-style, lunatic bohemianism."[15]

According to Dell, the date of arrival in the Village also became a measure of social prestige; those who arrived the earliest received the higher ratings. By 1916, Dell claimed, a "new Village had come into existence." Since he and Marjorie Jones had arrived in 1913, they were considered "among its first families." High status, however, entailed informal restraints on his behavior; he was expected to shun the new "immigrants," composed mostly of young people with "uncertain or unproved talents—or perhaps no real talents, but only artistic temperaments." When he became involved with a girl from this forbidden group, his affair was "subjected to a thorough and ruthless ostracism." Dell was not denied admission to the upper reaches of Village society, but his "sweetheart was not welcome there." In addition, Dell encountered hostility from the newcomers who judged him "one of the pillars of a hated Village orthodoxy." He was shocked to learn that they viewed his beloved *Masses* as "tame, old-fogy, stupidly conservative."[16]

Standards are necessary in any community to define social boundaries and provide stability. The Village intended to reduce rules to a minimum so that nothing would interfere with artistic endeavor or personal freedom. But if Dell's analysis is valid, Village rebels created their own social distinctions. Although Villagers rejected the crassness of business civilization, they reproduced stratification in their group.

The chance to escape from repression drew men and women to the Village, and romance became an essential element of the community. In comparison with conventional society, the Village appeared to be an island of freedom. Men and women were encouraged to seek out each other's company and interact as equals. Village morality proclaimed the joys of sex, defended birth control, and condemned the state's attempt to regulate sexual behavior. The Village intended to promote private happiness at the expense of public sham.

Isadora Duncan, the tunic-covered, bare-footed inventor of modern dance, symbolized the liberated woman who discarded social restraints. The Village revered Isadora as a Greek goddess freeing the dance and womankind from the burden of tradition. Her free-form dancing and flowing costumes were emblematic of women's liberation. Max Eastman said that Isadora and the young women in her troupe generated an "exaltation . . . that nothing else on stage had ever produced," and he was "passionately desirous of them."[17] For Eastman and other men, emancipation promised exciting companions for romance and rebellion. For them, the ideal woman had artistic talent and ambition; she was independent, daring, and wise about worldly affairs. Bobbed-haired women in casual attire were viewed as the vanguard of a more egalitarian society.

Many women migrated to Greenwich Village because it offered the opportunity to enjoy privileges usually reserved for men. A woman could smoke in public, drink in bars, and entertain men alone in her apartment. The informal atmosphere encouraged women to discard traditional norms in dress and behavior. "Here," Art Young related, "a woman could say 'damn' right out loud and still be respected."[18] Women were no longer custodians of morality, and the art of seduction was not restricted to men.

The traditional association of morality and taste with feminity generated in some women a rejection of middle class culture. The desire to be on her own and escape Mississippi plantation society brought Mary Kimbrough to the Village. "I realized by now that I did not like parasitic women. I was one myself, but I did not want to continue to be one."[19] In bohemia, Mary could dissociate herself from traditional roles. Similarly, Max Eastman described his wife, Ida Rauh, as a "truant from a family of rich Jews who lived uptown behind a brownstone front." Ida "renounced so hotly all the frills and luxuries of bourgeois life that she lived almost like a pauper" in the Village.[20] Ida and other women searched for a more meaningful standard of personal worth. They hoped that Villagers would accept this deeper self-estimation. They discovered, however, that physical beauty still mattered to liberated men. Henrietta Rodman angrily told Harry Kemp: "We choose our partners for their capabilities—but, as far as I've been able to observe, it's what you males call 'chickens'—pretty insipid girls that you choose as wives and sweethearts."

There were women who only wanted to find adventure and to mingle with artists. Ken Chamberlain recalled that Jewish girls from the Lower East Side took up with Village artists: "They were just daughters of little tradespeople; they weren't anything [sic] unusual, but they had warmth and sympathy."[21] A superficial engagement in bohemian life was sufficient for women sampling Village experiences. Harry Kemp described some of them as being of a "sequestered, demure cast—the kind who longed for life but never got into it":

They were generally of impoverished but genteel families; they dabbled a trifle in art, in poetry, in dramatics; they affected tall candles burning in heavily curtained rooms while day, unheeded, went on without [sic]; they received their friends in large, high-ceilinged rooms of old houses where massed chandeliers still hung in hundreds of glittering crystals.[22]

Kemp's portrayal of feminine dilettantes was corroborated by Michael Gold's story of an incident involving John Reed, an idol of Village women. Reed was sitting in the Brevoort Hotel on the night of his return from Russia when a "red-haired, moon pale, young actress" greeted him from her table:

'Hello, Jack,' she called, languidly.
'Hello,'
'I don't think I've seen you lately, Jack. What've you been doing?'
'I've been to Russia.'
'Why Russia?'
'There's a revolution there!'
'A revolution? I see. Was it interesting Jack?'[23]

In the minds of Village rebels, sex was the most carefully guarded taboo of the Victorian world; they considered, therefore, the rebellion against sexual conventions to be a revolutionary act. Besides, poets were thought to have a special need for love affairs; Harry Kemp insisted that he needed women for his "body," "soul," and "poetic inspiration."[24] Isolated from the social and economic problems of American society, the Villager could more easily rank sexual freedom with economic justice. For some, the pursuit of personal whims and sexual gratification represented the extent of their revolt.

Conventional morality dictated that women remain virginal until marriage and monogamous afterwards. Since society viewed men as animalistic, women were supposed to remain chaste in order to sanctify the home and family. Villagers, however, concluded that glorifying women as civilizing agents placed barriers between the sexes and denied women the chance for self-fulfillment. Village rebels demanded an end to feminine prudery, especially since birth-control measures were readily available.[25] If a girl should feel inhibited and guilty about premarital sex, Village men used various ploys and alcohol to get them into bed. Arguments from Edward Carpenter, Havelock Ellis, and other "modern prophets" were advanced to show, Dell recalled, that "love without marriage was infinitely superior to the other kind, and that its indulgence brought the world, night by night, a little nearer to freedom and Utopia." Dell claimed that he never resorted to trickery; he offered "companionship, talk, laughter, poetry," and picnic lunches "to salve a girl's conscience."[26]

Much of the Village's sexual ideology was derived from anarchist tenets that stressed individual freedom in sexual relations. Men and women, it was argued, should be allowed to live together without the approval of church or state. While free love combatted sexual repression, it was not supposed to promote promiscuity. The Village accepted sex as something natural, a pleasure to be indulged in without reproductive intentions. Sexual intercourse represented the highest form of communication and should be experienced only when sanctified by love. Hutchins Hapgood told Mary Heaton Vorse: "You feel very keenly the over-emphasis which the Puritan puts on the sexual act. He sees sex as just in that. The wide human permeating effect of sex he ignores."[27] In the war against lust and repression, Villagers intended to combine the "spiritual" with the "physical."[28]

Although Villagers expected sexual freedom to elevate relations between men and women, they could not insure that sexual intercourse would be more than physical gratification. The heroine in Dorothy Day's autobiographical novel says: "Anything short of absolute promiscuity is disregarded as long as you can speak of sexual relationships as love affairs." In theory the Village wished to free individual emotions from the tyranny of laws and social conventions; in practice it accentuated a preoccupation with sex and personal relations. Dorothy Day commented in her novel:

When they gossip you hear them say, 'Haven't you heard the latest. Beatrice has left Charlie, or do you think he left her. And now she's living with Bertram. I wonder how long it will last—Oh, wasn't she the one who lived with Jim Albright for three years.'
Or if you mention the name of some woman, somebody immediately speaks up—'Who is she living with now?'[29]

Despite its shocking connotations, free love was supposed to strengthen, not destroy, monogamy. The search for a perfect mate and, as Mary Heaton Vorse said, "the inner significance and mystery" of love, made sexual encounters necessary. Floyd Dell, who lived with several women, argued that "no matter how cynical our words or how apparently frivolous our actions, there was the ancient mutual if unconfessed desire for a permanently enduring relationship."[30] Testing compatibility before marriage vindicated the preservation of an institution men had traditionally misused. The heightened sensitivity to the privacy of marriage indicated how little community and family considerations counted in such unions. Decisions about potential mates no longer underwent parental scrutiny or approbation; even the ritual of courtship was greatly curtailed or discarded.

In some cases free love became indistinguishable from marriage. Floyd Dell recalled how the breaking up of his "illegal domesticity" with Marjorie Jones caused a shock amongst prominent circles in the Village: "Although there were those men in the Village who indulged in passing love affairs, something better was expected of me. . . . I was, though I had not realized it, an example to newcomers, one who could be pointed out as proof of emotional stability in our little world."[31] That the Village attached so much significance to one affair suggests that Dell's two-year relationship was the exception rather than the rule. It also indicates how respectable Villagers used conventional standards to distinguish themselves from promiscuous bohemians. Free love relationships were assessed on traditional grounds — the most valued were those that endured while the transitory were used to carry Village gossip.

To separate "true love" from other considerations, one entered into a relationship that could be terminated when one "fell out of love." Whether married or simply living together, partners were theoretically free to form new relationships whenever the impulse moved them. An affair was a means of testing the original relationship. "Strenuous lovers," Hapgood recounted, violated "all sex conventions in order to purify and strengthen the essential spiritual bond."[32] Partners were supposed to tell lovers or husbands of their unfaithfulness, for honesty and sexual equality, presumed to be uncommon in conventional society, were acclaimed as bohemian virtues. If a man or a woman took up with someone else, the mate was expected not to raise objections or become jealous because that was considered conventional. In practice, tolerance about infidelities was rare; individuals experimented, feelings were hurt, objections were lodged, and divorces or break-ups ensued.

Despite his adherence to anarchism, Hippolyte Havel remonstrated violently when Polly Holladay had affairs with other men. His emotional explosions sometimes led to physical abuse of Polly.[33] Nonetheless, their stormy and destructive relationship continued. At one point Polly complained to Hapgood that Hippolyte had not yet committed suicide: "He promised me over and again, but he just won't keep his word."[34] Similarly, Christine Ell, a bohemian restaurateur, told Hapgood how the relationship with her husband, Louis, drove her to adulterous affairs:

> Why is it that I must act as I do? I long to have a perfect lover, one that satisfies me. [Louis] doesn't know how to express himself to me. . . . It is only when he is jealous that he can express himself, and I want him to be near me all the time, and he cannot. When I see how far

away he is, I cannot stand it. I try to console myself with other men, but he, Louis, is always there in my thought, standing between me and them and making it impossible for me to realize the dream of my life, of an utter sympathy with some man. So I hurt him all the time, yet I know too that I help and stimulate him, that through me life is richer and more interesting to him.[35]

These conflicts might be dismissed as simply examples of neurotic behavior. If so, troubled individuals found a community in which they freely acted out their conflicts and pursued an active sexual life. While the most extravagant and colorful affairs were conducted by "off-beat" personalities, the behavior of the Ells, Havel, and Polly Holladay was not unique. Not only did the Village tolerate interpersonal conflicts, but the atmosphere and ideology encouraged its prevalence. Out of a desire to debunk conventions, the Village praised behavior that others believed destructive.

Frenetic quests for love and companionship were commonplace and the Village offered opportunities for romance. In raising hopes about the possibility of discovering an ideal partner, Villagers intensified their preoccupation with one another. Exaggerated expectations undoubtedly spurred some individuals to avoid permanent relationships. Idealistic notions caused men and women to put less effort into resolving the difficulties besetting marriages and love affairs. Instead, individuals sought a solution with someone "new." Harry Kemp, who called himself an "incurable" monogamist despite his involvement with numerous women, remembered the pain and boredom he endured in a fruitless search for the perfect girl:

Around and about on the continual, hopeless quest I whirled, seeking in every group I knew, a woman's intimate companionship . . . running hectically to parties . . . drinking, debating, philandering, reading aloud my latest poems; enduring the companionship of people whom I did not even like—all to alleviate the misery of my solitariness,—to find, perhaps this time, in some woman, more than a passing affair . . . a woman, the beautiful, golden-haired creature that obsessed the dreams of all my imagination.[36]

Kemp charged about the Village as a vagabond poet and irreverent bohemian seeking extraordinary lovers. His hope, that salvation could be attained in a relationship, was un-exceptional. Unable to find meaning and fulfillment in conventional arrangements, Villagers overemphasized personal relations.

Feminism became part of the bohemian ideology as romantic ideals merged with reformist urges. Men and women, eager for liberating experiences, called for a loosening of formal restraints. Unlike socialism, feminism seemingly presented a set of beliefs Villagers could implement amongst themselves. Insularity enhanced a fascination with interpersonal relations, which feminism promised to improve. Village men and women proclaimed their allegiance to feminist goals without fully understanding what that encompassed.

Given the heated opposition of conventional males to changes in the status of women, Village men exulted in their acceptance of women into the community. Dell argued that "men who were more interested in success than in ideas had but the slightest capacity for boon companionship" with the modern woman. Whereas the capitalist only wanted a "domestic prisoner" to cheer him up after business hours, Village men ("unsuccessful idealists") offered "sympathy and understanding to women who desired a life outside the home."[37] Since they were not employed in regular occupations, Village rebels had more time to spend with women.

In the early years Villagers shared a common optimism about the feminist movement. Men and women assumed that they were comrades fighting for the same ideals. Although women's suffrage and career opportunities gained widespread support in the Village, many men thought that social and sexual emancipation was the most important issue. This emphasis blurred the broader implications of feminism and brought to the movement male advocates whose commitment was as much to freedom for themselves as freedom for women.

Although confusion initially promoted a sense of solidarity, it became increasingly apparent that there were differences of opinion and significant gaps between theory and practice. Village men interpreted feminism as freedom from domestic roles and the expansion of artistic and professional careers. They thought that domesticity and capitalism were mainly responsible for female bondage. Since these rebels had little to do with patriarchal families or economic exploitation, they viewed themselves as liberators. They were, therefore, somewhat surprised and dumbfounded when women accused them of violating feminist principles. Some men protested their innocence, others reacted with hostility. But Village men failed to realize that they expected women to conform to their ideals of femininity.

Max Eastman considered himself a feminist even though he did not contribute or publish much in defense of the movement. Moreover, he criticized *The Woman Rebel,* a feminist journal, for displaying "a style of over-conscious extremism and blare of rebellion for its own sake." He particularly disliked the empty-headed "babydoll" or the "repressed and petty-minded" mother who "handed on, to sons and daughters alike, the limitations of her nature." He thought that a woman's involvement in community affairs would enhance her experience and intelligence. He maintained that liberation would somehow alter hereditary characteristics and change "the very kind of descendants we generate."[38] Eastman implied that rearing a family was the woman's most important task.

Harry Kemp called himself a feminist because he advocated sexual liberation. Like other Village rebels, he bragged of never having sex with a prostitute.[39] To his disappointment, however, he discovered that feminism did not mean the end of sexual dependency on women. He complained to Henrietta Rodman:

> Oh, you damned women don't know how we men suffer for lack of you —such of us as try to be good Radicals—such of us as don't have recourse to prostitutes—those amongst us who also detest the long, devious, hypocritic [sic], diplomatic sex-pursuit you drag us pitilessly through.[40]

Given Kemp's self-centered desire for compliant sexual partners, it is not surprising or unfair that feminists became disenchanted with their masculine allies.

Harold Stearns attested to the fact that some Villagers relied upon women for economic survival. Stearns found a girl, a fashion artist, and "she made more than her share of what was needed to keep up the semblance of a menage":

> She bought everything; she prepared some of my meals; she paid the bills and saw to it that I had new clothes when my old ones could not any longer be repaired—and all of this, as if it were the most natural thing in the world.[41]

If a woman undertook the role of breadwinner, her mate was supposed to apply himself to artistic endeavors. But men without talent or dedication accepted economic support from their lovers. Floyd Dell recalled disdainfully that "any tenth-rate free-verse poet could find a capable and efficient stenographer to type his manuscripts, buy his clothes, pay his rent, and sleep with him."[42]

Floyd Dell deplored the insincere lovemaking of other men because premarital sex often aroused guilt feelings in women. But the amount of mental anguish, depended to a large extent on the individuals involved. There were women who indulged in liaisons without fear or remorse. Edna St. Vincent Millay had numerous affairs with men who wildly competed for her affections. Alice Palmer, Hapgood reported, took pride in "the passionate vehemence of her unfaithfulness."[43] One female character, Billy, (inspired by Peggy Baird) in Dorothy Day's novel argued:

> 'Sex is a barrier between men and women keeping them from a complete understanding of one another. Barriers are made to be broken down. . . . Once there are no barriers and men don't want to get something out of women in the way of sex, there is complete freedom between the sexes.'[44]

If women, 'Billy' suggested, would discard chastity, they could end the cat and mouse game in which aggressive men pursued an elusive prey.

Some women, however, were unable to abandon the traditional sentiment that women were pure creatures defiled by men. Henrietta Rodman accused Village men of imposing on "the hearts and affections" of women who were trying to "live up to the new freedom of sex."[45] In her view, men used free-love unions to satisfy their sexual appetites. This attitude inspired a feminist revulsion against sexual gratification. According to Hapgood,

> women of character and personal charm and beauty, although they felt the quality of men and had their husbands and lovers like other women, yet felt that in so doing they were merely gratifying some of their commonplace instincts.[46]

In some instances, sexual attitudes came full circle: liberation produced a resurgence of "puritanical" attitudes.

Feminist propositions made women more self-conscious and more sensitive to real and perceived instances of male exploitation. Village feminists saw men, not patriarchy, as the cause of sexual injustice. Hapgood claimed that feminism persuaded Neith and other wives to demand "freedom from the ideal of monogamy." There were separations, he reported, especially after the War, "when something like sexual demoralization took place in the community."[47] Whether feminism promoted prudery or promiscuity, it contributed to the confusion of Village life and exacerbated personal relations.

Feminism was not a monolithic movement. If Henrietta Rodman denounced "free love," Margaret Sanger thought the abolition of marriage was essential for the liberation of women. There were women who did not need feminism to awaken their resentment of men. Some women liked to compete against and surpass their male rivals. Journalist Inez Haynes Gillmore confessed that she was jealous of men: "I am always comparing them with women, trying to prove to myself that some of their obvious superiorities are purely adventitious." In embarking on a career in journalism, Inez gained admission to worlds inhabited and dominated by men. When she forced her way into a boxing match, breaking the restrictions of conventional femininity, she found the experience exhilarating and commended herself for not showing alarm "at the sight of blood":

> One gets thrilling impressions, first of power and skill, then of courage and an extraordinary capacity for taking punishment. And as for beauty, again . . . I got that effect of a Greek frieze suddenly come to life, of two wonderful machines, perfectly adjusted, which had for driving-power something quicker than thought—intuition.[48]

A woman who could savor the brutal spectacle of two men fighting like harnessed machines was likely to deal with men on her own terms.

In Hapgood's view, Village men, "even the most advanced of them," suffered from "the woman's full assumption" of male privileges. The freedom of bohemian life, he maintained, brought out "the greater naturalness of woman's instinct." In the Village,

> she shows herself as indeed a part of nature. She remains herself, as does nature, in the recurring years, often with a new lover, leaving not even a memory of the old. . . . She had the power and the primitiveness of the earth. Woe to the more artificial male, dependent on the unconsciously remembered past and on willful desire to maintain the impossible structure of civilization—woe to this delicate spiritual organization if he gets in her way.[49]

To Hapgood's way of thinking, sexual roles had been reversed. Liberated women supplanted Victorian males while overrefined men emerged as the psychological descendants of the domesticated female.

Hapgood maintained that the feminist movement degenerated into a conflict between men and women. He believed that "The Heterodoxy," a club for "suffragists and professional women," was "moving toward the unknown hoped-for world of feminine predominance." Other men agreed with him. Initially Randolph Bourne had been sympathetic to the plight of women in American society. In his first book, *Youth and Life* (1913), Bourne denounced the prejudice against a girl performing useful work in society and called for the liberation of women:

> It is imperative that a girl be prevented from growing up into a useless, fleshy, and trivial woman, of the type one sees so much of nowadays. . . . The world never needed so much as it does today women of large

hearts and large minds, whose home and sphere are capable of embracing
something beyond the four corners of their kitchen.[50]

Bourne's assault on a social system that frustrated female maturity
predisposed him to bohemianism. Shortly thereafter he visited the
Village and discovered women who had thrown off the burdens of tradition. He liked what he saw, calling them "a most delightful group of
young women of decidedly emancipated and advanced" opinions. He
shared his enthusiasm with a friend:

> They are of course all self-supporting and independent, and they
> enjoy the adventure of life; the full, radiant, audacious way in which
> they go about makes you wonder if the new woman isn't to be a very
> splendid sort of person.[51]

He thought that these women would restore "equality and cam[a]raderie
and frank hearty delight in personality and all the charm, physiological
and spiritual, that goes with it."[52] The Village seemingly provided a community that freed women from domestic roles and nurtured their
development.

By 1916, Village experiences had eroded Bourne's optimism. In a fictional story, "Karen," Bourne revealed his disillusionment with the "new"
species and feminism. Karen, an attractive college girl, was more interested in males "as co-actors in a personal drama of her own devising
than as lovers or even as men." Gradually her attitude toward men
became bitter and paranoid. Feminism, Bourne concluded, had the effect
of intensifying her anti-masculine tendencies. "She was intimate with
feminists whose feminism had done little more for their emotional life
than to make them acutely conscious of the cloven hoof of the male."[53]
Detecting instances of male cruelty and releasing women from the bondage of marriage had become her personal crusade.

Bourne's disillusionment paralleled the reaction of other Village men.
Any man, Harry Kemp observed sourly, who "prated glibly of any ready
solution, orthodox or heterodox, radical or conventional, of the problems
of the relationships between men and women was worse than a fool, he
was a dangerous madman."[54] Floyd Dell reached a similar conclusion. He
had seen the harm caused by a "theory of marriage which genially encouraged outside love affairs," and he had experienced the pain and
frustration of "trial marriages."[55] He realized that "their feminism and
ours was unconsciously different," for women had gone beyond the wish
to be liberated "playfellows"; they wanted to be free of male hegemony.
"We were," he wrote,

annoyed by what seemed to us (though we gallantly denied the possibility of such a thing) an anti-masculine flavor in this later feminist spirit . . . . It was not the masculine cigarette they wanted so much as the abrogation of the masculine right to boss women around and tell them what they should and should not do.[56]

After assuming the responsibilities of marriage and fatherhood, Dell was critical of Village men, whom he accused of living "a prolonged holiday," in which "triviality" dominated their work and love affairs. Since men "weren't doing a damn thing" to improve conditions for women, he understood why feminists "went off by themselves in Women's Clubs to plot votes for women, factory legislation, and equal pay for equal work."[57]

If bohemian men harbored a narrow view of women's emancipation, the same criticism could be leveled against their female companions, who seldom immersed themselves in the larger movement for women's rights. This self-centeredness was reflected in Henrietta Rodman's plan for a "feminist apartment house," which would replace the patriarchal family with a more equitable arrangement. Owned cooperatively by the resident families, the apartment complex would have a staff of women trained in "mothercraft" to do the housekeeping, mending, washing, cooking, and baby-sitting. Since these "experts" would also feed, care for, and educate the children in the basement and on the roof, professional women could be freed from the burdens of child-rearing and the drudgery of housework. By relegating her children to the basement, the professional woman could retain her career. Henrietta argued that this organization would produce a more efficient family situation because "intelligent mothering" would supplant traditional "instinctive mothering." Instead of expending her time and energy on the child's physical well-being, the modern mother would act as a companion to the child. Calling housework a science would not, however, eliminate poor pay and low status for trained servant-girls. But for Henrietta, feminism was "a movement by women of the upper classes to save their own souls."[58]

Feminism was supposed to liberate Villagers from old-fashioned attitudes and establish open, trusting relationships between men and women. But there was no consensus on feminist goals and few rebels of either sex were capable of equality. As the differences between masculine and feminine views emerged, more discord was injected into the community. Instead of joining Villagers together in a common struggle, feminism heightened distrust and undermined social harmony.

Although Greenwich Villagers held diverse views on art and politics, they agreed that the individual should be liberated. To this end, they en-

couraged artistic freedom, violated conventional mores, and supported a
radical reorganization of society. Their goals, however, were never in-
tegrated into a coherent program, and little thought was given to the
problems of implementation. Although they assumed that self-expression
contributed to social reform, the history of the Village illustrates the conflict between living uproariously and working for political objectives.

By acting out a revolt against respectability, Villagers confirmed their
bohemian identity and generated a feeling of solidarity. Rebellious
gestures expressed a desire for freedom and a generalized hostility
toward prevailing rules. But Villagers overrated the significance of defiant behavior and underestimated its harmful effects. Free love and informal dress advertised the Village as a playground for the uninhibited.
The community became notorious for high jinks and sexual freedom instead of cultural achievement and radical politics. Given the conservatism of the populace and the power of established authority, it was
perhaps not so important that Villagers expend their energy in futile attempts to restructure and enlighten society. They might, however, have
been more serious about developing social criticism.

Existing without customs, institutions, family ties, and communal
responsibilities, bohemians inhabited a world that responded to intellectual fashions, artistic fads, and group pressures. Villagers were not so
much artistic innovators as they were popularizers of avant-garde
culture. Inspired by the bohemian ideal of unlimited freedom, they were
attracted to ideas that seemed to support liberation and offend conventional sensibilities. Village rebels propagated watered-down versions of
Freudian psychology and Marxian economics and ignored the work of
European social scientists, for example, Max Weber and Emile Durkheim.
Fascinated by symbolic gestures, Villagers overlooked the importance of
institutions and power. For all their sensitivity to social repression, they
preferred to denounce industrial and financial magnates instead of exposing the system that produced them. They lacked the information and
interest to formulate a penetrating critique of American business and its
practices. Their most important insights were simply intuitive, a sense
that much was wrong with society without an adequate understanding of
the causes.

In creating an enclave for nonconformists, Villagers expanded the
limits of behavior for men and women. Advocating private values over
public conventions, they affirmed the dignity and meaning of personal
life and suggested that there could be a purpose greater than the mere
accumulation of money. The emphasis on individual gratification over
familial and public responsibilities, the celebration of leisure over work,

and the preference for psychology over religion, in some measure foreshadowed the values of contemporary America. Their revolt against middle-class culture extended the diversity of American society and established a tradition of bohemian rebelliousness. Village rebels provided a mythology of immense importance to subsequent generations of youthful dissidents who wished to express their dissatisfaction and experiment with a freer mode of existence.

Even as the Village attracted more newcomers after the armistice, many of the first bohemians left the community. Max Eastman and John Reed pursued a revolutionary movement in Communist Russia, Hutchins Hapgood sought intimate friendships outside the Village, George Cook exiled himself to Greece, and Floyd Dell repudiated bohemianism for a more conventional life in Croton. Their departures signalled a disenchantment with bohemia. Originally they came to the Village anticipating that this community would appreciate their talents and support achievement in the arts. They hoped to make friends and fall in love with rebels who shared their ideals. They wanted to participate in the rebellion against traditional culture and overthrow the economic system that supported it. Extravagant expectations were bound to result in disappointment, especially for individuals who disliked compromise and ordinary accomplishments.

Although these rebels did not perceive it, their dissatisfaction was largely of their own doing. The goal of self-fulfillment was impossible for individuals whose pursuit of unbridled fantasies precluded a reasonable assessment of their talents and objectives. Political reform demanded a commitment that was inconsistent with the self-centered existence of bohemian radicals. The creation of an open and supportive colony required some sacrifice of individual interests to the needs of the group. But these five rebels from the provinces refused to impose restrictions on their behavior. Having learned in childhood that fantasies could protect them against loneliness and rejection, they were unwilling to relinquish or discipline their dreams. On the contrary, they celebrated self-gratification as a praiseworthy attack on social repression. The deficiency in their vision was not in wanting to replace conventional society with a better one, but in failing to see the magnitude of the task.

NOTES

1. Floyd Dell, "Out of the World," in *Looking At Life* (New York, 1924), p. 67.
2. Harry Kemp, *More Miles: An Autobiographical Novel* (New York, 1926), p. 309.

3. Floyd Dell, "The Rise of Greenwich Village," in *Love in Greenwich Village* (New York, 1926), p. 34. Dell, "Out of the World," p. 67.

4. Harold E. Stearns, *The Street I Know*, p. 126-129. Floyd Dell, "The Fall of Greenwich Village," in *Love in Greenwich Village*, pp. 307-308.

5. Floyd Dell, "The Rise of Greenwich Village," p. 36.

6. Floyd Dell, "Out of the World," p. 66.

7. Letter, Griffin Barry to Mary Heaton Vorse (October 16, 1916), Vorse Papers, Wayne State University Library.

8. Kemp, *More Miles*, p. 351. Letter, Randolph Bourne to Carl Zigrosser (September 12, 1915), Bourne Papers, Columbia University Library.

9. Letter, Randolph Bourne to Ester Cornell (August 10, 1917), Bourne Papers.

10. Floyd Dell, "Should A Young Writer Live in Greenwich Village?" undated, unpublished essay, Dell Papers, Newberry Library, Chicago.

11. Letter, K. R. Chamberlain to Robert Humphrey (March 18, 1974).

12. Floyd Dell, "Rents Were Low in Greenwich Village," *American Mercury* (December 1974), pp. 662-668.

13. *Ibid.*, p. 663. Harry Kemp recounted that a distinction existed between poor and prosperous Villagers. He was among those writers and artists, living in Patchin Place and [Milligan] Place, who were not "able to afford, unless invited, to spend their summers out of the City. They stayed on in New York, during the stifling months, scraping along, as in Fall and winter, on book-reviewing or by holding their day-long or part-time jobs." *More Miles*, p. 346.

14. Letter, Max Eastman to Norman Thomas, quoted in *Enjoyment of Living*, p. 548.

15. Dell, *Homecoming*, pp. 279-280, p. 148.

16. *Ibid.*, pp. 280-281.

17. Max Eastman, *Enjoyment of Living*, p. 266.

18. Art Young, *On My Way: Being the Book of Art Young in Text and Picture* (New York, 1928), p. 129.

19. Mary Kimbrough Sinclair, *Southern Belle* (New York, 1957), p. 76.

20. Max Eastman, *Enjoyment of Living*, p. 266.

21. K. R. Chamberlain, interviewed by Richard Fitzgerald (August 10, 1966).

22. Harry Kemp, *More Miles*, p. 361.

23. Michael Gold, "The Masses Tradition," *Masses and Mainstream*, Vol. 4 (August 1951), pp. 51-52.

24. Harry Kemp, *More Miles*, p. 132.

25. Greenwich Village was probably the best informed community in America on birth-control measures — condoms and diaphragms were the most popular devices. Conversation with K. R. Chamberlain (May 1976). If an unplanned pregnancy occurred, an abortionist could be secured. Of the central figures, only Mary Heaton Vorse gave birth to a child out of wedlock, and she subsequently married the father, Joe O'Brien.

26. Floyd Dell, *Homecoming*, pp. 288-289.

27. Undated letter, Hutchins Hapgood to Mary H. Vorse, Vorse Papers.

28. Randolph Bourne expressed this sentiment in a letter to Henry Elasser: "It is only because this Puritanical Policy of repression brings everybody up to an idea of the complete divorce of the spiritual and the physical, to a 'nice' girl as all spiritual. . . and of the prostitute as all physical that the double life is possible." (October 18, 1913), Bourne Papers.

29. Dorothy Day, *The Eleventh Virgin*, p. 167.

30. Floyd Dell, *Intellectual Vagabondage: An Apology for the Intelligentsia* (New York, 1926, p. 161).

31. Dell, *Homecoming,* p. 279.
32. Hutchins Hapgood, *The Story of a Lover,* p. 105.
33. Conversation with K. R. Chamberlain (May 1976).
34. Quoted by Hutchins Hapgood, *A Victorian in the Modern World,* p. 318.
35. *Ibid.,* p. 424.
36. Kemp, *More Miles,* p. 256.
37. Dell, *Intellectual Vagabondage,* p. 166.
38. Max Eastman, "Confession of a Suffrage Orator," *The Masses* (October-November 1915), pp. 8-9. Eastman, "Revolutionary Birth-Control," *The Masses* (July 1915), pp. 22-23. Eastman, "Inez Milholland," *The Masses* (March 1917), p. 22.
39. Ironically, however, Kemp idealized street-walkers as "ignorant working girls clutching at romance." He believed that the city's "special Vice Squad" employed "well-dressed, contemptible young agents to entrap girls who "didn't come across with enough graft." *More Miles,* p. 235.
40. *Ibid.*
41. Harold Stearns, *The Street I Know,* p. 127.
42. Dell, *Homecoming,* p. 288.
43. Hapgood, *A Victorian in the Modern World,* p. 321.
44. Dorothy Day, *The Eleventh Virgin,* p. 120.
45. Harry Kemp, *More Miles,* p. 94.
46. Hapgood, *A Victorian in the Modern World,* p. 377.
47. *Ibid.,* p. 395.
48. Inez Haynes Gillmore, "A Woman at a Prizefight," *The Century Magazine* (1914-1915), p. 783, p. 791.
49. Hapgood, *A Victorian in the Modern World,* p. 320.
50. Randolph Bourne, *Youth and Life* (Boston, 1913), p. 263.
51. Letter, R. Bourne to Prudence Winterrowd (April 28, 1913), Bourne Papers.
52. *Ibid.*
53. Randolph Bourne, "Karen," in *History of a Literary Radical: And Other Essays,* ed. Van Wyck Brooks (New York, 1920), p. 51, p. 54.
54. Harry Kemp, *Tramping on Life: An Autobiographical Narrative* (New York, 1922), p. 396.
55. Dell, *Homecoming,* p. 290.
56. Dell, *Intellectual Vagabondage,* p. 134.
57. *Ibid.,* pp. 141-142.
58. *New York Times* (January 24, 1915), 6, p. 9.

Select
Bibliography

PRIMARY SOURCES

Manuscript Collections

Randolph Bourne Papers, Columbia University Library
Neith Boyce Papers, Beinecke Library, Yale University
Louise Bryant Papers, Houghton Library, Harvard University
George Cram Cook Papers, New York Public Library
Floyd Dell Papers, Newberry Library, Chicago
Max Eastman Papers, Lilly Library, Indiana University
Susan Glaspell Papers, New York Public Library
Hutchins Hapgood Papers, Beinecke Library, Yale University
Mabel Dodge Luhan Papers, Beinecke Library, Yale University
John Reed Papers, Houghton Library, Harvard University
Carl Van Vechten Papers, Beinecke Library, Yale University
Mary Heaton Vorse Papers, Wayne State University Library

Published Writings

Anderson, Margaret. "Art and Anarchism," *Little Review,* 3 (March 1916), 3.

——. *My Thirty Years War: An Autobiography.* New York, 1930.

Anderson, Sherwood. *Sherwood Anderson's Memoirs,* Ray L. White, ed. Chapel Hill, 1969.

Bourne, Randolph. *Youth and Life.* Boston, 1913.

Boyce, Neith. *The Folly of Others.* New York, 1904.

Brown, Robert Carlton. "Them Asses," *American Mercury,* 30 (December 1933), 403-411.

Collier, John. *From Every Zenith: A Memoir.* Denver, 1963.

Cook, George Cram. *The Chasm.* New York, 1911.

——. *Company B of Davenport.* Davenport, Iowa, 1899.

——. *Greek Coins.* New York, 1925.

——, and Charles Banks. *In Hampton Roads.* Chicago, 1899.

Cook, George Cram, Ed. *The Provincetown Plays.* Cincinnati, 1921.

——. *Roderick Taliaferro: A Story of Maximilian's Empire.* New York, 1903.

——. *The Spring.* New York, 1921.

Cook, George Cram, Ed. *Suppressed Desires.* New York, 1917.

Cook, Nilla Cram. *My Road to India.* New York, 1939.

Davidson, Jo. *Between Sittings: An Informal Autobiography.* New York, 1951.

Day, Dorothy. *The Eleventh Virgin.* New York, 1924.

——. *The Long Loneliness: The Autobiography of Dorothy Day.* New York, 1952.

Dell, Floyd. "A Literary Self-Analysis," *The Modern Quarterly,* 4 (June-September 1927), 148-152.

——. "All About Love," *Pearson's Magazine* (December 1918), 76-77.

——. *The Angel Intrudes: A Play in One Act.* New York, 1918.

——. "Edna St. Vincent Millay: The Literary Spotlight," *The Bookman,* 56 (1922), 272-78.

——. *Homecoming: An Autobiography.* New York, 1933.

——. *Intellectual Vagabondage: An Apology for the Intelligentsia.* New York, 1926.

——. *King Arthur's Socks and Other Village Plays.* New York, 1922.

——. *Looking at Life.* London, 1924.

——. *Love in Greenwich Village.* New York, 1926.

——. *Moon-Calf.* New York, 1920.

——. "My Friend Edna St. Vincent Millay," *Mark Twain Journal,* 12 (Spring 1964), 1-2.

——. "Rents Were Low in Greenwich Village," *American Mercury,* 65 (December 1947), 662-668.

——. *Sweet and Twenty: A Comedy in One Act.* Cincinnati, 1921.

——. *Were You Ever A Child?* New York, 1921.

——. *Women As World Builders: Studies in Modern Feminism.* Chicago, 1913.

Eastman, Annis Ford. "Hide the Text: A Sermon for Children," *The Independent,* 48 (May 21, 1896), 704.

——. *Have and Give.* Elmira, N.Y., 1896.

——. *A Flower of Puritanism: Julia Jones Beecher.* Elmira, N.Y., 1905.

Eastman, Max. "Artists in Straight Jackets," *Modern Monthly,* 8 (August 1934), 445-447.

————. "Bunk About Bohemia," *The Modern Quarterly,* 8 (May 1934), 200-208.

————. *Colors of Life: Poems and Songs and Sonnets.* New York, 1918.

————. *The End of Socialism.* New York, 1937.

————. *Enjoyment of Poetry.* New York, 1913.

————. *Enjoyment of Living.* New York, 1948.

————. "Exploring the Soul and Healing the Body," *Everybody's Magazine,* 32 (June 1915), 741-750.

————. *Great Companions: Critical Memoirs of Some Famous Friends.* New York, 1942.

————. "Healing at the Shrine," *The Texas Review* (September 1915), 120-135.

————. *Heroes I Have Known: Twelve Who Lived Great Lives.* New York, 1942.

————. "Ignominy of Being Good," *Atlantic Monthly,* 107 (January 1911), 131-134.

————. *Journalism Versus Art.* New York, 1916.

————. "Lazy Verse," *New Republic,* 8 (September 9, 1916), 138-140.

————. *Leon Trotsky: Portrait of a Youth.* New York, 1925.

————. *The Literary Mind: Its Place in an Age of Science.* New York, 1931.

————. *Love and Revolution: My Journey Through an Epoch.* New York, 1964.

————. *Max, Lenin, and the Science of Revolution.* London, 1926.

————. "Mr. Er-er-er–Oh! What's His Name," *Everybody's Magazine,* 33 (July 1915), 95-103.

————. "New Art of Healing," *Atlantic Monthly,* 101 (May 1908), 644-650.

————. "New Masses for Old," *Modern Monthly,* 8 (June 1934), 292-300.

————. "Patriotism: A Primitive Ideal," *International Journal of Ethics,* 16 (July 1906), 472-486.

————. "The Poet's Mind," *North American Review,* 187 (March 1908), 417-425.

————. "Science and Free Verse," *The Seven Arts,* 1 (February 1917), 426-429.

————. *Since Lenin Died.* New York, 1925.

————. "Socialism and Human Nature," *The New Leader,* 25 (January 24, 1942), 5-6; *The New Leader* (January 31, 1942), 5, 7.

————. *Stalin's Russia and the Crisis in Socialism.* New York, 1940.

————. "Summation For the Defense," *Liberator Pamphlet.* New York, 1918.

————. *Understanding Germany: The Only Way to End War, and Other Essays.* New York, 1916.

————. "Unlimited Francise," *Atlantic Montly,* 108 (July 1911), 46-51.

————. *Venture.* New York, 1927.

————. "What Nietzsche Really Taught," *Everybody's Magazine,* 31 (November 1914), 703-704.

————. "Why All Should Enjoy Poetry," *Literary Digest,* 46 (May 10, 1913), 1060.

Flynn, Elizabeth Gurley. *The Rebel Girl: An Autobiography.* New York, 1973.

Freeman, Joseph. *An American Testament: A Narrative of Rebels and Romantics.* New York, 1936.

Gillmore, Inez Haynes. "Confessions of an Alien," *Harper's Bazaar,* 46 (April 1912), 170-171.

————. "Life of An Average Woman," *Harper's Bazaar,* 46 (June 1912), 383-384.

Glaspell, Susan. *Fidelity.* Boston, 1915.

————. *Plays*. New York, 1920.

————. *The Road to the Temple*. New York, 1927.

————. *The Visioning*. New York, 1911.

Gold, Michael. "The Masses Tradition," *Masses and Mainstream*, 4 (August 1951), 45-55.

Goldman, Emma. *Living My Life*. New York, 1934.

Hapgood, Hutchins. *A Victorian in the Modern World*. New York, 1939.

————. *An Anarchist Woman*. New York, 1909.

————. *Autobiography of A Thief*. New York, 1903.

————. *Paul Jones*. New York, 1901.

————. "The Picturesque Ghetto," *Century Illustrated Monthly Magazine*, 94 (July 1917), 469-473.

————. *The Spirit of Labor*. New York, 1907.

————. *The Story of A Lover*. New York, 1919.

————. *Types From City Streets*. New York, 1910.

Johns, Orrick. *Time of Our Lives*. New York, 1937.

Kemp, Harry. *More Miles: An Autobiographical Novel*. New York, 1926.

————. *Tramping on Life: An Autobiographical Narrative*. New York, 1922.

Kreymborg, Alfred. *Troubadour: An Autobiography*. New York, 1925.

Langner, Lawrence. *The Magic Curtain*. New York, 1951.

Luhan, Mabel Dodge. *Movers and Shakers*. New York, 1936.

McKay, Claude. *A Long Way From Home*. New York, 1937.

Mencken, N. L. *Letters of H. L. Mencken*, ed. Guy Forgue. New York, 1961.

Monroe, Harriet. "Two Poets Have Died," *Poetry*, 17 (January 1921), 208-212.

Reed, John. "Almost Thirty," *New Republic*, 86 (April 15, 1936), 267-270; *New Republic*, 86 (April 29, 1936), 332-336.

————. "America, 1918," *New Masses*, 17 (October 15, 1935), 17-20.

————. "A New Appeal," *The Revolutionary Age*, 1 (January 18, 1919), 8.

————. "Aspects of the Russian Revolution," *The Revolutionary Age*, 2 (July 12, 1919), 8.

————. "Back of Billy Sunday," *Metropolitan*, 41 (May 1915), 9-12, 66-72.

————. "Bolshevism in America," *The Revolutionary Age*, 1 (December 18, 1918), 3.

————. "The Causes Behind Mexico Revolution," *New York Times* (April 27, 1914), 4.

————. "Charles Townsend Copeland," *American Magazine*, 73 (November 1911), 64-66.

————. "The Colorado War," *Metropolitan*, 40 (July 1914), 11-16, 66-71.

————. "The Constituent Assembly in Russia," *The Revolutionary Age*, 1 (November 23, 1918), 4.

Reed, John. *Daughter of the Revolution: And Other Stories*, ed. Floyd Dell. New York, 1927.

————. "The Dinner Guests of Big Tim," *American Magazine*, 75 (December 1912), 101-104.

————. "The Englishman," *Metropolitan*, 40 (October 1914), 39-40.

————. "German France," *Metropolitan*, 41 (March 1915), 13-14, 81-82.

————. "If We Enter Mexico," *Metropolitan*, 40 (June 1914), 4.

————. *Insurgent Mexico*. New York, 1914.

————. "In the German Trenches," *Metropolitan*, 41 (April 1915), 7-10.

————. "The National Circus," *Metropolitan,* 44 (September 1916), 12-14.

————. "On Bolshevism, Russian and American," *The Revolutionary Age,* 1 (April 12, 1919), 6.

————. "The Origins of Worker's Control in Industry in Russia," *The Revolutionary Age,* 1 (November 23, 1918), 4.

————. "Sheriff Radcliff's Hotel," *Metropolitan* 39 (September 1913), 14-16, 59-60.

————. *Ten Days That Shook the World.* New York, 1935.

————. "This Unpopular War," *Seven Arts,* 2 (August 1917), 397-408.

————. "With Villa in Mexico," *Metropolitan,* 40 (February 1914), 72.

————. *The War in Eastern Europe.* New York, 1916.

Sanger, Margaret. *Margaret Sanger: An Autobiography* New York, 1938.

Sinclair, Mary Craig Kimbrough. *Southern Belle.* New York, 1957.

Sloan, John. *John Sloan's New York Scene: From the Diaries, Notes, and Correspondence, 1906-1913,* ed. Bruce St. John. New York, 1965.

Stearns, Harold. *The Street I Know.* New York, 1935.

Steffens, Lincoln. *The Autobiography of Lincoln Steffens.* New York, 1931.

————. "A Letter About Jack Reed," *New Republic,* 87 (May 20, 1936), 50-51.

————. *The Letters of Lincoln Steffens,* ed. Ella Winter and Granville Hicks. New York, 1938.

Sterne, Maurice. *Shadow and Light: The Life, Friends and Opinions of Maurice Sterne,* ed. Charlotte Mayerson, New York, 1965.

Tietjens, Eunice. *The World At My Shoulder.* New York, 1938.

Untermeyer, Louis. *Bygones: The Recollections of Louis Untermeyer.* New York, 1965.

————. *From Another World: The Autobiography of Louis Untermeyer.* New York, 1939.

Van Vechten, Carl. *Fragments From An Unwritten Autobiography.* New Haven, 1955.

————. *Peter Whiffle: His Life and Works.* New York, 1924.

Vorse, Mary Heaton. *Footnote to Folly: Reminiscences of Mary Heaton Vorse.* New York, 1935.

————. "Is the American Man a Failure?" *Woman's Home Companion,* 39 (January 1912), 10.

————. "The Importance of Play," *Woman's Home Companion,* 41 (March 1914), 23, 67-68.

————. "New Freedom for Little Children," *Woman's Home Companion,* 40 (October 1913), 8, 91-92; 41 (November 1913), 13, 62-63; (February 1914), 11-12, 58; 41 (April 1914), 13, 60.

————. "Standardizing Jimmy," *Woman's Home Companion,* 40 (January 1913), 6-7, 16.

————. *Time and the Town: A Provincetown Chronicle.* New York, 1942.

Wilson, Edmund. "15 Beech Street," *New Republic,* 51 (June 29, 1927), 150-151.

Wilson, Edmund. *I Thought of Daisy.* New York, 1929.

Young, Art. *Art Young: His Life and Times.* New York, 1939.

————. *On My Way: Being the Book of Art Young in Text and Picture.* New York, 1928.

Zorach, William. *Art is My Life: The Autobiography of William Zorach.* New York, 1967.

Newspapers and Journals

Chicago Evening Post.
Liberator.

The Masses.
New York Call.
New York Globe.
Tri-City Workers Magazine.

SECONDARY SOURCES

Aaron, Daniel. *Writers on the Left: Episodes in American Literary Communism.* New York, 1961.
Arens, Egmont. *The Little Book of Greenwich Village.* New York, 1919.
Baldwick, Robert. *The First Bohemian: The Life of Henry Murger.* London, 1961.
Bogard, Travis. *Contour in Time: The Plays of Eugene O'Neill.* New York, 1972.
Brill, A.A. *Psychoanalysis: Its Theories and Practical Application.* Philadelphia, 1914.
Brinnin, John. *The Third Rose.* Boston, 1959.
Brittin, Norman. *Edna St. Vincent Millay.* New York 1967.
Brooks, Van Wyck. *The Confident Years, 1885-1915.* New York, 1952.
———. *John Sloan: A Painter's Life.* New York, 1955.
Brown, Milton. *American Painting From the Armory Show to the Depression.* Princeton, N.J., 1955.
Cargill, Oscar. *O'Neill and His Plays: Four Decades of Criticism.* New York, 1966.
Churchill, Allen. *The Improper Bohemians: A Re-creation of Greenwich Village in its Heyday.* New York, 1959.
Clark, Barrett. *Eugene O'Neill.* New York, 1926.
Costa, Richard Haver. *H. G. Wells.* New York, 1967.
Cowley, Malcolm. *Exile's Return: A Narrative of Ideas.* New York, 1934.
Deutsch, Helen, and Stella Hanau. *The Provincetown: A Story of the Theatre.* New York, 1931.
Diggins, John. "Getting Hegel Out of History: Max Eastman's Quarrel with History," *American Historical Review,* 79 (February 1974), 38-71.
Draper, Theodore. *The Roots of American Communism.* New York, 1957.
Easton, Malcolm. *Artists and Writers in Paris: The Bohemian Idea, 1803-1857.* New York, 1964.
Eaton, W. P. *The Theatre Guild: The First Ten Years.* New York, 1929.
Egbert, Donald, and Stow Persons. *Socialism and American Life,* vol. 1, Princeton, N.J., 1952.
Farnham, Emily. *Charles Demuth: Behind a Laughing Mask.* Norman, Okla., 1971.
Foner, Philip. *History of the Labor Movement in the United States,* vol. 4, New York, 1965.
Gelb, Arthur, and Barbara Gelb. *O'Neill.* New York, 1962.
Gelb, Barbara. *So Short A Time: A Biography of John Reed and Louise Bryant.* New York, 1973.
Gilbert, James. *Writers and Partisans: A History of Literary Radicalism in America.* New York, 1968.
Glackens, Ira. *William Glackens and the Ashcan Group.* New York, 1957.
Grana, Cesar. *Bohemian Versus Bourgeois: French Society and the French Man of Letters in the Nineteenth Century.* New York, 1964.
Hackett, Francis. *American Rainbow: Early Reminiscences.* New York, 1971.
Haftmann, Werner. *Painting in the Twentieth Century,* vol. 1, New York, 1965.

Hahn, Emily. *Romantic Rebels: An Informal History of Bohemianism in America*. Boston, 1967.

Hale, Nathan. *Freud and the Americans: The Beginnings of Psychoanalysis in the United States, 1876-1917*. New York, 1971.

Hansen, Harry. *Midwest Portraits: A Book of Memories and Friendships*. New York, 1923.

Harris, Neil. *The Artist in American Society: The Formative Years, 1790-1860*. New York, 1966.

Hart, John. *Floyd Dell*. New York, 1971.

Hoffman, Frederick, *Freudianism and the Literary Mind*. Louisiana State University Press, 1945.

————, Charles Allen, and Carolyn Ulrich. *The Little Magazine: A History and a Bibliography*. Princeton, N.J., 1947.

Homer, William. *Robert Henri and His Circle*. Cornell University Press, 1969.

Hunt, Edward. "Prophets of Rebellion," *The Outlook*, 139 (March 18, 1925), 411-415.

Kenton, Edna. "The Provincetown Players and the Playwrights' Theater," *The Billboard*, 34 (August 5, 1922).

Kramer, Dale. *Chicago Renaissance: The Literary Life in the Midwest, 1900-1930*. New York, 1966.

Kramer, Hilton. *The Age of the Avant-Garde*. New York, 1974.

Kuhn, Walter. *The Story of the Armory Show*. New York, 1938.

Lasch, Christopher. *The Agony of the American Left*. New York, 1969.

————. *The New Radicalism in America, 1889-1963: The Intellectual as a Social Type*. New York, 1965.

Lowenthal, Leo. *Literature, Popular Culture, and Society*. Englewood Cliffs, N.J., 1961.

May, Henry. *The End of American Innocence: A Study of the First Years of Our Own Time, 1912-1917*. New York, 1959.

Moore, Jack B. *Maxwell Bodenheim*. New York, 1970.

Morris, William. *News From Nowhere*. London, 1920.

Murger, Henri. *Vie de Boheme, trans. Norman Cameron. London, 1960*.

O'Connor, Richard, and Dale Walker. *The Lost Revolutionary: A Biography of John Reed*. New York, 1967.

Parry, Albert. *Garrets and Pretenders: A History of Bohemianism in America*. New York, 1933.

Poole, Ernest. *The Bridge: My Own Story*. New York, 1940.

Preston, William. *Aliens and Dissenters: Federal Suppression of Radicals, 1903-1933*. Cambridge, Mass., 1963.

Ray, Man. *Self Portrait*. New York, 1963.

Rose, Barbara. *American Art Since 1900*. New York, 1967.

Rosenstone, Robert. *Romantic Revolutionary: A Biography of John Reed*. New York, 1975.

Schlissel, Lillian, ed. *The World of Randolph Bourne*. New York, 1965.

Shattuck Roger. *The Banquet Years: The Origins of the Avant Garde in France*. New York, 1968.

Sheaffer, Louis. *O'Neill: Son and Artist*. Boston, 1973.

————. *O'Neill: Son and Playwright*. Boston, 1968.

Sochen, June. *The New Woman: Feminism in Greenwich Village, 1910-1920*. New York, 1972.

Street, Julian "A Soviet Saint: The Story of John Reed," *Saturday Evening Post*, 203 (September 13, 1930), 9-10, 65.

Swanberg, W. A. *Dreiser*. New York, 1965.

Tanselle. G. Thomas. "Realist or Dreamer: Letters of Sherwood Anderson and Floyd Dell," *Modern Literary Review*, 58, 532-537.

Thompson, E. P. *Morris: Romantic to Revolutionary.* London, 1955.

Tornquist, Egil. *A Drama of Souls: Studies in O'Neill's Super-Naturalistic Technique.* New Haven, 1969.

Vilhauer, William. "A History and Evalution of the Provincetown Players," unpublished dissertation. University of Iowa, 1965.

Ware, Carolyn. *Greenwich Village, 1920-30.* New York, 1935.

Waterman, Arthur. *Susan Glaspell.* New York, 1966.

Wilenski, R. H. *Modern French Painters,* vol. 2. New York, 1966.

Williams, Albert Rhys. *Journey Into Revolution: Petrograd, 1917,* ed. Lucita Williams. Chicago, 1969.

Index

Anderson, Margaret, 103, 214, 228
Anderson, Sherwood, 103, 216-218
Armory Show, 14-18, 22, 34

Banks, Charles, 94
Barry, Griffin, 238
Becker, Maurice, 25, 33, 39, 41, 78, 170, 174
Berkman, Alexander, 32, 146, 151
Bodenheim, Maxwell, 103, 239
Bolshevism, 149-154, 192, 195-196, 198
Bourne, Randolph, 25, 238, 249-250
Boyce, Neith, 31, 33, 61-64, 66, 68, 71-73, 75, 79-81, 108, 138, 248
Boyd, Fred, 75, 134
Boyesen, Bayard, 31, 36, 38, 76
Brill, Abraham A., 38, 173, 227
Brubaker, Howard, 4
Bryant, Louise, 109-110, 120, 142-144, 147-149
Bullard, Arthur, 4, 178

Carlin, Terry, 67
Chamberlain, K. R., 25, 78, 174, 238, 241
Coleman, Glenn, 4, 25, 41
Communist Labor party, 152-153
Cook, Edward, 86-87, 94
Cook, Ellen Dodge, 76, 86-89, 91-92

Cook, George Cram, 11, 22, 72, 76-77, 84-115, 210-211, 214, 219, 253
Copeland, Charles, 126-127
Cowley, Malcolm, 8
Crane, Stephen, 4
Currey, Margery, 213-215, 218

Dasburg, Andrew, 31-32, 36, 38, 153
Davidson, Jo, 16, 35-36
Davis, Stuart, 4, 41, 43, 72
Day, Dorothy, 243
Dell, Floyd, 5-6, 8, 11, 23, 37, 40-42, 49, 99-100, 103-105, 109, 146, 170, 190, 207-232, 237-238, 243, 246-247, 250-251
Demuth, Charles, 76, 144
Deshon, Florence, 182, 189, 197
Dewey, John, 166, 178
Dodge, Edwin, 29-31
Dodge, Mabel, 8, 10, 14, 17-18, 21, 26-38, 50, 71-73, 77, 79, 133-134, 137-139
Dreiser, Theodore, 10-11, 218, 220, 239
Duchamp, Marcel, 15-16, 144
Duncan, Isadora, 221, 240

Eastman, Annis, 159-165, 168-169
Eastman, Crystal, 162, 166-167, 169, 180, 191

265

Eastman, Max, 5-6, 11, 19-20, 31-32, 37, 39, 40-41, 49, 73, 76, 129, 153, 158-201, 220, 240-241, 246, 253
Eastman, Samuel, 160-161
Edwards, Bobby, 43-44
Ell, Christine, 110, 244-245
Ellis, Charles, 112
Evans, Donald, 31, 36-37

Ferrer School, 5
Ficke, Arthur, 215, 217, 218, 222
Fineshreiber, William, 210, 213, 219
Freudian psychology, 41, 165, 173, 176-177, 200, 227-229, 239, 252

Gillmore, Inez Haynes, 39, 170, 239, 248-249
Glackens, William, 4, 16-17
Glaspell, Susan, 72, 101-102, 105, 108-109, 111, 113, 219, 228, 239
Gold, Michael, 242
Goldman, Emma, 5, 24, 32-33, 146, 151

Hackett, Francis, 212
Hallinan, Charles, 103, 214-215
Hapgood, Charles, 55-56, 58
Hapgood, Hutchins, 11, 17, 19-23, 27, 31, 33, 34-38, 54-81, 104, 109, 228, 243-244, 248-249, 253
Hartley, Marsden, 31, 36, 143
Havel, Hippolyte, 24, 31-32, 73, 143, 239, 244-245
Haywood, William, 18, 20-21, 32-34, 69, 132, 171
Herbst, Josephine, 198
Holladay, Paula (Polly), 24, 26, 73, 76, 244-245
Huffaker, Lucy, 73, 102, 144, 214
Hunt, Edward, 126, 131, 134

Industrial Workers of the World, 18-19, 22, 68

Jelliffe, Smith Ely, 38, 173, 227
Jones, Marjorie, 103, 216, 220, 222, 240, 244
Jones, Robert Edward, 21, 31, 36, 38, 108, 133

Kemp, Harry, 19, 20-21, 24, 26, 31, 37, 78, 104, 237-239, 241-242, 245, 247, 250
Kenton, Edna, 106, 112, 214, 218
King, Pendleton, 108, 114
Krylenko, Eliena, 198-199

Langner, Lawrence, 26, 217
Lee, Arthur, 31-32, 36, 139
Lee, Freddie, 36, 139
Lenin, Nikolai, 49, 160, 162, 184, 194-196, 199
Liberal Club, 5, 10, 14, 23-26, 38-39, 50, 105, 227-228
Liberator, 152, 191-194, 197-198, 230
Light, James, 110, 112
Lippmann, Walter, 31, 38, 127, 177
Luhan, Antonio, 38

Masses, 9-10, 14, 22, 38-50, 108, 142, 148-149, 170-171, 178, 180, 186, 188, 190, 201, 219-220, 229, 231, 239
Masters, Edgar Lee, 107-108
Mencken, H. L., 10, 25, 227
Milholland, Inez, 167-168
Millay, Edna St. Vincent, 198, 224-225, 229-231, 247
Minor, Robert, 41, 196
Monroe, Harriet, 103, 129
Mother Earth, 24, 99
Murger, Henri, 3

Nordfelt, B. J. O., 109, 216
Norton, Grace, 23

O'Brien, Joseph, 20, 36, 104, 109
O'Carroll, Joseph, 76
O'Neill, Eugene, 10-11, 84, 106-113, 143-144, 147
Oppenheim, James, 227

Paterson strike, 14, 18-22, 34
Potter, Grace, 218, 244
Price, Mollie, 96-102, 211
Provincetown Players, 77, 84, 105-115, 223
Psychoanalysis, 225-226, 228

Rand School, 5, 39
Rauh, Ida, 31, 73, 105, 109, 111-112, 114, 167-169, 173, 176, 182, 241

Reed, Charles, 119-123
Reed, John, 11, 22, 35-38, 40-41, 49, 72,
    106, 108, 119-154, 184, 190, 230, 242,
    253
Robinson, Boardman, 40-41, 140-141, 149
Rodman, Henrietta, 23-24, 241, 247-248,
    251
Rogers, Bobby, 143
Roosevelt, Theodore, 16, 18, 121-122, 143,
    181

Sanger, Margaret, 21, 31, 34, 248
Shaw, George Bernard, 103, 178, 211
Shostac, Bee, 21, 34
Sinclair, Upton, 36, 151-152
Sloan, John, 4-5, 17, 21, 39-41, 170, 239
Stearns Harold E., 237, 247
Steele, Wilbur, 20, 72, 104, 108
Steffens, Lincoln, 23, 31-33, 37, 59, 121-
    123, 127
Stein, Gertrude, 18, 29, 31, 34-35, 59
Stein, Leo, 38, 59
Sterne, Maurice, 36-38, 77
Stieglitz, Alfred, 5, 10

Tannenbaum, Frank, 44-45, 108

Thomas, Norman, 194, 239
Throckmorton, Cleon, 112, 114
Tietjens, Eunice, 103, 214
Trotsky, Leon, 150, 158, 199-200

Untermeyer, Louis, 5, 25, 39-40, 227,
    231

Van Vechten, Carl, 27, 31, 33-37, 133
Villa, Pancho, 134-137, 154
Vorse, Mary (Heaton), 6, 20, 23, 31, 39-40,
    72, 76-77, 170, 238-239, 243

Walling, William, 4-5, 31-32
Washington Square Players, 105
Weber, Max, 34, 36
Whitman, Walt, 98, 166, 211
Williams, Albert Rhys, 149-150, 198
Wilson, Woodrow, 137, 146, 152, 160, 162,
    164, 170, 172, 180-184, 186-188, 192-
    193, 195-196, 229

Young, Art, 5-6, 39, 41-42, 45, 170,
    190, 239, 241

Zorach, William, 16, 104